WALKING

Fortunately, the daring Thayer, age 63, fights nature and common sense for us, giving readers a fascinating account of her 1,600 mile journey with her husband, Bill, 74...Despite the hardship, Thayer is a sure and steady guide; this harrowing travelogue reads like a nail-biting adventure, sure to enthrall fans of Jon Krakauer and Bill Bryson.

—Publishers Weekly

"Helen Thayer is a survivor: not just of daily slings and arrows, but of polar bear attacks and Arctic storms, close calls with piranhas and crocodiles, the stings of hundreds of wasps and even an ambush by armed illegal gold miners."

—Shape magazine

"Helen Thayer is a remarkable woman whose accomplishments make her sound like a character dreamed up by the fertile imagination of a fiction writer."

—Autograph Times

"Thayer is an explorer-naturalist of a breed that in a modern age is more threatened than wolves. She is not a millionaire, an academic, a government scientist, or the sponsored face of a large corporation. In the beginning, she wasn't even a writer. Instead, she's a self-taught, self-financed, and self-effacing woman whose chief interest in life has been to do difficult and interesting things. Her adventures are a mixture of climb-it-because-it's-there feats of endurance and quasi-scientific efforts to satisfy her own curiosity."

—The Washington Post

It's the stories of smugglers in the night, a camel temper tantrum that cost a week's worth of water, and sightings of a wild desert bear that make this book irresistible.

—Rocky Mountain News

A tightly written and quick-moving account of [a] perilous journey.

—The Herald, Everett, WA

Helen Thayer shows not only her sense of courage and adventure, but also her talent as a writer and, through her words, her love of the desert and the culture therein...Thayer deserves applause not only for her incredible life as an adventurer, but also for her mastery of language that brings us on the journey with her...Thayer's writing pace turns this eighty-one day excursion into a journey readers can experience in just a few hours—preferably in the comfort of shelter, food and water.

—Indigo Editing

Walking the Gobi provides easy access into a world most Westerners know only by its exotic history.

—The Seattle Times

A 1600-MILE TREK ACROSS A DESERT OF HOPE AND DESPAIR

WALKING THE GOBI

HELEN THAYER

THE MOUNTAINEERS BOOKS

THE MOUNTAINEERS BOOKS
is the nonprofit publishing arm of The Mountaineers Club, an organization founded in 1906 and dedicated to the exploration, preservation, and enjoyment of outdoor and wilderness areas.

1001 SW Klickitat Way, Suite 201, Seattle, WA 98134

Copy Editor: Sherri Schultz
Cover, Book Design, and Layout: Mayumi Thompson
Cartographer: Moore Creative Designs

All photographs by the author unless otherwise noted.
Cover photograph: *Bactrian camel on dunes.* © George Steinmetz/ Corbis

Library of Congress Cataloging-in-Publication Data
Thayer, Helen.
  Walking the Gobi: a 1600-mile trek across a desert of hope and despair / Helen Thayer.—1st ed.
      p. cm.
  ISBN 978-1-59485-064-X(hardcover)
  ISBN 978-1-59485-112-4(paperback)
1. Gobi Desert (Mongolia and China)—Description and travel.
2. Mongolia—Description and travel. 3. Hiking—Gobi Desert (Mongolia and China) 4. Hiking—Mongolia. 5. Thayer, Helen—Travel—Gobi Desert (Mongolia and China) I. Title.
DS798.9.G63T54 2007
915.17'3—dc22
                                                2007023416

*To Bill, for his unfailing support,
and to the nomads of the Mongolian Gobi Desert*

CONTENTS

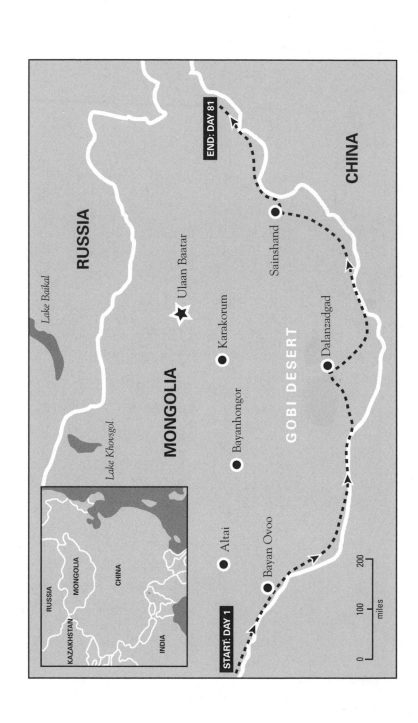

INTRODUCTION: DREAM

I first learned of Mongolia at age thirteen during a lecture by our teacher, Miss Carpenter, at Pukekohe High School in New Zealand, the country where I was born. As I listened to her describe Mongolia and its mysterious Gobi Desert, I knew this was a place I had to explore. Even after learning that the Communist government had closed the borders to foreigners, I kept the dream alive.

I acquired a taste for adventure at an early age. I often imagined myself climbing mountains, or in some far-off place exploring where few others had been. Long before society accepted the idea of women challenging themselves with long treks across polar ice caps and deserts, I yearned to test myself, to push myself to the limit, and to associate with little-known cultures. With the money I earned helping my father with farm chores, I began to accumulate an impressive collection of travel books.

I started climbing mountains at nine, when I summited New Zealand's 8,258-foot Mount Taranaki in midwinter with my parents, whose unfailing encouragement urged me to set my goals to infinity. Eventually such explorations would become my life. In 1988 I founded Adventure Classroom, an educational program for students from kindergarten to grade twelve that allows me to share the splendor of my expeditions with youngsters who might learn from my experiences. Since then, sometimes alone and sometimes with my husband Bill, a retired helicopter pilot, I've trekked from the Arctic to Antarctica and from the Amazon rain forest to some of the world's greatest deserts in a quest for knowledge of distant lands.

But always there, at the edge of my expedition plans, was that unfulfilled childhood dream, the Mongolian Gobi Desert.

AN ANCIENT LAND

Mongolia, an ancient land, is a country of enchanting, hospitable people, windswept open spaces, and unexpected extremes. Its approximately three million people live in one of the least-populated and highest-altitude countries in the world, sandwiched between two political giants, Russia and China. More than half of all Mongolians still live in traditional felt tents, called *gers*, and many follow a nomadic lifestyle that has remained unchanged for more than a thousand years.

Most visitors shun Mongolia's Gobi Desert as a scorched wasteland, devoid of anything worthwhile. It is a world of blinding sandstorms, oven-like heat, and desolation so entrenched that in most places even the hardiest trees refuse to grow—a treacherous void that swallows the careless traveler.

But a closer look reveals a Gobi that has been home to nomad families for hundreds of years. They hold on to life with hands gnarled by hard work. Their round *gers* shelter families who share laughter and dreams of spring rains that grow needed grass to fatten their animals. In winter they endure severe winter storms, or *zuds*, that bring heavy winter snow and temperatures that may plunge to 40 below zero, killing their camels, sheep, and goats. In summer, temperatures soar well above 100 degrees. Clearly, these are a resilient and hardy people.

The fierce fighting nomads of Mongolia conquered an empire on horseback beginning in 1206. Led by the revered Genghis Khan, who united four hundred tribes and was feared by his enemies more than any other leader, the Mongolians showed no mercy to the conquered. Throughout Asia and Europe, Khan and his descendants in the thirteenth and early fourteenth centuries defeated one army after another.

But by the late twentieth century, the empire was long gone. The nomadic herdsmen who traveled from place to place to follow food and water, as their ancestors had for centuries, became victims of Soviet Communism, which nearly buried the country and its people in a torrent of war and greed. Nomads were forced to collectivize their herds, monks were killed or sent to labor camps, and monastery treasures were pillaged. The Soviets took over the country, making it the world's second Communist stronghold, and held it in their iron grip for seventy years, beginning in 1921. During this period, expeditions crossing the Gobi Desert were forbidden.

WINDS OF CHANGE

In the 1990s, the winds of political change swept through Mongolia as Communism collapsed throughout the Soviet Union and Eastern Europe. The consequences for Mongolia were mixed. During the Soviet occupation the Mongolian economy was overwhelmingly dependent on a steady supply of Soviet money and imports, but when Communism collapsed, the money flow stopped. Russian soldiers and technical advisors went home, Soviet-run factories closed, and shortages of jobs, fuel, and food ensued.

Mongolia was saved from financial collapse when the World Bank, the United Nations, and various other international organizations stepped in with infusions of money and advice for the inexperienced political leaders. Buddhist monks returned to restart the country's religious movement, which had been halted during the Soviet purges. Thus this landlocked country with no real industrial infrastructure, although it still relies on foreign aid and food shipments, is now slowly advancing toward a prosperous future.

Politically, the changes were more positive. Elections created a parliamentary democracy in Mongolia. And most significantly for us, the laws relaxed. In 1996 we were told we would receive our long-sought visa, so that our dream of walking across the Gobi Desert from west to east, a distance of 1,600 miles, might at last become a reality. But because our intended route would take us deep into the Gobi along the Chinese border, a place normally off-limits to non-military personnel, Mongolian Embassy officials told us that we would have to apply for special permission in person in Ulaan Baatar, the capital of Mongolia.

PREPARATIONS

To prepare for the harsh conditions of a summertime Gobi Desert expedition, we first made a 1,500-mile trek through Death Valley and other major American deserts, followed by a 4,000-mile trek across the Sahara. Thus it would be the year 2000 before we were ready to travel to Mongolia to seek permission for our Gobi trek.

The difficulties of crossing the Gobi in summer were made even more complicated due to our being the first to attempt such a daunting task. To ensure success, we were methodical in our research and planning of every detail, such as how much food, water, and other supplies we would need and how we would carry it. We decided to separate the trek into four segments, each one a self-contained journey of approximately twenty days. This put the long weeks and miles into a perspective that our emotions could better handle. We would carry a first round of supplies with us and receive a resupply by air at the end of the first, second, and third segments.

In addition to our long desert treks, we continued training in the craggy Cascade mountain range near our home in Washington state. We hiked hundreds of miles in the summer with heavy packs, and skied and snowshoed in the winter. Our home basement gym was a busy place of exercises and weight training six days a week, while the steep hills of our farm were perfect for strenuous early-morning runs. Our herd of goats often ran and frolicked with us at first, although they would give up after the first few laps.

Finally, in the summer of 2000—the year of the Iron Dragon, according to the Mongolian lunar calendar—we traveled to Mongolia to finalize our logistics and apply for permission to return a year later to walk across the Gobi.

We flew into the capital city of Ulaan Baatar, which means "Red Hero." Sadly, the capital of this beautiful country is a dismal collection of poorly constructed, Soviet-type cement apartment buildings with questionable plumbing set among blocks of equally drab government offices. Two ramshackle coal-driven power stations, with tall, blackened chimney stacks belching smoke, dominate the city's skyline. White canvas *gers*, surrounded by stockade-like wooden fences, encircle the city, housing people who refuse to live in apartments.

MONGOLIAN NAMES: Mongolians have only one given name, which serves as both first and last name. Sometimes the father's name, often reduced to a single letter, precedes a given name to distinguish an individual from others with the same name. In pre-Soviet days, families kept records of family names dating back hundreds of years, to clans in ancient feudal days. Centuries of history were eliminated, however, when the Soviets destroyed the records to end the clans' political power and abolish titles of the noble class.

In a society that values the macho male, men's names often describe "manly" qualities, while women are named after flowers, gems, and virtues such as wisdom and peace. In generations past, when someone became famous within his own tribe or region, others would copy his name and pass it on to their children. This practice, along with the fact that many men chose "manly" names (such as Baatar, meaning "hero"), has caused some names to become very common. Bat, meaning "strong," frequently precedes a man's name, for instance.

At the modern, newly upgraded airport, we met the local pilot who had been recommended to us by a friend who made frequent business trips to Mongolia. The pilot's name was Chuluubaatar, meaning "Stone Hero." He would fly our resupplies to us and help with logistics. We were relieved when he asked us to call him Chuluu, as it soon became obvious that our unpracticed tongues had difficulty wrapping themselves around Mongolian names.

Friendly and organized, Chuluu spoke excellent English and was a typical Mongolian—easygoing, pleasant, slow to anger, and always operating with the notion that somehow things would all work out. He had been recommended as someone who was not only reliable but also punctual—a rarity in a country where time is measured more by the passing seasons, or at best in days or weeks, rather than by a time on a clock. Indeed, if a Mongolian neglects to turn up for an appointment at all, it is not considered unusual.

Chuluu took us to his small, three-room, Soviet-built apartment, a sunny place with dark green and yellow carpets and lace drapes at the windows. On a small table sat a statue of Buddha on a blue cloth amid a circle of white candles. In the kitchen, the bare wires of the electric stove dangled precariously. In answer to our concern Chuluu said, "They are okay; just don't touch them." Loud drumming sounds bounced off the walls when we turned on a faucet. The place reminded me of the apartments I had visited in Moscow—unsafe and a daily adventure to its occupants.

This little apartment would be our base before our departure, and while we were on our trek Chuluu would provide our only link to the outside world. A pilot experienced in desert landings, he would fly our resupplies of food and water into the desert in his small airplane at critical intervals during our journey. He had already chosen two healthy camels for us from his family's herd of fifty beasts, which lived on lush pastures in central Mongolia. We planned to lead them across the desert carrying our supplies.

A SKEPTICAL OFFICIAL

After finalizing the details of the expedition logistics and the three resupplies, Chuluu directed us to the busy heart of the city, where we would visit the official from whom we needed permission to begin our journey across the desert. We knew that he had several reasons to be skeptical of our plans.

Because of the proximity of our intended route to the Chinese border, there was concern that we might unintentionally cross the sparsely marked frontier and venture into China, which was strictly against Mongolian and Chinese law and could result in our being jailed in either country. In addition, smugglers from both countries posed a serious danger to us. Although scattered outposts of border guards watch for them, smugglers frequently drive across the border and have been known to shoot anyone they consider a threat.

In addition, there was no written record of anyone having walked the entire length of the Mongolian Gobi before. In 1941 seven escaped prisoners and one woman from Siberia had walked north to south across the narrowest part of the desert, a distance of about three hundred miles, on a journey into China and beyond; but two of them, the woman and one of the men, had died in the terrible heat midway through. Another expedition had traveled partway along the northern edge of the Gobi in cool fall temperatures, following a route of government water wells that had been drilled by the Soviet military. But Bill and I would be the first to challenge the entire 1,600 miles of the Gobi on foot in summer, taking a route through the heart of the desert's driest, most water-deprived and desolate plains and mountains.

We climbed the chipped cement stairs to the second floor, our footsteps echoing in the dark stairwell, and entered an office littered with boxes of books and papers covered with a liberal layer of dust. An unsmiling man in his fifties, wearing a crisp dark suit, greeted us in fluent English. He waved us to two chairs at the side of his desk, which was adorned with several family photos and a six-inch-tall white ceramic Buddha alongside an overflowing ashtray.

We didn't have to wait long for a verdict. After listening to our plan, the official was adamant in his refusal: "No one can walk all the way across the Gobi. In most places there isn't even a track to guide you, and water is nonexistent in many places. And if you get into trouble there are enormous areas where no one lives, and there will be no one to help you." Even after we told him of our 1,500-mile trek across Death Valley and other American deserts, and our 4,000-mile walk across the Sahara, he still shook his head. "The Gobi is different. Water is always a problem where there are no villages. Desert wells can be dry and are never marked on maps. The answer is no; it is too dangerous." Not to be defeated, we retreated to plan a more persuasive approach.

The next day, armed with new tactics, we tried again. We explained that the desert trek was an essential part of our plan to produce an educational program about Mongolia for our Adventure Classroom. We intended to first travel for several months and 4,000 miles throughout the entire northern and central region of the country, covering the steppes, mountains, and lakes, then return the following year to walk across the Gobi. We emphasized the necessity of trekking the desert's total length to produce a complete picture of Mongolia.

This new tactic seemed to induce a slight change in the official's demeanor. Adjusting his rimless glasses for the hundredth time, he looked squarely at us. After a long pause, his voice rising in an attempt to drive home his concern, he said, "It might work. But what will you do when you walk for days, and perhaps weeks, through areas where there are no people and there is no water? What about sand and dust storms?" As we described our plans for resupply via aircraft, he began to relent. He stood up in order to better study our maps and air charts, then picked up our compasses and GPS units.

We reminded him of the two camels that would carry our water, food, and equipment, but at the mention of the camels his resistance returned. "It takes experience to handle camels. There are no camels in America."

16

"We used camels in the Sahara and learned to handle them there," I countered.

He leaned back in his well-worn chair, which creaked with every move. With hands locked behind his head, he thoughtfully studied the cracked ceiling. My heart beat faster in the heavy silence.

Finally, pointing a finger for emphasis, he leaned across the desk. "Two foreign men walked into the desert two years ago, trying to cross north to south, a far shorter distance than your route, and they were found months later, dead of thirst. West to east is far too long. I'll give you permission to go north to south."

"No," Bill replied. "We must cross the entire Gobi Desert west to east—or, if you prefer, east to west."

The official leaned back in his chair with a long sigh, as if he had at last run out of objections. After a few tense moments of silence, he jolted us with one last burst of inspiration. "Go by Russian jeep, and you might make it." Then he remembered that a group had tried that and had broken down, run out of water, and been found by nomads, barely alive.

Stifling his impatience at the flow of endless objections, Bill reminded the official that because we would walk all the way, we wouldn't have to worry about engines breaking down. "Good point," our official said. With a resigned shrug he took a pen and wrote a few lines of permission, signed it with a flourish, and then ushered us into the hallway with one last warning.

"Just remember: people die in the Gobi."

EXPLORATION

I was thrilled: Finally, the next year at age sixty-three, my fifty-year dream would come true. Exhilarated by our success, we set off to explore northern and central Mongolia for the first part of our Adventure Classroom program. For two months we drove 4,000 miles in a rented Russian jeep across rolling green steppes, over high snow-crested mountains, and around pristine lakes surrounded by emerald green tamarack forests where cuckoo birds entertained us with their distinctive song.

Along the way, we fell in love with the country and its smiling, hospitable people. Mongolians invited us into their *gers*, sharing their food and stories. Bill mastered the essential salutations and left the interpreting to me. With the assistance of a phrasebook, a language tape, and considerable prompting, my Mongolian gradually improved as I worked to master the unfamiliar sounds, which are distantly related to Turkish and several languages of central Asia. Ultimately we amassed two thick journals of notes, 2,000 slides, and several hours of video as we traveled over most of Mongolia outside the Gobi Desert.

After we completed our explorations and returned to Ulaan Baatar, Chuluu flew us across three hundred miles of the central Gobi Desert to prepare us for its desolation and enormity. After landing smoothly on a sun-baked plain, we stepped into stifling 112-degree heat. In all directions the land was devoid of people, animals, and water. I picked up a handful of dirt, gravel, and sand and let it fall through my fingers as I thought ahead to the deprivation we would experience. We walked to a low, rounded hill and looked east and then west. The barren desert stretched to a horizon of dancing mirages. It had a pristine, lonely beauty despite its killing heat.

We wondered what unknowns awaited us, and hoped that the ten months of training we had left would be enough.

DISASTER

Filled with anticipation, we returned to our farm in the mountains, continuing to train and to fine-tune our plans for the expedition. After only two months, however, disaster struck. While we were stopped in traffic on a bridge north of Seattle, a fast-moving van rear-ended us. The impact propelled our vehicle forward, and my laced-up running shoe was wrenched off my left foot. Searing pain, greater than any I had ever felt, shot through my back, left hip, and upper leg. My seat belt stopped me from being thrown through the windshield. It took a moment for the shock of the impact to pass, and then I thought, *Oh no, I'm not hurt. I can't be!*

Bill, clutching his shoulder, heard my cry of shocked pain and anxiously asked if I was all right. "I'm hurt, but I think I can walk it off," I replied.

In a lifetime of sports and expeditions, I had rarely suffered even a minor setback. But when I tried to take a step, my left leg crumpled and barely held my weight. A policeman who had pulled over asked if I wanted an ambulance. I told him no. The next morning I was due to leave for Banff National Park in the Canadian Rockies to guide a group of *National Geographic* clients for a week of heli-hiking. If they held me overnight in the hospital, I'd miss my 7 AM flight. I refused to consider that my injuries might jeopardize my guiding assignment, let alone my future expedition plans.

We left the next morning right on schedule, and after an uncomfortable journey arrived at Banff. We applied cold packs and massages overnight to our injured bodies, which caused the pain to subside to a barely tolerable level. Thanks to help from Bill, who was struggling through torn shoulder ligaments, and the helicopter that transported our group from ridge to ridge, I was able to do a reasonable job of guiding. But that week in the mountains was a nightmare.

When I returned home, I went through a series of X-rays and scans. The news was bleak. It seems that during the impact, in spite of my seat belt, I was thrown forward and twisted awkwardly, injuring my lumbar spine and tearing the ligaments of both sacroiliac joints. Impinged nerves in my spine radiated pain through my hip and down my left leg. Ligaments stabilizing my left hip were severely torn, putting the joint cartilage at risk. My right hip was moderately injured, and my right Achilles heel had ruptured. My left front thigh, or quadriceps muscle, was torn, and my left knee and hip received deep bone bruises. Internally, the left psoas muscle, alongside the spine, had torn.

I was told that future walking expeditions would be impossible due to the severity of the injuries, especially the destabilization of joints in my back and hip. I was devastated: I could not comprehend life without extreme activity. This would be an-other challenge, I resolved, no different than my solo trek to the magnetic North Pole among polar bears twelve years before. I would somehow walk pain-free again.

I found medical professionals to work with, and the long and painful road to recovery began. Eight months later, however, only a month before the start of our expedition, I was forced to rec-ognize reality. Although improved, I still limped, and with every step my hip and left leg radiated intense pain.

I asked myself if I could endure the pain of walking 1,600 miles. Should we cast aside our dream of walking across the des-ert, or perhaps, if I recovered completely, go another year? At first the latter seemed to be the answer, but Mongolia, which had been closed to foreigners for seventy years, had at last opened its frontiers. We had, after a struggle, obtained permission to walk the Gobi and we might not have another chance, especially if unstable politics closed the borders again.

The thought of abandoning a fifty-year-old dream and five years of planning was unbearable to me. And there was Adven-ture Classroom, a project that had become a large part of Bill's and my life and that depended on the information we gathered from our expeditions. The Gobi trek would provide students with a wealth of knowledge of an ancient culture. I reasoned that if I gave it my strongest effort and still failed, at least I would have done my best. If I didn't try, I would always wonder if I could have made it. I wasn't prepared to spend the rest of my life knowing that I had given up without a fight.

And so Bill and I agreed: we would depart for Mongolia as planned.

In 2001, the Year of the White Snake, we returned to Mongolia to begin our adventure.

Timing is crucial in the Gobi. We wanted to avoid winter's arctic weather and frigid Siberian winds, but we also knew that the transition from winter to spring is the most dangerous season of all: when warm air clashes with the receding winter cold, weather can turn treacherous. Sudden blizzards following a thaw can freeze the melting snow into a sheet of rock-hard ice that animals cannot break through to find food. The phenomenon, called *zud*, often kills a season's newborn animals. Then, as spring advances, horrific sand and dust storms accompanied by howling winds change day into night.

We chose a late May departure, hoping it would enable us to escape most of the unpredictable springtime conditions. Although our journey would take us through the worst of the summer heat, our projected mid-August finish would allow us to avoid the last few weeks of high temperatures. The danger of encountering armed nighttime smugglers along the border persuaded us to travel by day. Even so, we hoped that smugglers would avoid established border posts, so we could travel at night in those areas and gain at least some relief from the debilitating temperatures. After our twelve-hour flight from Seattle to Seoul, South Korea, we flew another two hours to Ulaan Baatar, arriving tired and thankful to leave behind us the bustle of busy international airports. Our three-month supply of expedition equipment and food was unloaded into the center of the main terminal. Obviously far beyond the average two suitcases of the average traveler, the untidy pile drew curious stares. Our assistant, Chuluu, would not arrive till the next day, so we hired two ten-year-old boys to guard our belongings while we looked for a couple of taxis large enough to carry our gear from the airport to Chuluu's apartment.

After haggling with us over their fee for guarding our stockpile, the boys finally settled on ten dollars each for a half hour, with a tip if we found everything intact upon our return. Ten dollars was considerably less than the ambitious figure of five hundred dollars with which they'd begun their negotiations. With one boy sitting atop the pile and the other on guard with his best macho stance, Bill and I left to find transportation.

Outside we found two taxi drivers named Baatar and Ching, who cheerfully hauled our pile piece by piece out of the airport. Several men joined in—mostly, we suspected, to satisfy their curiosity as to why foreigners would have so much luggage. Soon everything was jammed into the vehicles.

Bill and I sat beside Baatar on the worn front seat with duffel bags in our laps, and we roared away in a van that had long ago lost its muffler. With Ching following close behind, Baatar, his eyes fixed ahead in absolute concentration, drove at top speed, as we shuddered and swerved our way around two-foot-deep pot-holes. Occasionally, after hitting a hole, we would fly for several feet before plunging to earth with such a jolt that our heads hit the padded ceiling. After the first crack of my head I timidly sug-gested that we slow down, but Baatar was a man possessed. A speedy ride was part of the service. A half hour later we screeched to a halt at our destination.

The building security guard, a woman bent from years of hard work, regarded us with deep suspicion. After poking the various bundles and shaking one or two, she finally allowed us to pass. Baatar and Ching helped carry everything up the single flight of narrow, barely lit, spotlessly clean cement stairs to Chuluu's apartment.

Our compact one-burner cookstove was the most interesting item to the drivers. They were incredulous that we could actually cook an entire meal on it. After learning of our plans to walk across the desert, Baatar immediately offered horses to ride. They belonged to his cousin, who lived on the green steppes not far from the city. Both men assured us that our plan was insane and that riding horses was safer than walking. Since they were mem-bers of a society that learns to ride horses before learning to walk, we could understand their reasoning, but we adamantly kept to our pedestrian plan. After giving us directions to the "best market in the city," they wrote their names and phone numbers down for us to call if we needed help.

About midafternoon, after negotiating several potholed streets and skirting gaping manholes with missing covers, we ar-rived at the market. A horde of shoppers filled the aisles between makeshift shacks and tiny one-person stalls full of life's necessities. Raw meat, sprinkled with flies, hung from posts and rafters. Other booths were piled high with sacks of flour, sugar, and salt. Mon-golians love bright colors, and shouting vendors enthusiastically shoved red and orange fabric into our reluctant hands, right next to merchants offering potatoes and carrots. In the pressing crowd we couldn't see our feet as we stumbled into yet more holes in

23

the packed dirt aisles. As we shuffled along, shoulder to shoulder, from booth to booth, our foreign looks drew stares of curiosity. We gradually filled our shopping bags with fruit, vegetables, and two-foot-long rolls of processed meat.

An hour later we escaped to the relative quiet of the street, only to be accosted by a couple of vodka-laced drunks, who lounged unsteadily outside the market walls. One approached Bill, stumbling with an outstretched hand, asking for money. Another, dressed in grease-covered jeans, blue shirt, and orange baseball cap, wove his uncertain way in our direction, offering us a drink from his half-empty bottle. We quickly hailed a passing taxi, tossed our shopping bags inside, and fled to the apartment. The solitude of the Gobi seemed more inviting than ever.

For the rest of the day we sorted supplies and divided them into four piles, one for each stage of the trek. We would take the first pile with us, and Chuluu would deliver one of the other three every twenty days. The first aid kit held an assortment of necessities for desert travel. For foot problems, we carried rolls of moleskin to protect our feet from blisters. Other essentials included bandages, antiseptic ointment, iodine, burn cream in case of a stove fire, two splints for sprains and broken bones, and wide elastic bandages. We added a liberal supply of sunscreen, a nighttime cream to combat the dry air, lip salve for split lips—and a generous supply of pain pills, most of which I would use as a barrier against the pain in my hip and leg.

As always, travel to remote places with sanitation problems and unfamiliar food required various medicines to treat stomach ailments. In addition, in the months before leaving home we had received a variety of vaccinations. In case of serious mishap, we carried international medical insurance to ensure our evacuation to a competent hospital in Russia or China—a necessity in Mongolia, where hospital treatment, if it is available at all, is woefully antiquated. Because I am trained as an emergency medical technician, we included extra first aid supplies in case we were called upon to help others. And to avoid leaving any mark on the desert, we carried black plastic bags in which we'd store our daily garbage to be flown out by Chuluu when he arrived with a resupply.

After packing, we filled ten-gallon plastic containers with water, testing and retesting the leakproof caps. Two fifty-pound sacks of ground maize and a twenty-pound bag of plain vanilla cookies were added for camel food and treats. On each of our three resupplies, we would exchange our empty water containers for full ones.

Several times while we sorted gear, the security woman, who normally sat at the front entrance to keep nonresidents out of the building, wandered in to watch the proceedings. The Mongolian custom of entering without knocking meant the woman's first appearance took us by surprise. Bill, dressed only in his underwear, scurried to the protection of the bedroom; he reappeared a few minutes later, embarrassed but dressed for company. The woman showed no sign of having noticed his lack of garments and continued to examine various items with curiosity. As silent as a shadow, she suddenly left without a word, only to return an hour later with another woman. Now both continued the examination of our gear. After a few giggles and nudges, they finished their inspection and sat quietly on the sofa watching us.

To fill the silence that they seemed not to notice, I offered them tea, American style. One or two polite sips later, they both put their cups down and once more left without a word. In a few minutes they returned, this time with a thermos of Mongolian *suutei tsai* (salty tea). They filled our cups and then sat back with satisfied smiles to watch us drink "real" tea. It was only after we drank three cups each, and protested that we could drink no more, that they left with wide smiles, obviously satisfied that they had provided valuable education on the subject of tea drinking.

Later I jumped in surprise when a young girl silently appeared at my side in the apartment. With a bright smile of expectation, she offered ten hard-boiled eggs for sale. I paid her the equivalent of one dollar for the lot, and she went happily on her way.

I soon discovered my mistake. The ease with which she sold

her entire supply of eggs to these unwitting foreigners encouraged her to round up all her egg-selling friends. As they giggled their way up the stairs, we realized that in our ignorance we had become an easy target. Bill sprang to lock the door, barely in time. We were about to be offered enough eggs to fill a henhouse. But the girls, ever the determined saleswomen, were not discouraged by a mere locked door. They pounded and kicked the door for the next hour until finally giving up. We had learned our lesson. We should have bought no more than two eggs at a time and given the girl half her asking price.

That evening we loaded our first-stage supplies onto an aged truck with a large enclosed container, which Chuluu had left parked on the street outside the apartment building. But there was no way to secure the rusty locks, which had long since given up the struggle for survival. Rather than risk losing our precious supplies to thieves, we decided to drive to the airport, sleep in the truck, and wait for Chuluu's arrival in the morning. The worn truck, though unwilling and tired, finally managed to sputter its weary way to the airplane hangar.

Sleep was almost impossible in the cramped cab, which tortured our bodies and smelled like burnt oil. Longing for daylight, we cheered as the sun peeked over the surrounding low mountains. It was with immense relief that we watched Chuluu roar in, in his single-engine plane. Tall for a Mongolian at almost six feet, he greeted us with a typical wide Mongolian smile that quickly faded when he saw our untidy pile of gear, food, and water. He looked doubtful as he slowly circled the pile, shaking his head.

"This is a lot of stuff."

We assured him that we had weighed everything, and we were certain that it would all fit and that we could take off and fly safely.

"Okay, let's try," he said.

As we handed objects to Chuluu, he loaded the plane to keep it balanced. An hour later, he was surprised to find that everything did indeed fit, although just barely. Meanwhile, a friend of

Chuluu's arrived and gave our gear a skeptical look. He opined that if we rode horses we wouldn't need all that, and then insisted that we drink a bowl of salty tea to start our journey. He poured from the ubiquitous thermos that seems to accompany all Mongolians wherever they go. Finally, after drinking two bowls each, we climbed aboard the plane, jammed ourselves into the hard metal seats, and buckled the safety belts.

Bill, his caution and piloting background coming to the fore, remarked, "It would be a mess to try to get out in an emergency."

To which I replied, hoping I sounded convincing, "At least we'd be well padded in a hard landing, with all this gear."

Chuluu eased his tall, slender frame into his seat and started the engine. After a short warm-up, we taxied to the end of the runway. He turned into the wind and gunned the engine. The heavily loaded plane vibrated down the runway and labored into the light breeze on a cloudless morning.

The crumbling concrete buildings, potholed streets, and crowded markets of Ulaan Baatar dropped away behind us as Chuluu set a southwestern course, which would take us to the far western edge of the desert on the Chinese border.

A golf course–like carpet of undulating steppes rolled beneath our wings. Round white canvas *gers* dotted the landscape. The green vegetation gradually faded to tans and browns, and before long we were flying over the famed Gobi Desert. We looked across an immense space. Chuluu flew low, following the first third of our intended route over the parched rocky land that showed not a glimmer of welcome. It looked far more forbidding than the Sahara.

Until this moment, crossing the Gobi in summer on foot had been a dream composed of statistics, plans, and hope. Now the fearful immensity of the sandblasted wilderness began to imprint itself firmly on our minds. We no longer saw *gers* or any sign of nomads or their herds. It was late spring, and the water wells and ponds were rapidly drying up. For the next two months our route would cross mountains and endless plains where, in many places, no one dares live in summer.

As I took in the burnt landscape, the scope of what we were about to attempt suddenly became all too apparent. I knew that my injured leg and hip would make it impossible for me to resort to riding a camel, even in an emergency. Was I expecting too much of myself? Was it possible to cross the entire length of this desert using only the most primitive means of transportation? Was it just some romantic but impractical idea that had begun when I was thirteen years old and should never have been pursued?

Or was it an idea born of the desire to challenge myself, as explorers before me had done all over the world? To travel on foot without the aid of accompanying vehicles, and without riding a camel or horse, may seem impossible in a world of extravagantly financed and publicized expeditions. But Bill and I found the idea of a "back-to-basics" expedition compelling. We enjoyed the simplicity of a trek in a world drowning in convenience and easier methods of travel.

As the empty land dropped beneath the plane's wings, any doubts faded as the excitement of the desert's challenge resurfaced. It was the same sense I had experienced so many times in the past, at the start of other expeditions into the unknown. It was true that this time was different because of my physical impairment, but the same old excitement was still there. I had committed myself. Although there would be difficulties ahead, we were confident of success. Our meticulous planning, along with our long Sahara and American desert treks, had prepared us mentally for the heat, loneliness, and exhausting miles we were about to confront.

I tapped Bill on the shoulder, pointed down, and shouted above the din of the engine, "What do you think?"

"Tough going, but we can do it," he shouted back with an enthusiastic thumbs-up.

Two hours later we arrived at the Chinese border. The aircraft's global positioning system (GPS), which relies on satellites that circle the earth, read 90 degrees 41 minutes east longitude. Two camels and the waving figures of their owners waited below us. Chuluu circled, guided by the smoke from a fire that had been lit as a wind indicator, looking for a smooth place to land.

Here the desert was softened by a shadow of springtime green as the last of the plants bravely held on in the rising heat. Chuluu touched down with only the slightest bump, and taxied to a smooth stop amid a cloud of dust and flying gravel. The camels reared back on their tethers in alarm as the red-and-white bird descended into their world, but quickly calmed after the engine shut down. Relieved to leave the cramped seats, we straightened our protesting legs and passed our equipment out to Chuluu and the husband-and-wife camel owners, who stacked everything in a large pile.

Chuluu introduced us to his brother Batbaatar, or "Strong Hero," and Batbaatar's wife Sarantsetseg, "Moonflower." They were accompanied by a little girl, Sarantuya ("Moonbeam"), whose parents called her Saran. She peeked at us shyly from behind her mother's dark blue full-length *del*, a one-piece traditional garment, basically the same for men and women, that reaches from neck to ankles, with flared sleeves that roll down to cover the hands in winter's severe cold. The waist of Sarantsetseg's *del* was cinched with a wide yellow band, and delicate golden embroidery adorned the stand-up collar at her neck.

Batbaatar, dressed in plain dark pants and shirt, was tall, athletic-looking, probably in his twenties. His name suited him. Sarantsetseg was an elegant, slender woman with soft dark eyes and a serious face. Sarantuya, although shy of strangers, was a lively and independent four-year-old. She informed Chuluu that she would be "a pilot like you one day."

Batbaatar, who seldom stopped smiling, introduced us to the two camels that would carry our gear. His smile diminished slightly as he asked, "You'll take good care of them, won't you, and get them home safe? It's a long way, and dangerous."

"You can depend on it," I quickly assured him.

Bill answered by showing him the large sack of cookies we had brought to give the camels as treats and rewards. "Camel cookies," he said.

29

Batbaatar looked into the sack in disbelief. "You must be kidding. Never heard of giving cookies to a camel."

The two larger-than-average gelded males, mature at six years old, were muscular and among the best we had so far seen in Mongolia. We had leased them from Chuluu's family for only two hundred dollars each. With their winter wool shorn to ready them for the hot journey ahead, both camels stared placidly as we stroked their gray, naked bodies. Without winter coats they resembled prehistoric creatures.

The two-humped camel, or Bactrian camel, of the Gobi Desert is a member of a varied species that includes the more common one-humped camel, or dromedary, of the Sahara. The Bactrian camel was domesticated by nomads several thousand years ago and is closely related to the wild camels of the Gobi Desert. Each hump consists of fibrous tissue and fat, a reserve used in times of starvation, and produces not only energy but also water as a by-product of metabolism.

Under extreme conditions camels can live ten days without water and thirty-five days without food, which accounts for their ability to live in arid regions. When water is available they gulp down as much as twenty-five to thirty gallons at one time. These camels' humps stood tall and firm, indicating good health. When food and water are scarce, the humps become limp, empty sacks that flop to one side.

These magnificent beasts towered over us. They weighed more than 1,700 pounds each and stood seven feet tall at their humps. To keep out blowing sand, camels' eyelashes are long, their ears fur lined, and their narrow nostrils uniquely adapted to close in sandstorms. Their feet resemble snowshoes, with smooth soles and two clawlike nails in the front to prevent them from sinking into the soft sand.

Camels are not the world's most lovable creatures. They typically hold their heads high, giving them a haughty look. Their breath odor is a challenge. Bill once declared in the Sahara, "A camel's breath can wilt the finest rose at two hundred feet." As they age, their teeth turn yellow-brown; their vocal demonstration of grunts and bellows leaves human eardrums vibrating. A camel's digestive tract is a formidable affair, processing even dry sticks that appear impossible for any animal to consume.

When their camels are young, owners insert a sharp-pointed, six-inch wooden peg under the main nose cartilage, where it is least likely to tear. Though this seemed unduly harsh to us at first, we came to realize that camels are powerful animals, at times stubborn and cantankerous. The nose peg and lead are sometimes the only way to regain control of an unruly beast in the midst of a temper tantrum. If used with care, the peg appears to produce no discomfort.

The one-humped camels of the Sahara can sometimes be stubborn and rebellious in the face of the harsh treatment they often experience. These personality traits, combined with their intelligence, make them a challenge to train. But these two Bactrian camels came from a background of gentle handling. They proved to be intelligent hard workers, and as they grew to trust us they became playful companions, always on the watch for a handout.

Even so, they retained a certain haughty, opinionated attitude— as if God had put them on this earth to rule all others—for the entire journey.

Batbaatar gave us a lesson on camel loading. First, he pulled on the leads to make the camels "whoosh," which seems to be the universal term among camel tenders for having them sit on their thick, callused knees, which protect their joints. Then he laid a handwoven red pad between the two humps. As he loaded the duffel bags and water containers, both camels grumbled. Soon, with mouths agape and yellow teeth on full display, the sounds became full-fledged bellows, a challenge to the Richter scale. Bill and I exchanged quick glances. *Our eardrums will never survive this daily onslaught,* I thought.

Batbaatar laughed at our reaction and yelled above the awful noise, "Don't take any notice, it's only for show." He was right: once the loading was completed, as if on cue, the racket stopped.

31

Then it was time for us to depart. Sarantsetseg brought out a one-gallon thermos painted with red and yellow flowers, full of salty tea. After we each drank a full bowl, the family prepared to head for home, a hundred miles away. Batbaatar took a long length of hose and siphoned fuel into the gas tank from a drum on the back of the truck. They would be leaving the desert to travel across the roadless rolling steppes, which meant they would be dependent on the uncertain gas supplies in the scattered villages. Who knew whether the gas supply truck may have broken down on its way over the rutted tracks from Ulaan Baatar?

As the truck was refueled, I was reminded of our previous year's two-month tour of Mongolia by jeep, when we had spent an entire day in one small village looking for gas. We were told that none had been delivered in a month, but that one man had hoarded enough to sell. Following vague directions, we eventually found his *ger* on the edge of town, surrounded by a five-foot-high wooden fence. As we approached, a serious man of few words met us and asked if we needed gas.

"Yes, five gallons if you have it," I said and passed our metal gas container to him. We watched as he filled it, one cup at a time, from a large blue metal drum he kept inside his *ger*. Although he charged double the normal price, we were so relieved to be able to buy gas at all that we hardly noticed the highly inflated price.

Gas had been a constant problem on that journey. Whenever we arrived at a town, we would ask directions to a gas pump and would usually be directed to a cement shed with a tank locked inside. It was up to us to find the man in charge of pumping it.

After searching the town, we might find him at his *ger* drinking tea, or at the local market chatting with friends. He would say, "I'll be there soon." After an hour or so he would arrive, often on a motorbike, to pump our needed gas, usually by hand. In Mongolia no one hurries, and patience is a basic necessity of life.

After a few protesting sputters, Batbaatar's truck started with a noisy rumble. With cheery good-byes (*"Bayartai!"*), they drove off across the wilderness in a cloud of dust, following their instincts rather than maps. Earlier, when we had inquired about his lack of maps, Batbaatar had given us a puzzled look. After a long pause he said, "Maps don't always show the right direction." I was glad we hadn't shown him ours. Whatever would he have thought of our topographical maps, air charts, and satellite desert images, combined with our two pocket-sized GPS units and three compasses? They probably would have made us look like hapless beginners to him.

As the truck disappeared, Chuluu went over our route and the three resupply plans. He would fly to our prearranged meeting place in twenty days. If we weren't there, he would backtrack along the route we had traced on his map until he found us. If we arrived early, we would wait. A simple, straightforward plan.

Chuluu refueled from the reserve drum he carried, then gave us both one last hug. With an enthusiastic "Good luck!" he climbed aboard, gunned the engine, raced across the dusty earth, and took off. He circled once, dipped the wings in a farewell salute, and then flew through a narrow pass in the northern mountains. We watched as our only lifeline grew steadily smaller, then vanished.

Alone in a vast wilderness, swallowed by a silence so profound that our own voices sounded too loud, we looked around us, our eyes adjusting to the openness, feeling isolated and vulnerable. Statistics declare that Mongolia is one of the world's most sparsely populated countries, but that bland phrase didn't do justice to this vast empty region, where the sight of a tiny gecko lizard would become a notable event.

It was just Bill and me, the camels, and the desert.

DAY 1 > It was 11 AM. The sun, already high in the sky, sent the temperature to 90 degrees Fahrenheit—a balmy hint of the much higher temperatures to come as summer progressed.

We'd aimed to dress as coolly as possible. Our lightweight shirts and pants were treated with an anti-ultraviolet substance to help block the sun's rays. As added protection, we kept the long

33

sleeves of our shirts rolled down most of the time. Wide-brimmed hats, fitted with chin straps for windy days, provided us with a bit of shade. Lightweight boots with flexible soles, coupled with well-padded, moisture-absorbent socks, preserved our feet amid the daily punishment of walking over rocky plains. Sunglasses were so important that we carried three pairs each. Bandanna masks and special close-fitting goggles would protect us from the flying grit of sandstorms. And a fleece jacket, our only warm garment, would keep us warm during the cooler nights.

We checked our maps and tracking devices, happy to see that our position, already marked on the maps to coincide with the aircraft GPS, agreed with our handheld units. The terrain matched our charts, which were largely blank except for the thick black line we'd drawn to indicate the route we intended to follow. According to the contour lines and satellite images, it seemed to be the most reasonable path across the rolling terrain and around and over the mountains. The far southwestern corner of the Gobi—in Khovd aimag, or province, on the Chinese border—was our starting point.

I had two trekking poles to provide extra support for my injured left side, but before we headed out, I had to solve the problem of how to hold a pole in each hand while leading a camel. Doing some awkward experimenting, I succeeded in jabbing my foot. Then, just as I thought I had discovered the right combination, I tripped and stumbled into a surprised Tom, who stared down at me with a perplexed look. I patted his shoulder in apology, then looped the lead with plenty of slack around my right wrist. It worked. I could swing my arms as I walked and at the same time lead a camel.

"Onward and upward," Bill exclaimed enthusiastically, with a dramatic flourish of his trekking pole, as we started out side by side, our two camels following. We sang the energetic hymn "Onward Christian Soldiers" in shameless off-key unison in time with our steps.

The magnitude of the journey was almost too much to contemplate as we covered the first few miles, a mere half-inch on the map. After our singing start, conversation became sparse as we individually dealt with our thoughts and adjusted emotionally to the task ahead and the prospect of being exposed to loneliness, wind, and extreme heat. The fact that the nomads had already abandoned the area to find water, as we'd observed from the air, was disquieting. We were traveling into the inferno they had moved away from.

Two plodding hours later, we stopped to snack on peanut butter–covered crackers, regroup, and remind each other of our twenty-day strategy—to think of the journey ahead in four manageable segments rather than a single seventy-six-day odyssey. "After all," Bill lied, "twenty days will go by in a flash."

However disingenuous, our method seemed to work. Our emotional world brightened, and the desert didn't seem as empty or the miles as long, as we discussed our resupply and the prospect of seeing Chuluu again.

As we walked, we adapted to the wondrous scale of the vast horizons and rejoiced that we would have no e-mail or phone to answer. No television or newspapers to spew negative news of world conflicts. Released from the time schedules and bustle of modern Western existence, we were free to enjoy the simple things in life and become one with our surroundings.

To the north lay the towering rocky peaks of the Altai Mountains, with the highest peak, Mount Khuiten, reaching 14,346 feet into a deep blue sky. Still snowcapped, these mountains are home to the shy and endangered snow leopard. To the south lay a barren gray mountain range, the only thing separating us from China. Ahead lay a vast rolling void of emptiness.

Solitary mountains rose a few hundred feet above the dry plain like lonely Egyptian pyramids in an ocean of gravel. The tortured earth was already dry and dusty, and consisted mostly of pale, fine gravel; a thin scattering of plants no more than two inches high, barely green, spread across the forlorn setting.

Now and then, a plate-tailed gecko scurried by. They hardly noticed us, and in their hurry they even ran across the toes of our boots. We came upon the new skeletons of a camel and three sheep, surrounded by a few scattered clumps of fur and wool. A hundred feet away lay the older, sun-bleached bones of a goat.

"Not an encouraging scene," I said.

Bill, stoic, shrugged and walked on.

Our altitude was just over 5,000 feet, and in the first days of the journey we expected to cross a 7,000-foot mountain pass. The altitude and high summer temperatures combined to make the air so dry that our sweat dried instantly. At night, electric blue flashes sparked when we moved our hands rapidly through the air.

Measured against the depths of geologic time, deserts are relative newcomers. Enormously powerful geomorphic and climatic processes have, over time, changed the face of the earth. The same forces that have turned areas into wet bog lands have also created dry deserts.

Among the factors that have created the great Gobi Desert is the sheer remoteness of the landlocked area. The oceanic winds that reach the Gobi travel across mountain ranges and vast expanses of land; by the time they arrive, any moisture has long since been wrung from the air, leaving only cloudless skies and dry winds that often exceed thirty miles per hour, raking the desert with the world's most hellish sand and dust storms.

In the low humidity, the sun penetrates the atmosphere and pounds the earth into a dry, listless landscape. The accumulated daytime heat then dissipates at night, dropping temperatures by as much as thirty degrees. Sculpted by sand and dust storms, the predominantly stony desert has only about 3 percent of its surface covered by sand, a fact we considered a blessing because it made our walking easier. Later on, sand would become a detested enemy.

In the first day's afternoon temperature of 94 degrees, Tom and Jerry followed quietly behind us, easily carrying their loads. Because of the absence of trees or any other shade, we used two large blue-and-white golf umbrellas, which were to become some of our most valued pieces of equipment as the weeks went by, even though any current stronger than a breeze turned them into writhing, inside-out parachutes seemingly intent on escaping from us.

At first the camels were chary of the raised umbrellas and swung their rumps away from them, trying to put as much distance as possible between themselves and the strange objects. After we grew tired of being led by camels going backward, we put the umbrellas away until we could develop a new strategy. Later, to better accustom the camels, I tried carrying a closed umbrella in my hand and opening it briefly now and then. It seemed to work; at least Tom and Jerry weren't rearing backward, trying to escape these fearful items.

Marching at a steady pace, we used the first day to accustom ourselves to the routine of leading camels in our new environment. We didn't eat a proper lunch; instead, at one- or two-hour intervals, we snacked on peanut butter–covered crackers, dried fruit, cookies, and cold chocolate drink to provide a constant flow of energy.

As the sun slid across the western sky, we neared a small group of low mountains to the south where a gully led into the interior of the bronze, steep cliffs. It looked like a place worth exploring.

"There might be water higher up the gully," Bill said. Although we had a plentiful supply, we always kept watch for wells or springs where the camels could drink to save our precious liquid. At the gully entrance we found a dry creek bed where two-foot-high green saxual, or *zag*, shrubs grew, fed by springtime snowmelt that flowed from the mountainsides. The saxual, a slow-growing gnarled shrub with woody branches, is collected by nomads for their cooking stoves and is also prized for its ability to combat bubonic plague.

Occasionally, the marmots that live along the kinder northern edge of the Gobi carry fleas that infect the stout rodents with a bacillus which causes the plague. Powered by their inherent instinct for survival, the infected marmots travel into the desert in search of the tiny saxual leaves and small twigs, which they then carry back to their burrows for their medicinal properties.

Mongolians consider marmot meat a delicacy. Thorough cooking readily kills the bacillus, but if a person (such as a curious and unsuspecting child, for instance) touches a plague-infested marmot, the disease can leap from marmot to human and cause an outbreak. When that happens, Mongolian health authorities will quarantine the area until all danger of further infection has passed. Happily, plague-related deaths are rare.

We hobbled the camels and left them to graze on the saxual twigs as we walked into the gully in search of water. Besides the wells dug by nomads, the most likely place to find natural springs in the Gobi is in crevasses close to the cliffs. Long ago, as the mountains were thrust upward, the water tables also sometimes moved upward, resulting in springs that flowed to the surface through the fractured rocks.

Deeper into the gully, we found no springs but instead discovered evidence that this place had been the wintering-over area for a nomad family. We saw round, hard-packed areas of earth where two *gers* had sat side by side. Close by, tucked into the mountainside, piles of dung indicated where sheep and goats had wintered. Farther away were piles of golf ball-size dung from camels that had lived apart from the rest of the herd. The bones of butchered animals lay in a two-foot-high pile in a rocky cleft. All signs indicated that the family had left several weeks ago, but returned every winter to take advantage of the natural shelter the gully provided from the icy blast of wind and driving snow. For us, savoring the shadow of the gully that protected us from the hot sun, it was difficult to imagine the area covered in snow and ice.

The camels were still munching happily on the saxual bushes when we emerged and began making camp close by. Their ankle hobbles prevented them from wandering far, yet gave them the freedom to graze overnight on whatever they could find. The hobbles were two padded loops that fastened around both back legs, although sometimes we hobbled them with one back leg attached to a front leg to give them even less mobility. Not only did the hobbles keep them close by so they would be easy to find the next morning, but the camels' closeness to our tent also helped prevent any roaming wolves from attacking. Because the camels had fed well, we gave each one only a small handful of maize, keeping the rest in reserve for when there would be little available food. They had already drunk their fill from a water supply on the truck they had arrived in, so they would have no need for water until the next day.

Our two-person red tent, easily seen from the air in case of emergency, was a freestanding model that anchored securely into the ground with stout pegs and was designed to withstand the anticipated high winds and dust storms. My height of five feet two inches, and Bill's of five feet five, allowed us ample room in the tent, along with plenty of space to stow our gear inside, where it would be safe from prowling nighttime scorpions and snakes.

After erecting our tent and tossing our lightweight sleeping bags inside, we prepared dinner using our one-burner propane stove. Over forty-six years and several thousand miles of trekking together, we've fine-tuned our system of packing food and gear. Everything goes into numbered nylon stuff sacks, which are each color-coded and labeled with a list of contents. These get loaded into colored duffel bags. On this trip, a food duffel bag held one week's meals. A black duffel bag contained the stove and fuel. Even in the worst of storms, the system eliminates fumbling through bags to find the right one.

Our sleeping bags had an established place, too: mine on the right, Bill's on the left. Our clothing duffel bags, one each, were placed beside the sleeping bags. Camp was set up exactly the same way, day after day, in about ten minutes. Only then did we cook dinner. Bill doesn't mind if things are all over the place, but I insist on a tidy organized camp, and he goes along with it to avoid being called sloppy.

Our diet consisted of 4,000 calories a day, but as the summer heat steadily increased, we would eat less and drink more. Our first dinner started with packaged soup of unknown origin, bought in Ulaan Baatar. The soup was followed by a large helping of rice covered with a creamy herbal sauce, to which we added dried pieces of mutton, the most common meat in Mongolia. Cheese would last for only the first few days before being reduced to an oily paste, so we ate several large pieces that first night, trying not to notice the oil that had already separated during the heat of the day. We followed this with dried fruit, mostly apples and raisins, then cookies and two cups of hot chocolate to finish the meal. Not a gourmet dinner, but high in calories and energy. For the first few nights we also enjoyed the luxury of chunks of sausage-like meat cut off two-foot-long rolls. We spread a mysterious Mongolian-made jam on our limited supply of bread, but as hard as we tried, we could never figure out what fruit it came from.

We ate our first Gobi dinner under a cloudless sky filled with stars that were brighter and larger than any we'd seen in our previous travels. In the pristine air, the stars twinkled against the inky black night and seemed so close that we were tempted to reach up to touch one. A shooting star dashed across the sky and disappeared over the horizon. A new yellow moon glided into view, and I realized this same moon would be shining down on our family and friends, far away at home. Suddenly the desert seemed not quite so lonely.

I was encouraged by the day's trek. My leg and hip, although painful, had performed well enough for me to look ahead with confidence. I was certain that if I stayed optimistic and resisted the doubts that pain can produce, I could manage the discomfort. Of course I knew I could also rely on Bill, who had never failed in his support of me as I fought to recover in time for the expedition. Our love, our bonded friendship, and our respect for each other had enabled us to surmount countless obstacles and survive danger again and again during past expeditions.

A welcome chill settled over us as the temperature dived to 42 degrees, a full 52 degrees below the daytime high. We snuggled into our warm fleece jackets.

After a final check on the camels, which were quietly grazing nearby, and a last look at the stars, overpowering in their brilliance, we climbed into our sleeping bags to spend our first night under the Gobi sky. We lay awake talking about what had gone well that day, and soon drifted off to a contented sleep. Around midnight, a lone wolf howling broke the silence. Instantly awake, we listened, aware that wolves often attack camels. Two wolves howled in reply, a long distance away, their melody rising and falling, fading and fading, and then silence.

CHAPTER 2 **SANDSTORM**

DAY 2 > At 5 AM the sun's first rays climbed above the Altai Mountains. The barren slopes glowed a deep bronze as our camp warmed after the cool night. The fragrance of sage-scented *agi*, a ground-hugging gray-green plant, drifted on a gentle breeze. Geckoes headed for their burrows to escape the oncoming heat.

We felt an invigorating energy rising from the empty plains spread beneath a big sky. There was no trace of human passage, no hint of an outside world. Here Bill and I would live by our wits, depending on ourselves as we marched toward a goal so distant that it was almost lost in our imaginations. I felt liberated, ready for whatever unknowns lay along our path.

The Mongolians had made camel loading look easy, assuring us that we just had to survive the bellowing and grumbling. In the days ahead, however, we were to learn that our confidence in our camel-handling skills was somewhat misplaced. At first we were often forced to stop and reload when something shifted or dangled out of place. It took us a few days of practice to learn how to get the water containers to sit evenly. Whenever something went awry, the offended camel would refuse to take another step until everything was comfortable again. We soon learned to take our time and get it right the first time, rather than make lengthy adjustments later.

As nomads don't name their animals, we decided to call our camels by the names of the cartoon characters Tom and Jerry. The service they provided to us was no laughing matter, though. These big, powerfully built specimens were able to carry seven hundred pounds each and walk as fast as a man. Their peculiar back-and-forth rolling gait consumed the miles with ease. Each day one camel carried the plastic water containers, which when full weighed seven hundred pounds, while the other carried equipment and food packed in canvas duffel bags—a total of three hundred pounds. The second camel also carried four gallons of emergency water. Each animal would have a heavy day followed by a rest day, carrying the lighter load.

Although we were scheduled to be resupplied by Chuluu every twenty days, we carried twenty-five days of water and food, just in case. Past expeditions in other deserts had used a long train of several camels, but we chose to use only two. That meant fewer animals to care for, but it also meant a no-frills expedition of simple supplies and lightweight equipment, and walking rather than riding.

We began the day's trek by skirting a group of three-hundred-foot-high hills that rose straight up from the flat desert. The perpetual winds had scarred their gray summits into jagged sentinels, guarding the path to a plain startling in its limitless space. A withered springtime carpet of barely green blades of thin grass covered the bleak land.

Later, as we walked ever deeper into the hostile desert, we

crossed the western boundary into the Gobi B Strictly Protected Area, a *takhi* (wild horse) refuge. Gobi B, also known as Zuungarin Gobi, is actually part of the Great Gobi Strictly Protected Area, which was created in 1975 and designated as an international Biosphere Reserve by the United Nations in 1991. The even drier part, Gobi A, or the Southern Altai Gobi Nature Reserve, lay almost two hundred miles farther east. Together they make up 20,670 square miles. Both parts differ not only in size but also in the intensity of human use. Although Gobi B is an arid area of windblown sand and rocky mountains and plains, it also contains a few water points, which encourage grazing by nomadic herds.

The previous year Bill and I had visited the site of the reintroduction of Przewalski's horse, aka *takhi*. These pale yellow horses with a distinctive black stripe became extinct in the wild in the 1960s. Drawing from a pool of only thirteen individuals, *takhi* were bred in captivity overseas. In 1992 the first group of zoo-born *takhi* were flown to Mongolia and into Gobi B, where they continue to flourish.

A murmuring breeze first sent thin wisps of white cloud skittering across the sky, then gradually hardened into a fifteen-mile-an-hour wind. Menacing dark clouds billowed above the horizon. Tom and Jerry nervously raised their heads and offered low, restless grunts. Focused on making progress, we pressed on as the rising wind increasingly blasted us with sand and grit.

Two hours later, a bank of black clouds at least fifty miles wide swept west, filling the sky all the way to the southern mountains of the Chinese border. A sudden stab of lightning, followed by the rumble of distant thunder, stopped us.

Could this have been what Chuluu had meant when he warned us of the "black days"? He had spoken of violent storms that turn a bright day into inky night, and accompanying lethal winds that can knock camels off their feet or shred a tent. They occur with the spring thaw, as rising temperatures cause a dangerous transition from frigid winter temperatures. In the year 2000, dust from one powerful Gobi storm traveled thousands of miles across China and the Pacific Ocean and into the western United States.

Momentarily mesmerized, we watched a dark wall of clouds rapidly bear down on us as a brown dust dome leapt hundreds of feet toward the sky. It was Bill who broke the spell. "Kneel the camels and use them as shelter!" he yelled over the now deafening gusts, hanging onto Jerry's lead with both hands.

But the camels had already turned their backs to the wind and gotten on their knees. Bill grabbed their tie-down stakes and tossed one to me. With the storm almost upon us, we frantically screwed the sharp stakes into the ground, beat them down with mallets, and fastened the leads to the stakes as choking dust engulfed us.

We shoved on close-fitting goggles and bandanna masks as fast as our fingers could move, but our eyes were already watering from the blasts of sand and dust. Screaming wind slammed into us. Lightning struck the earth, and thunder cracked close behind.

We dove behind the camels' humps just as the first enormous drops of wind-driven rain pelted us, stinging our backs with their force. I shoved my right arm through Tom's tie-down rope, grabbed another, and held on with all my strength to avoid being blown away. Bill, protected by Jerry, hung onto two ropes.

"Don't let go!" he shouted above the din.

I started to reply, but choked on the dust as my words were swept away.

The camels, our lifesaving anchors, were still as stone, heads close to the ground to screen out the blinding fury. They were well equipped for this weather. But we had no such natural protection, so their bodies were our only shelter.

Jagged streaks of lightning flashed, some so close we smelled the odor of burned air and earth. Sparks jumped whenever I shifted my hands on the ropes anchoring me to Tom. I was terrified. *We can't end it all here*, I thought. Time dragged and my fatigued hands began to slip from the ropes, but each time another gust hit, I dug deep and found a new surge of energy to hang on.

The constant roar of the storm blocked all thoughts except those of survival. I prayed that Bill was safe. Unable to communicate with him above the bedlam, I tried to ease forward to see him, but the angle was too great.

The rain, suffocating dust, and wind raged on, engulfing everything in its path. The gritty air rasped our bodies like sandpaper. Darkness grew as the storm moved directly overhead. Slowly the rain passed, leaving in its wake a wild dust storm that made us gasp for air.

We guessed the wind exceeded eighty miles per hour, with even stronger gusts that almost sent me flying. With gritted teeth, I managed to hang on—except when one strong gust pulled me into the air and then slammed me down on the hard earth. Gusts hit Tom too, but he was too heavy to budge.

After three hours, the wind finally let up and we staggered to our feet, shaking. Enough sand still swirled about to make each breath a challenge, but slowly the sky cleared and daylight returned. Both the camels and their loads were covered in dust, with more than two feet of coarse sand piled on the windward side of their bodies.

Sand was everywhere else too: down our necks, inside our clothes and boots, even in our pockets. The masks and goggles had helped protect us, but nevertheless our eyes were so swollen that we could hardly see. Bill had been slammed to the ground too and had skinned his elbow, and flying stones had bruised both our backs.

The camels had fared much better: Jerry was unscathed, and Tom escaped with only a shallow two-inch cut in his tough hide from a wind-driven rock. We dressed his wound with antiseptic, then wearily set up camp, shaking sand out of our clothing bags and sleeping gear. Next we tackled the camera equipment. Sand had rendered one 35mm backup camera useless, but the rest were in plastic bags that so far remained inviolate.

With the passing of the tempest, the temperature rose to a withering 93 degrees. We longed to close our painfully swollen eyes that stung cruelly in the bright light, so we decided on an early night with a cold supper.

DAY 3 > The next morning we rose with the first light, ready to make up for seven hours of lost travel. Overnight our eyes, although still sensitive to light, had improved. During breakfast, we discussed our plans. The spiraling summer temperatures were a worry. Our bodies had already adjusted to the over-90-degree heat, but days of energy-sapping exertion lay just ahead.

Bill calculated that with my injury-dictated slower pace, we should aim for fifteen-hour days of thirty miles each to keep us on schedule until the first resupply on Day 20. The mountains would slow us, but we hoped to make good time on the rolling plains. After Day 20 we would have to reduce our hours and mileage to survive the oncoming heat, which would stay consistently over 110 degrees.

We were off by 6 AM, following the dark line we had drawn on our maps. We set a compass course that led us around a looming rock ridge to a 6,000-foot pass of loose gravel that crumbled at every step. My hip and leg, which had been fairly quiet for the previous two days, screamed in protest this morning.

At the summit, shortly after catching our breath, we passed an *ovoo*, a six-foot high pyramid of stones sprinkled with offerings. *Ovoos* are found throughout Mongolia, especially in mountain passes and on hilltops. At this one, vodka bottles, bits of metal, and several pieces of blue *khadag* (silken material) fluttered in the light breeze. A *khadag* expresses the highest form of respect, and blue represents Tengger, the ancient god of the sky. It is believed that pleasing Tengger keeps storms at bay.

Chuluu, a deeply religious man, had requested that we always honor the gods. Here we followed his instructions, not only out of respect for him but also in deference to Mongolian customs. We approached from the left, walked clockwise around the pyramid three times, and then added a few stones to the heap. *Ovoos*, which date from the age of the ancient shamans, are said to summon

48

spirits to watch over travelers' safety in return for their offerings. This centuries-old shamanism seems to coexist comfortably with Tibetan Buddhism, the predominant religion of Mongolia today. Many Mongolians believe that male shamans (boo) and female shamans (udgan) can cure illnesses caused by the straying of a body's soul. The shaman also protects a family's livestock from evil spirits. The Great Sacrifice, a shamanist ceremony held on the third day of the Lunar New Year, is of major importance, especially to the older people of the steppes and desert.

The ovoo was the first sign of human life we had seen in three days. As I added two small stones to the pyramid, I thought of the generations of travelers who had passed by in this ancient land. Picking up a scrap of blue cloth, I wondered who had laid it there. Perhaps a thirsty nomad had prayed that water would not be far away. Or perhaps a herding family moving their animals had wished to soon find fresh pasture. Following Bill across the crest, I felt a new connection to the souls who lived in this harsh place.

49

Descending from the summit, our sure-footed camels smoothly stepped across the rocks, while Bill and I fought to stay upright without twisting our ankles. The task before us was deceptively simple: follow an easterly route as set by our compasses, and we should arrive at our destination in about seventy-six days. What our compasses and other navigational aids couldn't communicate, however, was the harsh reality of an environment where over many generations, only desert nomads had figured a way to survive.

I wrote our coordinates on the map, and then looked out across a trackless panorama stretching without relief. A good twenty miles distant stood two barren pyramid-shaped hills. Nothing taller than two inches grew anywhere. There was no sign of human presence, and nothing stirred. The plain appeared eerie and devoid of life, as if all had fled some pestilence.

As we walked on, however, I began to see a simple beauty in the forbidding wasteland. A mosaic of browns, tans, and blacks merged to form abstract patterns across the scorched earth. Heat waves danced under a soft blue sky. The desert has not only perils and discomforts, I realized, but also a wild splendor and a quiet mystery.

Only when a forbidding environment is accepted on its own terms, I think, is it possible to experience the allure that attracts us to it. I would remind myself of this many times in the coming weeks.

Stepping with care, we moved down the steep slope until we reached the plain. A pile of yellow-brown dirt sat slightly south of our route, marking a twenty-foot-deep well with an open top. It was almost dry. Bill lowered a worn wooden bucket on a long camel-wool rope until it reached the dirty water at the bottom. Our camels noisily slurped two buckets full and then shook their generous floppy lips in our direction.

"Gross!" Bill yelled as we wiped camel water and green saliva from our faces, resolving to duck next time.

Being sprayed was better than being spat on, of course. Camels, when annoyed, regurgitate their food and spit a foul-smelling green slime at the offender. George, one of the two camels on our Sahara expedition, would spit on us whenever he was moody, as if to show us who was boss. But he and Henry, our other camel, carried our supplies for about 4,000 miles, so what could we do but forgive him?

As we prepared to leave, we noticed an area of packed earth where a *ger* had stood. The people who lived on these western plains in winter had undoubtedly only recently moved to find more water and food. In the extreme isolation that Bill and I both felt, I was moved to place my hand where the *ger* had been, as if to contact its inhabitants.

Over time the camels would become accustomed to the golf umbrellas we carried for shade. But that afternoon, as I pulled mine from the top of Tom's load, he reared and jerked his lead from my hand. I dropped the umbrella and dove for the lead, but a panicked Tom loped off. I had no chance of catching him as I stumbled over the uneven ground, pain grabbing my injured leg.

Bill ran to my side as Tom headed south, his load of food and equipment swaying in time to his lurching gait. He paused and looked back as if to return, then continued on his way. We walked on, pretending to leave him, hoping he wouldn't abandon Jerry. Sure enough, when we were a half-mile away, he loped back to Jerry's side. I slowly approached, holding out a sweet vanilla cookie, trying not to spook him. As he took his treat, I quietly picked up his lead.

Six cookies later, we were on our way again, with Tom and Jerry walking happily behind us. For now, the offending umbrella was stowed out of sight.

Later we detected movement and puffs of dust to the southeast. We squinted into the bright glare and faintly made out a group of black-tailed gazelle, or *khar suult zeer*, as Mongolians call them. With bounding leaps they sped away, raising more miniature clouds of brown dust. We couldn't imagine what they could find to eat. All around us was only barren gravel and sandy dirt.

Soon more gazelle crossed our path, close enough for us to get a good look at their magnificent long-necked bodies, which seemed to float over the ground on their stick-thin legs. A small group watched us for a few moments until suddenly their streamlined bodies, built for instant flight, raced into blurred motion. As they streaked away, we could see why even wolves find it difficult to catch gazelle. Acceleration and blazing speed are their protection.

In the past, along with the eastern white-tailed gazelle, these athletic animals had been hunted by the thousands to feed Russian troops. Gazelle are now protected, but poaching still continues—even by the Chinese, who cross the remote southern border and then retreat undetected.

Gazelle are well suited to life in the water-deprived climate of the desert. As a rule, they do not need to drink; they obtain all their moisture from plants, preferring to eat them in the early morning, when dew may coat the vegetation. To help conserve water, their body temperature rises during the day and they do not need to perspire. They recycle urine internally, and their feces are almost completely dry. Only during the last stages of pregnancy and shortly after calving do females need to drink, and then only in meager amounts. Like all animals, they know where the occasional spring lies hidden—perhaps in crevasses at the base of the mountains.

Chuluu had told us that gazelle would be the most common large animal on our trek. "If they cross your path at right angles," he said, "you'll have good luck for the rest of your journey." Several did, but only time would tell our fortune.

Later, as we watched another group of gazelle, Bill suddenly whispered, "Wolf to the left."

Two hundred yards away, a large gray male trotted with easy strides behind an unsuspecting cluster of gazelle. He saw us and stopped. Standing motionless as only a predator can, he locked gazes with us. Then he spun and raced toward the herd, which by now had disappeared into the desert haze. He couldn't possibly catch those gazelle, but would likely make a meal of others later that day.

Gray wolves live in many parts of Mongolia. Whenever possible, they feed on gazelle, which often easily outrun them. Much easier prey are small rodents and even the rare wild Bactrian camel.

Wolves hold a lofty place in Mongolian folklore. Many Mongolians consider themselves "sons of the blue wolf," who descended from heaven and took as his wife a fallow doe. Mongolia's great leader, Genghis Khan, is thought to be a descendant of the "blue wolf." To Mongolians a wolf's tail is sacred, and seeing a wolf in January brings good luck for the entire year.

A man we met in Ulaan Baatar claimed that he and his hunting companions hunted wolves to drink their fresh blood and eat the still-warm liver. He said the practice brings good health and, of course, proves the hunter's bold spirit. We could think of many things this diet might cause, but good health and courage were not among them.

We skirted a low mountain on the sloping plain ahead, closing in on the unmarked border of the Gobi B Park. The existence of large expanses of land designated as parks in a sparsely populated country such as Mongolia, and especially a forsaken place such as the Gobi, at first seemed absurd.

But as we came to better understand the people, we realized that their closeness to nature, and indeed their dependence on nature, was an integral part of their survival. By creating parks, they attempt to protect the land and endangered species. As harsh and unforgiving as the climate is, Mongolians, especially the nomadic herders who often live on the edge of survival, have made their peace with it. If the winter snows are deep and the sweeping Siberian cold dips too low, their herds die and then the people die. They accept nature on nature's own terms. Among many other things, our journey taught us that Gobi herders could be described as true ecologists.

DAYS 4–6 > The next few days took us over a firm surface of sand mixed with gravel. One night we camped on a low ridge, a mere wrinkle on the surrounding plain. Two geckoes dashed inside our tent to take up residence. We tried to drive them away, but they darted just out of reach.

Stepping outside, I announced that I would not share the tent with a lizard. "You can't stand outside all night," Bill advised, quite sensibly. "The scorpions and spiders will get you."

Upon further reflection, I decided he was right: lizards were more acceptable tent mates than scorpions, and far better than the desert spiders, which grew to four or five inches across, with thick gray bodies and long legs that produced surprising spurts of speed and jumps of impressive distances.

Resigned, I returned to the tent and slipped into my sleeping bag, but then immediately jetted out of both. My bare feet had felt something move in the bottom of my bag! I pulled it outside and tipped it upside down. Out tumbled two gray lizards. They dove into separate holes in the earth. Bill couldn't stop laughing.

Even this early in our journey, we had become desert nomads of sorts. We packed up camp each morning, walked throughout the day, and camped again at night, always carrying our home and belongings with us, always looking ahead for the easiest route. We used our compass and maps to point the way, checking our

53

position every few hours with the GPS as we crossed arid plains that appeared devoid of any plant life.

On long treks, we've found, our sense of time evaporates with the ceaseless miles, and it's especially easy to lose track of the date. I had worked out a fail-safe solution to this problem on my solo trek to the magnetic North Pole in 1988. Immediately before taking the first step of the day, I would say the time and date aloud to Charlie, my canine companion. He really didn't care about such matters, but the verbalization imprinted the date on my mind.

Now, on this journey across the Gobi, Bill and I used the same tactic, in unison, at the start of each day. We also carried a small calendar in the back of our journals to mark off the days at bedtime. We soon understood the nomad's expansive sense of time. Appointments made on the hour seem nonsensical to a culture that tells time by darkness and daylight, and Westerners' habit of constantly checking a watch to "be on time" seems an odd, unnecessary habit.

One morning a thick veil of dust rose in the distance. A large caravan with horses and riders leading heavily loaded camels slowly approached, trooping north to summer pasture, driving ahead of them a herd of about six hundred sheep and goats. Two large black dogs ranged along the flanks of the flock, discouraging any cavorting goats from straying too far. We were excited to catch our first glimpse of the people who spend their whole lives in this forbidding landscape.

Within a half hour, our routes converged. The entire group sat astride black or dark brown Mongolian horses the size of ponies, with streaming tails and manes. The riders, who sat atop their mounts with nonchalant ease, stopped in bewilderment. Three families totaling seventeen people—six adults, six teenagers, and five children—stared in wonder at the two sweaty, dusty Westerners who were actually walking.

The flock, a flowing river of woolly white and brown animals, streamed around and past us, catching us in their dust. Eleven camels carried everything the families owned, including their dismantled *gers* and four wooden clothes dressers painted orange and red. The men and boys wore pants and shirts of subdued grays and browns, while the women and girls wore long pants fully pleated at the waist and ankle, topped with bright multicolored blouses and matching head scarves.

No one spoke English, so it was time to practice my Mongolian. *"Sain bainuu,"* I hesitantly said in greeting.

They nodded and murmured in response, then continued to stare in silence while the youngest children giggled. I couldn't tell if I had been understood, and wondered if my accent was the cause of the tittering. I looked to Bill for help, but all he could do was spread his hands wide in a gesture which clearly explained that he spoke not a word of Mongolian. I tried to remember where I had packed my Mongolian phrasebook. Why hadn't I put it in my pocket? I resolved to find it and practice every day as I walked.

Wilting under so many inscrutable stares, I plucked up the courage to plunge right in and hope for the best. Ignoring my carefully memorized prepositions and conjugations, I told them in somewhat muddled shorthand Mongolian that we were walking all the way across the Gobi. *"Bid—nar—Gobiig—yavganaar—tuulj—baigaa—yumaa."*

Obviously understanding me, they glanced at each other in disbelief. A straight-backed, gray-haired man with deep-set eyes and dark, weather-beaten skin, apparently the family patriarch, seemed particularly dumbstruck. Evidently, our plan was so outlandish that he needed time to absorb it. The group discussed our chances of reaching the other side of the desert. To their minds, "the other side" was an unimaginable distance away. After all, this is a country where the distance to a point is measured in the time it takes to get there, rather than in miles.

The Mongolians spoke to each other in clipped sentences that were difficult for me to follow, but as they rolled their eyes, shook their heads, and giggled, it was clear that they had never heard of such a crazy idea.

55

The elderly man finally spoke. Centering his gaze on me and speaking slowly, as if to a child, he said, "Mongolians travel to find water and grazing for their animals. We walk only if a horse drops dead or becomes so lame it can't go on. Why do you walk when you could ride your camels?"

I explained with increasing confidence, even using complete sentences, that due to my injuries I couldn't ride. He examined me somberly from head to toe, then gave a barely perceptible nod. Their mountain spring had run dry, he told us, and they were traveling north to find water and grazing. They expected to move three times during the summer. Later, after the first snows arrived, they would return to the southern desert for the winter.

The deeply lined faces of the adults reflected a life lived under the dry Gobi sun. As the older man spoke, a younger man nudged his horse to the front to better assess us. He gave us a friendly smile that showed gaps where teeth were missing, but he and his diminutive wife said little.

"How many animals do you have in America?" asked their oldest girl, a round-faced teenager.

"Not as many as you," I said.

It took a while for this information to sink in. In the desert, where wealth is measured by how much livestock you own, my answer wasn't impressive. A man with a moon-shaped scar across his cheek asked if we owned the camels.

"No," I said.

"Nice camels, but they aren't from around here," he commented, as he looked them over with an expert eye.

"They're from the north." My answer warranted only a slight nod. Switching topics, I asked about the weather. "Will we see many more black storms?"

He believed the weather was all up to the gods. When I told them of our storm experience, the group collectively shook their heads. "People die in those storms," the older man told us. "Very dangerous." He summoned his wife, a tiny smiling woman, from the back of the group and told her to touch our heads with a piece of blue silk to ensure our safety from storms.

She dismounted, and as she gently placed the cloth on our heads, she brushed our cheeks with her own. Then, noticing my limp, she bent to lightly touch my knee with the silk.

After the short ceremony, she remounted her steed. As they left to catch up to the flock, they all took turns saying *bayartai*, good-bye, and wishing us *sain yavaarai*, a safe journey.

In a few minutes the wife galloped back, a smile etched across her face, and spun her mount to circle us. She tossed a small amount of milk into the air from a tiny bowl—another custom to ensure safe travels. As the droplets sprinkled us, she slapped her mount's flank and galloped back toward her family. Still clutching the blue silk, she turned and waved to us. We waved back and watched until they were only specks in the distance.

CHAPTER 3 **CANYONS**

DAY 7 > On this day, as on so many others, we were out of our sleeping bags and had eaten a substantial breakfast and filled our water bottles before the crack of dawn. We led the camels back to camp, where they had been nibbling on scattered low plants. We fed them a breakfast of maize and then began to load them with our supplies. Their customary bellowing stopped as soon as both were on their feet and had received their morning cookie bribe.

After a last check of our compass and GPS, we started walking as the sun rose, turning south toward the broad shimmering sweep of the distant Takhlyn Shar Mountains. Although our other maps showed no sign of a trail, our satellite image map indicated one etched by migrating animals. Leading east through the mountain passes and canyons of barren rock, it would take us well north of the Chinese border.

Rough-hewn, reddish tan mountains blocked our way to the east, so finding that trail, just a broken thin line on the map, was crucial. Not only was it forbidden to make an unauthorized crossing of the frontier, but there was a danger of meeting smugglers, who use remote stretches of the border to travel between Mongolia and China in their illegal trade of items ranging from drugs to endangered animal parts.

In a silence made heavy by the oppressive heat, the only sound was the steady plodding of camel feet and the crunching of our own boots. A winding animal path took us through an area of two- to three-foot-high scrub. Gazelle tracks and wolf prints zigzagged back and forth, later joined by the rounded, solid hoofprints of the eight Asiatic wild asses, or *khulan*, that we would see grazing not far ahead.

Khulan, which look like the domestic donkey, can gallop at least thirty miles an hour. Having recently suffered a serious decline due to poaching for food and skins, they are now protected in Mongolia's many national parks. We kept the camels between them and us as we crept closer, but we managed to snap only a few photos before the *khulan* detected our presence and raced away, disappearing in a cloud of dust raised by their pounding hooves. Traveling through the dust of *khulan*, according to local superstition, will bring good luck for a year, so we eagerly followed, hoping that a sprinkling of the magical dust would help us along our way.

When the temperature rose to a scorching 103 degrees, I began to complain. "Wait until later, when we really begin to fry," Bill said. The picture that came to mind was not a pretty one and so, as if using the remote on a television, I switched channels to an air-conditioned room with luxurious sofas, perfect for lounging.

My thoughts of comfort were interrupted by the desert's creatures. First we saw group after group of gazelle, darting into the distant haze. Then a bunch of five *khulan* stood watching us approach, but at the last moment they sped away toward the mountains, their flying hooves beating a tattoo into the dusty earth. Just before they disappeared into the low shrubs, we caught a fleeting glimpse of two wolves traveling together.

The sight of wolves always alarmed the camels. They stopped and searched ahead for danger, heads held high and tails nervously twitching. So far no other desert species seemed to alarm them, but wolves always gained their immediate attention, and it was only after these two disappeared that Tom and Jerry resumed their easy plodding. Mongolian gray wolves typically hunt wild animals, but the domesticated herds are highly vulnerable, especially at night, when herders rely on their guard dogs to keep determined predators at bay.

Although tempted to keep walking to make good daily mileage, we stopped for two hours around midday to allow the camels to graze on the abundant bushes. Because we never knew where we would find good foliage next, we encouraged grazing at every opportunity. The camels didn't waste a minute. These efficient eating machines tore at the branches and chewed the rough wood and tiny leaves. A camel's well-hinged jaws move sideways in wide circles, and their large teeth make short work of even the thorniest of shrubs, while their strong digestive juices can take on woody branches and even dry sticks they pick up along the way.

While listening to the loud munching and the rumbling of digestive organs, we relaxed under our umbrellas, to which the camels had by now become accustomed. As Bill lay back to nap, I wrote in my journal:

> *Our surroundings are pristine and natural. No soda bottles carelessly tossed into the bushes or candy wrappers left on the trail. No sign of the dark shadow of civilization—its endless chatter, noisy contraptions, and trail of litter. Only the quiet of the desert and the sounds of animals whose forebears have inhabited these places for hundreds of years. The dust*

*beneath our feet, the mountains, and the vast blue sky could
tell us tales of simple, uncomplicated survival and death on
the plains that encircle us. The peace and serenity reaches
deep within. It seems a pity to break the spell and move on.
Here I float on a cloud of tranquility that buoys my spirits.*

My thoughts returned to the present, though, when the camels, now restless with full bellies, were ready to leave. Rising to our feet, Bill and I shook the kinks out of our muscles, picked up the camel leads, and set out, still following the narrow trail.

Suddenly Tom trumpeted loudly and came to a complete stop. He promptly sat as we inspected his load. Nothing seemed out of place, so I pulled his lead to get him going again, while Bill pushed from the rear. But all the pushing and pulling only produced more roars of defiance. He would not move until we solved his problem. Only a more detailed inspection would do.

Just as we were ready to give up, I noticed that the tip of the umbrella was positioned so that with each stride it would jab his shoulder. While I loosened his tie-down rope, Bill repositioned the offending object. Then, without a murmur, Tom rose, ready to resume the journey. The crisis was over.

An hour later, with the scrub desert behind us, we beheld in the distance a beautiful wide carpet of green grass covering several acres. As we drew closer, we saw a large herd of sheep and goats grazing along with several horses. Four *gers* stood on a low, rounded hill overlooking the herds, and we caught the glint of water in a stream no more than two feet wide, winding its gentle way across the green plain. Our weary, bloodshot eyes rejoiced at the sight. We had come across one of the water points in Gobi B. Surely there would be someone here who could give us directions to the so-far invisible trail that headed east into the mountains.

After the camels had drunk their fill from the stream with loud slurping sounds, we stepped across it and headed toward the *gers*. Several people of various ages spilled out of their houses to greet us as though we were expected. And indeed, they had been watching us for some time as we traveled through the scrub. Embarrassed by my disheveled appearance, I smoothed my rumpled shirt and brushed the dust off my hat, while Bill hastily tucked in his shirt.

An elderly woman, who turned out to be the respected grand-mother of the eleven children scampering about, told us they had noticed gazelle and *khulan* running, then saw us walking behind the dust clouds raised by the alarmed animals. Their first ques-tions were the same ones asked by the nomads we had met earlier: "Where are you going?" "Why?"

Those were followed by the comment we were to hear many times during our journey: "No one does that."

This large extended family was even more amazed at our plans than the nomads had been. After they recovered from their incre-dulity, they all burst out laughing, shaking their heads, pointing at us, and even slapping a neighbor on the back. Apparently our journey was the funniest thing they had heard of in a long time.

Theirs was the innocent laughter of unpretentious people who see things as they really are. It was impossible to take of-fense at their merriment, which held no malice or ridicule. We managed self-conscious grins, and finally, after everyone regained their composure, they became the perfect hosts. Two teenage boys took the camels to graze on the green grass, while others escorted us toward the center *ger*.

In the lifestyle of nomads, there is a right and a wrong way to do nearly everything. Religious and superstitious customs have been followed for hundreds of years, even though the origins of many practices have been forgotten. Every *ger* is set up the same way. The single doors always face south for protection from the cold winter weather, which races south across Mongolia from Siberia.

It is important to never step on the threshold of a *ger*, which, according to folklore, is to step on your host's neck. (In historical times it was a crime punishable by death for a commoner to touch the threshold of a nobleman.) Instead, you must duck your head to get through the low, shoulder-high wooden doorway, while at the same time remembering not to step on the entrance, which often has a foot-high board placed across it at ground level to keep wind and sand out. It takes practice to lift one's feet to negotiate the board while at the same time remembering to duck.

I had hoped to regain our hosts' respect by observing correct *ger* etiquette, which we had memorized before leaving home. But my dreams of an elegant entry were dashed when I hit my head on the top of the doorway with a resounding *whack*, which caused me to stumble over the board and lurch through the doorway, as out of control as any village drunk. Bill's entry, right after mine, was no less disastrous: he and the family guard dog crossed paths just as he stepped across the doorway, causing him to fall into the room as well.

Now I was lying on my side, having narrowly missed the stove, with Bill draped over me in the center of the *ger*. Not only had we both failed our first etiquette test, but we had also committed the forbidden act of stepping on the threshold. Feeling foolish, we untangled ourselves and scrambled to our feet, not knowing what to expect. The facial expressions all around us were politely noncommittal.

With a gracious wave of his hand, as if nothing unusual had happened, a soft-spoken, rake-thin older man, the family patriarch, ushered us to our places of honor on the visitors' stools. I silently vowed to restore some measure of dignity.

Tradition requires that upon entering a *ger*, the men and visitors move to the west, or left, to remain under the protection of Tengger, the sky god, while the women move to the east to be protected by the sun god. Visitors sit on tiny, very low wooden stools. The *ger*'s patriarch sits beside the visitors toward the back of the *ger*, in a sacred place called the *khoimor*, where the respected elders sit, usually on the floor. Behind them, on a dresser painted in eye-popping shades of red, yellow, and orange, sit a statue of Buddha, other religious artifacts, and ancestral photos.

On the women's side hang pots, pans, and cooking utensils, while in the male area saddles and harnesses are tucked away. Beds are pushed close to the walls. Brightly colored wooden dressers fill the remaining space, with a neatly stacked pile of suitcases stashed between them. The vivid colors represent the sun and do indeed turn the *ger* into a sunny place.

Nomads do not own any more than they absolutely need, a practice essential to families who move several times a year. Their house is just twelve feet in diameter, a fact that automatically discourages the Western habit of hoarding items "in case we need them someday."

A black iron stove, its long chimney protruding from the white canvas roof, sits in the center of the house. During storms, the chimney is lowered and a protective cover pulled across the roof opening (*tonoo*). Two wooden poles, painted orange, support the roof. A lattice-like expanding wooden framework extends all around the circular walls and is covered on the outside by a thick layer of warm felt made from sheep and camel wool, which in turn is covered by weatherproof white canvas. In the heat of summer, the lower two feet of the walls are rolled up, and the stove is sometimes moved outside. When nomads move, the expanding walls close accordion-style, ready to load onto a camel's back.

Wall hangings, often of wild sheep, cover the inside walls, while floors are carpeted. The carpets are often packed away until winter to make moving easier. Often a slab of very ripe mutton hangs just inside the doorway, which presents another challenge to those entering the *ger*. After hitting my head in the doorway, I was almost smacked in the face by a smelly slab of mutton.

We were about to experience generous hospitality in a deprived wasteland where, although the search for sustenance is an obsession, guests are always well fed. Our hostess, a tiny woman in a pale blue *del*, her features delicately beautiful, wore a radiant smile that seldom faded. She gently took my hand and squeezed it, as if to ease my concern over our unusual entry.

Turning to the stove, she tossed dried saxual twigs onto the fire. After pouring goat's milk into the pan of hot water, she added a handful of salt. Cheap black tea, sliced off a pressed-tea brick, was dropped into the mixture and stirred. With a long-handled ladle, she lifted spoonfuls high in the air and then let them drop back into the bubbling pan, explaining that this purified the tea of bad spirits. Then, with her right hand only, she handed us bowls with no handles, filled to the brim with salty tea. We in turn were careful to accept with our right hands, knowing that Mongolians consider the left hand unclean.

At first the salty tea seemed to defeat the purpose of a drink, to quench one's thirst; but in fact, it replaced valuable body salt lost due to sweating.

Moving as quietly as a shadow, the woman then mixed some goat's-milk yogurt (*tarag*) and gave us a brimming bowl. We soon learned that it was useless to ask for "only a little." A bowl must be filled to the brim to show proper respect for a visitor. The mouth-puckering *tarag* tested our taste buds to the limit, but after our undignified entry into this family's *ger*, we were determined to show that we had at least a few manners. As the sour yogurt hit my stomach, it almost came back up, but I willed it to stay down.

We were ten in number, crammed into a hot space. The merry grandmother we had first met sat opposite us, drinking tea, her twinkling eyes watching our every move. Several of our hosts' relatives had piled into the *ger* right behind us and squeezed themselves into a tight circle. We were a novelty, and they weren't about to miss anything. Feeling like zoo exhibits, we smiled as we accepted the food and drink. The audience clapped and nodded. It clearly pleased them that we consumed all that was put before us. A relaxed, jovial group, most wore traditional *dels*, their wide green waistbands showing that they belonged to the same family. There were frequent long silences, since Mongolians feel no need to fill gaps in conversation.

After an hour of drinking tea and eating a second bowl of yogurt, we were eager to leave. Sweat ran down our faces and dripped from our chins. We were close to being overwhelmed. I noted that the Mongolians, judging by their sweat-free appearance, seemed not to notice the rapidly rising temperature caused by many bodies in a cramped space.

I dislodged myself from the crowd to present our gifts of soap and salt to the grandmother, the most senior member, as custom demands. Observing the traditional approach called *zolgokh*, which a younger person must always use when interacting with an elder, I placed my hands under the grandmother's forearms and elbows, providing gentle support. After I brushed each of her cheeks with mine, I stepped back and with both hands gave her the gifts, which she in turn accepted with both hands and a wide smile that made her eyes almost disappear. After considerable bowing, smiling, and head nodding to everyone, we eased out the door, remembering not to turn our backs on the sacred altar at the back of the *ger*. Although the outside temperature was in the high 90s, we felt instant relief in the fresh air.

Asked for directions to the easterly trail, the older man pointed to two distant mountains that rose like pyramids from the southern plain. "Go to the right of the main one, and not far ahead you will see two dead sheep. The trail to the east begins there. It's narrow and faint, but don't miss it, or you'll cross the Chinese border and you might be shot. We never go there. It's trouble if the guards catch you."

After making sure we had understood the directions correctly, especially the part about being shot, we took the camel leads from the two beaming preteen boys and with a good-bye, *bayartai*, took our leave. Our hostess appeared with a bowl of milk and a ladle, and tossed milk into the air to speed us on our way. As the white drops fell to the ground, everyone wished us luck and good health. After we crossed the narrow stream, we stopped and looked back for a final wave, but everyone had already disappeared into the *gers*, no doubt to discuss the very odd couple they had just met and their even stranger journey.

This family was more fortunate than most. The stream and green grass allowed them to remain year-round. Never owning any land, herdsmen usually move several times, traveling the same traditional route their family has followed for generations. Each generation hands down vital information concerning water sources and adequate grazing. Those living close to the desert's northern edge occasionally visit a nearby village, but the nomads who live deep in the dry interior know almost nothing else but the vast baking desert.

Soon the green plain and herds of fat animals were only a memory, and we were once again traversing barren ground that unfolded toward mountains. As instructed, we kept to the right of the central mountain and scanned the surrounding area for the two dead sheep. These unusual directions seemed reasonable here, in a place where roads and signs were nonexistent. Our apprehension grew, however, when we had arrived within a mile of the mountain and still saw no sign of the sheep. "A short distance past the mountain," the man had said. We began to wonder about the wisdom of accepting estimates from nomads living in such immense spaces, who would inevitably have a different sense of distance than ours.

In a half hour we entered smooth, rounded foothills, which rose to meet a massive mountain range of jagged barren rock. We had still not found the sheep. But there was something on the ground not far ahead.

We were relieved to see that it was indeed the two dead sheep, along with a dead camel. And a faint trail nearby led into the mountains, as promised. Our satellite map showed a more easterly trail than the one etched into the dry soil, but since this was the only trail around, we determined that it must be the correct one. A lesson we had learned long ago was that maps of remote regions must be read with a certain artistic license.

A hot breeze had sprung up earlier, but there was no sign of an approaching storm. The famous Gobi wind blows most of the time and dries up what little moisture there is in the air. The sun was already close to the horizon, so rather than search for a camp spot in the mountains in the dark, we decided to erect our tent in the foothills for the night.

After securing the camels' hobbles to their back legs, we began preparing dinner on our backup stove, which required white gas. Chuluu had obtained a small supply of the scarce fuel in the capital. But as I was about to place a saucepan of water on the burner, a flash of flame erupted. Instantly the stove was on fire, with two-foot-high flames reaching for the tent walls.

I grabbed the large piece of flameproof Kevlar that always laid alongside the stove and threw it over the flames, then tossed the stove through the door. It landed several yards away from the tent. The flames quickly extinguished themselves, and an inspection of the fuel tube revealed a leak in a gasket. The stove survived its rough treatment with only a couple of dents. After Bill replaced the faulty gasket, he cautiously lit the stove, this time without mishap.

Around midnight we awoke to the sound of wolves howling close by. Our first thought was for the camels' safety. Bill unzipped the tent door and we fell into the night, still groggy from a sound sleep. The camels emitted nervous, guttural grunts a hundred yards away. Seeming to understand that we represented security, they settled down as we led them closer to the tent and tied their leads to ground stakes.

Suddenly both camels stared into the darkness from which the howls had erupted. Straining to see, we barely made out three shadowy wolf figures circling about two hundred yards away. Determined to protect our camels, we yelled and threw rocks. The wolves skirted us silently and then disappeared into the darkness. Ignoring the possibility of a scorpion visit, we dragged out our sleeping bags and spread them on top of foam pads to spend the rest of the night outside, close to the camels.

Although we awoke often to listen, the night passed peacefully. Once, long before daylight, we were awakened by a chorus of wolf song floating on the still air from the east. The wild symphony of many lupine voices grew louder as they approached, unseen, in the blackness. When they were perhaps only a hundred yards away, the voices waned, then retreated into silence. The camels had tensed up, but they relaxed after it was evident that the wolves had left and there was no longer any danger.

In the dry, dust-free air of the 36-degree night, a breeze barely whispered its way under a magnificent canopy of twinkling stars. They seemed so large and close that we might have plucked them from the sky. Almost overhead, the bright stars Vega, Altair, and Deneb formed the "navigator's triangle." The Great Square of Pegasus sat farther east, while the familiar Big Dipper stared down at us and Scorpio rose from the south. It was a magnificent sight that we will never forget.

DAY 8 > As the night slowly gave way to a gray dawn, we yawned away the cobwebs of sleep and stirred the camels. Morning chores finished, we headed southeast, confident that we were taking the right trail.

We entered a diverse kind of country, one that turned our senses on end. The barren rolling slopes soon turned to gaunt, steep canyons as the trail, which had widened somewhat, led us deeper into the Takhlyn Shar Mountains, whose jagged summits reached over 9,000 feet. The rock walls, brilliantly colored in bronze, red, and rust, allowed us no way to proceed except forward or back.

Numerous sheep, goats, cattle, and camels lay dead along the trail. There was no water, and nothing to eat. The animals had died of thirst, but we couldn't imagine why herdsmen would allow their animals, which are so vital to their existence, to wander here. We kept to the center of the trail, as if to escape the doom we saw on the sides.

The dizzyingly high canyon walls radiated heat, trapping us as the trail twisted and turned. The walls of rock gradually narrowed and became steeper and more rugged by the mile. A GPS reading, to our horror, found our position to be only the width of the canyon wall away from China. We contemplated going back, but we had traveled for hours through these hot dry canyons in temperatures that rose to 106 degrees. Turning back would be an unthinkable loss in miles and time. Trusting our intuition that the trail would turn north, we pressed on.

With anxiety stalking our every step, we rounded the next curve and were confronted by the sight of two dying camels. Their water-deprived, shrunken bodies were almost at their end. We tried driving them ahead in case we might find water later, but they stood lethargic, so weak they could barely hold their heads up. We offered them water from our supply, but they sipped only a little and turned away, already resigned to their fate.

Our camels seemed troubled. Tom nudged the shoulder of the closest one, as if in sympathy, and Jerry made soft mewling sounds. The strangers gazed back through uncomprehending, mournful eyes. As a last resort, we tied ropes to their nose pegs and attached them to Tom and Jerry, hoping they would follow. We shoved, pulled, and shouted, determined that these animals would not die, but no amount of persuasion would budge them. Tears of frustration rolled down my dusty, sweaty face, and Bill wiped his sleeve across his eyes, trying to conceal his own deep emotion.

Finally, admitting defeat, we untied the ropes. It seemed wrong to leave them to suffer, but there was nothing more we could do. I picked up Jerry's lead and followed Bill and Tom, forcing myself not to look back.

We passed more dead animals, and still the trail led us through silent rock walls. This wilderness of unyielding canyons, deprivation, and death seemed to be closing its jaws around us. I was desperate to escape. I could no longer ignore the bodies of the dead animals; I imagined their desperate search for water, their last agonizing hours. I reached up to pat Jerry's neck to reassure him that he would never go thirsty. Bill noticed my anguish and reached out his hand to me. "We have to get out of this graveyard before we go mad," he said, tears in his eyes.

But still there was no way through the high walls of sheer rock surrounding us. The heat rose to 112 degrees. Our pace slowed as moisture was sucked from our bodies. Until now the pain in my leg and hip had been manageable during the day, with more painful flare-ups over difficult terrain and at day's end, but now my entire left side throbbed in pain as I leaned even more heavily on my two trekking poles. *Will we ever find an exit from this hellhole?* I stepped to the side of the trail with Jerry to allow Bill to pass. *It might help if I follow, without the need to watch ahead for the route.* As we wordlessly changed places, Bill's discouraged countenance mirrored my thoughts.

We rounded a bend. Heads down, plodding forward like robots, we at first didn't notice that a wide-open black gravel plain stretched before us, rolling south into the desert of northern China. Then, at the sudden realization that we had at last broken free, we simultaneously punched our fists to the sky and yelled to the heavens, "Yeaaahh!" Free of the hot canyons, we luxuriated in the brush of wind on our hot skin.

After a few gulps of water to slake our thirst, I looked around and with a start saw a new problem. Motioning to Bill, I pointed, speechless, at the four-foot-high rock cairns marking the Chinese border a half-mile to the north. We were in China! The track we had followed was an animal migration trail that disappeared south into the Chinese desert.

Anxiety blossomed anew. Another animal trail before us curved north into Mongolia. With no border patrol stations close by, we were so far undetected. Water bottles hastily stowed and hearts pounding, we rushed across the roughly marked border, praying that the guards were nowhere near. In a short time we were back in the right country, but our troubles weren't over.

When we had been granted permission to cross the southern desert, the official had been explicit in his warning that even with our special permit to travel close to the Chinese frontier, we were required to stay at least a mile north of the border. "Only the border patrol has permission to travel along our frontier. The border is a no-man's-land to everyone else. If they find you crossing into China, the penalty will be severe. You'll be treated as smugglers and will suffer the consequences."

Our fatigue forgotten, we hurried along the easterly trail at the base of the mountains, just barely on the Mongolian side of the rock markers. Our bloodshot eyes searched for a way north. A mile later we rounded a sharp bend in the trail and there, a quarter mile ahead, was an alarming sight: a cluster of white concrete buildings that marked a border patrol station. Behind the station, a lookout tower stood high on the mountainside. My stomach turned to ice as Bill exclaimed, "They'll see us from that tower! No use going back."

Seeing no way out, I agreed. "All we can do is try to talk our way out of the mess we've walked into," I said, hoping that I sounded more confident than I felt. Before we left Ulaan Baatar, Chuluu had warned us that we should stay away from border patrol stations at all costs. Alarmed by the seriousness of his tone, I had asked why. He told us that as a woman, I might be assaulted by soldiers who had lived in isolation for too long, and if we mistakenly crossed the border, they might jail us. "Jails in Mongolia are places in hell," he had said ominously.

As Chuluu's words rang in my mind, I tried to bolster my confidence, wondering aloud whether a sympathetic border official would understand our mistake. "If they speak English, I'd better do the talking," Bill said. "If there's any threat, stay in the background. Remember what Chuluu told us."

A bright light flashed from the tower to signal the soldiers below, who ran out of the station to wait for us.

In a few minutes, with hearts pounding, we reached the border patrol station's tall, rusting iron gate, where two stern uniformed guards stood with revolvers drawn and pointed at us. Our finest smiles of innocence vanished as an officer strode forward with a rifle and roughly shoved it against Bill's chest. Immediately escorted into a large courtyard, we shuddered as the ominous crash of the ten-foot-high green steel gates slamming behind us echoed off the mountainsides.

A captain, in an immaculate dark navy uniform and shiny black riding boots, marched with military precision from a whitewashed cement building and informed us in perfect English that we were to be detained indefinitely. "You're obviously smugglers from China," he said, and delivered the chilling news that smugglers could be shot on sight. We suspected that he would be delighted to pull the trigger. Considering the acute scarcity of non-Chinese travelers in the region, we guessed that we were his first Caucasian victims. This was his big moment.

Two guards led our camels to an enclosure with a water trough beside a well. After we retrieved our passports from Tom's load, the soldiers escorted us to an interrogation room and left us alone there. The worrisome sound of the door being locked behind us did nothing to bolster our confidence. "At least the firing squad hasn't arrived yet," I said to Bill.

"Not funny," he mumbled.

It was a sparse, concrete-walled room with not much to look at. Two iron-framed beds covered with thin mattresses and one gray blanket each pushed against the grass-green walls. A long, narrow table sat in the center of the room, covered with a tattered plastic yellow cloth. A window, its glass painted white, cast a dull light into the depressing room, aided by a single weak bulb hanging over the table. Trapped in this tiny end-of-the-world outpost, we tried to bolster each other, but our conversation trailed off into dejected silence.

Half an hour later the officer returned. In a tone that held the power of a coiled snake ready to strike, he told us that we could not leave until his investigation was completed. Bill gave him the letter of permission we had received in Ulaan Baatar. Still standing, the captain shouted down at us that the letter did *not* give us permission to travel closer than a mile from the border. "You've broken the law and must pay a penalty—perhaps prison, or a fine, or both." Clearly meaning to intimidate us further, he tossed the letter onto the table, snatched up our passports, and left.

Soon an older woman, avoiding eye contact and ignoring my greeting, placed a flower-decorated thermos of salty tea and a bowl of fat on the table. She silently filled two bowls with tea and left. Later the officer and two guards joined us with their own tea and bowls. It looked as if we were in for a long session.

"We searched your belongings and found nothing," said the

officer. "If you're not smugglers, what are you doing here?" We told him how we had reached the border by mistake. It seemed prudent to avoid telling him we had actually crossed into China already.

We showed him our intended route on the map. After several minutes of intense scrutiny, he told us that the map was not accurate. I showed him the satellite map. "Ha," he said, "a picture from space!" He showed us the faint white line several miles north that was the indistinct trail we had missed.

Again he inspected our passports and noted our ages. "You don't look so old," he said. Then, as if to satisfy his pride and demonstrate his authority, he asked more questions that we had already answered at least twice.

When all avenues had been explored and no incriminating evidence found, he switched subjects and, as if as an afterthought, asked where we were going. My answer left him speechless. Taking a moment to compose himself, he leaned across the table and said, "You're going *where?*"

Bill repeated my answer. The officer interpreted for the guards, and their expressions clearly indicated that they thought we were crazy. The officer's mood changed. He now delivered questions in a softer tone, perhaps one more fitting for the truly insane. We explained our plans in more detail, and in the more amiable atmosphere, I carefully reminded him that because we were innocent and as his seniors, Mongolian custom required that we be shown respect. Taken aback, he gazed out the window, contemplating this latest development.

Then he sighed, as if reluctant to give up his victims, and told us there appeared to be no reason to detain us further. We would have to wait, however, while he wrote a letter of permission that would allow us to travel along the border. An hour later he returned with the letter, and in an obvious attempt to gain our good opinion of him, he reminded us that the letter gave us "a very special privilege" and that it was highly unusual to allow nonmilitary personnel to travel within the buffer zone, let alone right along the border.

He instructed us not to leave the trail, which would lead us to the next border patrol station, about sixteen miles away. We should present the letter to the officer in charge and then proceed on to Bayan Ovoo, where we would be questioned by the authorities, "who will decide what to do with you." We inquired as to what they might do with lost travelers. "It could be jail, or they might fine you." Then, as an afterthought, he added that because we were seniors, we might just be interrogated. The first two options were not reassuring, but certainly seemed preferable to being shot.

Now that it had become evident that the captain and the soldiers would do us no harm, I couldn't leave without asking a favor. Would they consider taking water to the two camels about a mile back in the canyons and leading them to safety, if we left some grain for them? There was a thoughtful pause before he nodded his agreement, then told four soldiers to carry a drum of water and two ropes in the back of a jeep and lead the camels back to the station.

I reminded him that they wouldn't budge for us. He pointed to an older guard. "He's an expert government camel handler. He knows how to make them drink. Once they take water they'll walk, and we'll feed them hay and grain here." The camels would become government property and would ferry loads between border patrol stations. Judging by the other government camels munching hay in the courtyard, any additions would be well cared for.

Shaking our hands with his iron grip, the officer thanked us profusely for our concern about the camels. The dead animals we had passed along the trail were owned by herdsmen, he said, who never ventured into the canyons to seek wandering animals. "If a herdsman is caught, his herd would be confiscated, and he could be shot without interrogation."

Advising us to watch out for smugglers, the officer directed a guard to open the gates and allow us to leave with Tom and Jerry. We departed with a huge sense of relief, not only for ourselves but also for the two abandoned camels.

Our ordeal had lasted more than five hours. It was late, but we were anxious to camp as far as possible from the border post, just in case anyone changed their mind about releasing us.

The narrow, deeply rutted trail led us east across somber black plains that stretched as far south into China as we could see. After three miles the flat plain became rolling hills, empty of human life. At the post they had told us that no one lives in the black hills because nothing grows and there is no water. That assessment seemed correct; even the moon would have more to offer than this grim landscape. As the light dimmed, we rounded a curve, the post now out of sight. A flat place about two hundred feet north of the road made a perfect tent site.

It was 10 PM before we had fed the camels and eaten dinner in a rapidly increasing wind filled with dust. Soon the blackness of another storm engulfed the moon and stars. The tent quivered, snapped, and groaned as the tempest gained strength. Gale-force winds bombarded our tent with sand and pebbles for most of a night that seemed years long. The furious flapping of the walls and the worry that a sharp pebble might rip the thin nylon at any moment made sleep impossible.

Around midnight a tie-down rope tore loose from its peg. In the howling wind we crawled on hands and knees trying to protect our bodies from the flying missiles, without much success. The tent rope flailed in the wind as if possessed, and it took a wild lunge from Bill to grab it. Thoroughly exhausted, we returned to our sleeping bags to continue an uneasy night, kept awake by the wrath of the siege around us.

CHAPTER 4 **INTERROGATIONS**

DAY 9 > Fear darkened our morning as we talked about the threat of being jailed in Bayan Ovoo. Trying to hide my worry over the mistreatment we might be subjected to in a Mongolian jail, I said nothing about my innermost fears of abuse and rape. Bill, unusually quiet, was obviously worried. As the first light seeped over the horizon, we ate an unappetizing breakfast of cereal with a liberal helping of grit that didn't help our despondent mood. We loaded the camels and headed into a dust-filled wind. The black rolling plains still surrounded us like a cloud of gloom in an abandoned world. My injured leg and hip sent messages of stabbing pain as I limped forward, doing my best to make progress.

So engrossed were we in our battle with the wind that we didn't see the vehicle approaching from China until it was almost upon us. Two men in a battered jeep rattled across the border and stopped a few feet away. The driver's door was held in place with a frayed rope, adding a rakish look to a vehicle that could have easily been at home in a junkyard.

With no hint of surprise at seeing foreigners on foot leading two camels, a young Chinese man in a dark shirt and pants—the color almost obliterated by dust—blurted out in Mongolian, "Which way to Bayan Ovoo? We're lost!" I told him he was going in the opposite direction, and Bill used our map to show him where he was. After we had warned him of the border patrol station behind us and the one ahead, he and his companion launched into a nervous, arm-waving torrent of Chinese, obviously panicked to find themselves so close to a border patrol station. Uneasiness crept down my spine. They appeared desperate to avoid authorities. I caught Bill's eye and saw a suspicion that mirrored mine: these might be smugglers bringing illegal drugs from China.

With a polite nod from Bill and a "Good luck on your trip" from me, we smiled our good-byes. Feigning ignorance of what the two men represented, we walked on without looking back. In minutes the jeep clattered off, but instead of following the track to the next border station and on to Bayan Ovoo, the only village anywhere within many miles, they charged north across roadless country, apparently seeking to escape detection.

Not wanting to meet any more suspicious types, we stepped up our pace. We even looked forward to arriving at the next border patrol station. If nothing else, it would represent safety from dubious characters like the ones we'd just met.

Around noon a gray border patrol jeep approached from the rear. It had barely screeched to a stop when two soldiers jumped out and, in a ridiculously dramatic half-crouched battle stance, pointed pistols at our heads as though facing the most desperate of criminals.

"We have permission to go to the next station," I said in a voice that wavered ever so slightly.

Cautiously, Bill eased his hand into his pocket for the letter of permission, then handed it to the soldier with the most stripes on his sleeve. There was a heavy silence as the soldier, by his puzzled expression, gave away the fact that he could not read. Trying to conceal his dilemma, he rudely tossed the letter on the ground at Bill's feet, and in a surly voice told us to go to the next station. With that they lowered their guns, scrambled back into their jeep, and drove off, leaving us in a cloud of dust. Although the incident lasted no more than five minutes, it left us wondering what else might be in store for us down the road.

"I can't wait to see the last of this blasted border," Bill exclaimed angrily as he picked up the letter, dusted it off, and shoved it back into his pocket. "Too many rude people running wild around here."

What a contrast to the gentle hospitality we had received earlier from the herdsmen and their families. As we reflected on the day's events, we concluded that the overreaction of the border guards was no doubt due to their being outnumbered by smugglers and poachers, who have no regard for borders or laws. What to do with two foreigners found walking and leading camels in a place that was meant to be off-limits to them must have been a dilemma with no ready solution.

During the next few hours, the wind gradually calmed as we scanned ahead for the border post. After twenty-four miles we had almost given up on ever finding it when we rounded a low bluff and there it was before us, overlooked by a five-hundred-foot hill topped with a cement watchtower featuring a uniformed guard with binoculars.

Bracing ourselves for the worst, we arrived at the green iron gate, where we were pleasantly surprised to meet a polite soldier who waited to take our papers. He disappeared into a white cement building with more green doors and a darker green patched roof. Green seemed to be the color of choice in this desert, perhaps because there was so little green vegetation anywhere.

The barred windows of the border station looked formidable enough. Outside the station, in a ramshackle courtyard of wind-blown sand, was an exercise area complete with weight-lifting apparatus, chin-up bars, and a long jump pit. Everything was covered in dust and sand that reached two feet high against the sides of the buildings. A few soldiers lounged outside on narrow green benches: some smoked cigarettes, but most simply stared out at the blankness surrounding them on all sides. No one looked as if they had the energy or the ambition to use the exercise equipment.

This desert post did not appear to be a place where soldiers would clamor to spend their year of compulsory military service. The dismal mistreatment of soldiers in rural military barracks had become a well-documented national scandal. Many men in the larger cities dodged their year of service by paying off officials or claiming disability, but those without the financial means to meet bribes were forced to comply.

We stood in the hot sun waiting, growing increasingly anxious that we might be detained again for questioning. Fifteen long minutes later, an officer approached us. His knee-high black riding boots displayed a state-of-the-art shine, and his uniform was perfect down to the last crease. His shoulders were military square, and his back was so straight that I could not imagine him bending, even ever so slightly.

I could hardly breathe. But miracle of miracles, everything was apparently in order. With a polite bow and salute, the officer handed us our papers and quietly reminded us that we were expected in Bayan Ovoo for further interrogation, so would we please keep to the track that would lead us there? He bid us a safe and happy journey, turned on his heel, and marched back toward the white building.

Then, as if as an afterthought, he turned and marched back to us. He looked more closely at our camels. "Would they care for water?" he asked.

"Thank you, yes," I said.

He snapped his fingers, and immediately two soldiers leapt to their feet and ran to his side. He told them to take the camels and allow them to drink all the water they wanted.

Again he snapped his fingers, and two more soldiers ran to get tea for us. One returned with the tea, and the other carried the tea bowls. The officer poured with a dramatic flourish and handed us the bowls. Then, with a bow and another salute, he once more marched away and disappeared inside the building. This man's incredible talent for showmanship was wasted in the desert.

The two soldiers hovered over us, refilling our bowls. We were experiencing roadside service beyond compare. It was quite the saltiest tea we had so far been pressed to drink, but nonetheless it felt good to chase the dust from our mouths and throats. After two bowls, I told the soldier who appeared to be in charge of pouring that we had had enough. "Only one more," he insisted. A soldier returned the camels just in time to save us from more tea. Tom and Jerry were still shaking the last drops of water from their lips as we said our final good-byes to the soldiers.

It was 8 PM and the red disk of the sun, suspended behind a veil of dust, sank toward the horizon. It was time to find a camp spot, but when we looked back and saw that we were still within range of the watchtower, we decided to travel through the brown gravel hills, till we were out of sight of the prying eyes that we knew watched our every move.

An hour later we erected our tent, thankful that the day's sixteen-hour, thirty-two-mile march was over. Taking our boots off was sheer pleasure. Fresh socks were a joy to our hot, aching feet. My leg had been screaming for relief for the past four hours, but I had ignored it as best I could until we were out of sight of the tower.

We calculated our progress. In the last nine days, we had traveled 209 miles, averaging more than twenty-three miles per day. Our one-day high of thirty-two miles kept our average up in spite of the border delays.

After we plotted our position on the maps and entered our journal notes, we ate dinner and bedded down for the sort of dreamless sleep that only true fatigue can produce.

DAY 10 > After a calm morning, the inevitable wind sprang up by noon. Dust and sand had by now penetrated everything we owned, necessitating a daily struggle to keep our camera gear clean. We couldn't keep the camera at the ready, around our necks or hanging from the camels' loads, in case a photographic moment presented itself; we had to store everything in sealed plastic bags. When changing film, to protect the exposed camera gear from the blowing sand and dust, we would crouch under a jacket thrown over our heads.

Sand was also the enemy of our tent zippers. Every day, before we took the tent down, we brushed the sand and grit from between the zipper teeth with a soft brush.

Although we checked the compass regularly and the GPS less frequently, it was the rutted vehicle track that stretched between the border and Bayan Ovoo that led us onward. The struggle to walk another six miles into the fierce dust-laden wind, knowing that at Bayan Ovoo we would face a final interrogation that could end our journey and even send us to jail, was difficult.

Bill was especially worried that we might land, as he put it, "in some dingy jail where we would be separated." That prospect weighed on my mind too. To be jailed together would be bad enough, but to be jailed separately was unthinkable.

As we walked on, Bill's mood continued to plunge. It was always more difficult for him to express his deepest thoughts when worried; his tendency was to bury them. But when he accidentally let the word "rape" drop into the conversation, I suddenly realized with a jolt what he as a husband dreaded most. Jail conditions from hell, as Chuluu had described them, were bad enough, but what might happen to his wife was worrying him unbearably.

All morning I had pushed the worst possibilities from my mind and concentrated on the positive side. After all, I told myself, the soldiers at both border stations had been nothing but businesslike. But at the sound of the word "rape," my mind froze too.

Eventually, though, I recovered my optimistic outlook and common-sense attitude, which had enabled me to successfully face down so many fears and dangers on previous expeditions. Although some officials had been harsh and unbending, I reminded Bill (and myself), the Mongolians we had so far met had been honorable people with strong Buddhist beliefs. We had received only generous hospitality at the last border post. It was also customary for Mongolians to respect people older than themselves, I noted. Deep down, I believed that even if we were jailed, we would be fairly treated because we were seniors and foreigners.

My optimistic words seemed to make us both feel better, and Bill visibly brightened. The track twisted its way east, forcing us to climb in and out of massive holes and ruts, some three feet deep. Eventually a new vehicle track branched off and paralleled the old one. Walking was easier then, as we followed the dusty ribbon cutting through the rocky desert.

Another *ovoo*, this one consisting of a few rocks and an incredible number of vodka bottles, stood close to our path. After seventy years of Russian tutelage in the art of vodka—*arkhi*—drinking it has become a necessity for Mongolians of all walks of life. Throughout the country, vodka distilleries both legal and illegal blossomed after the Russians left.

Last year, when our jeep hit a cavernous pothole during our tour of Mongolia, one of our tires disintegrated. As we stood wondering where we could find a replacement, a truck lurched through the potholes and rumbled to a stop. Four men tumbled out of the cramped cab and, after a short discussion, decided to travel twenty miles to a village and return with a new tire.

But first, a bottle of vodka appeared. The men sat on the

ground in a tight circle and passed a silver cup around as each took a sip. A half hour later the short ceremony was over, and they sped back to town and returned with the promised tire. After installing it, they again sat in a circle and shared another bottle of the fiery liquid. An hour later, as the last drops were consumed, the men, who by now were in a very happy state of mind, shook our hands, gave us pieces of dried meat, and drove off. We later learned that many Mongolian men carry a bottle of vodka and a silver cup in a cloth bag, always ready for a special occasion that can arise on the slightest whim.

A short time after passing the *ovoo*, we found a well only three feet deep, with just a few inches of water at the bottom. We could see all manner of indescribable filth floating on the surface. Sensing water, Tom and Jerry pressed forward with moans of pleasure, bending their long necks and drinking as if the water were the sweetest in existence.

"They'll shake that stuff all over us when they come up for air," Bill warned. I beat a hasty retreat and Bill followed just in time as the two heads came up and shook vigorously, casting a vast shower in all directions and just missing us.

Overall, Tom and Jerry were faring well. So far they had been watered at reasonable intervals, and the food they'd found in the scrub desert and the green oasis had been more than enough to sustain them, when supplemented with their nightly ration of maize.

Soon Bayan Ovoo came into view. The small community of about three hundred people was overlooked by the usual frontier-lookout hill topped with a cement tower. Situated in the province, or *aimag*, of Gov-Altai, the town is the administrative center of its district, or *suum*. Many *suums* make up each *aimag*, and there are twenty-one *aimags* all together. They are overseen by the democratically elected president, who also heads the country's national government, known as the Khural.

A closer inspection revealed Bayan Ovoo to be a dismal place dominated by crumbling Soviet concrete buildings well on their way to oblivion. The coal-blackened smokestack of the town's power plant towered above a silent, closed-down building that no longer produced power. On the edge of town sat an open water well, overflowing, surrounded by a wide variety of broken bottles and unusable buckets. The danger of a child or animal falling into a coverless well seemed to be of no concern to anyone. A few scruffy, roughly shorn young camels drank noisily from puddles as we passed.

Four soldiers in full uniform, complete with knee-high riding boots, dug a ditch in the hot sun. One dug in slow motion, while another pointed to where the shovel should go. The remaining two offered advice but seemed to have opposing opinions. Wholly absorbed, they appeared not to notice us as we walked by.

We asked another soldier, who was smoking a cigarette as he leaned on a low fence that went nowhere, for directions to the government headquarters. Without turning to look at us, he raised a heat-weary hand to point toward a large building on the other side of town. Reflecting on the contrast between these bored soldiers and the lively desert nomads we'd met previously, we surmised that most normal, active young Mongolian men, many of whom were nomadic animal herders before their compulsory service, likely found the relative inactivity of military life mind-numbing and tedious.

Dust-covered, tired, and hungry, we walked across what passed for the town square, artfully dodging the deep holes that had been dug there, the purpose of which escaped us entirely. We passed a cluster of tiny shops. While Bill held the camel leads, I looked inside a shop that I thought might sell bread. The shelves were almost bare, with no bread in sight. Then I spied some chocolate bars, but by then my unwashed foreign appearance was attracting curious stares. I hastily retreated, and we continued along the dusty potholed street.

The entire town looked as if it were about to disappear under a blanket of dust and sand. After the wide-open, uninhabited space we had traveled through these past ten days, the village seemed crowded and noisy.

The concrete government headquarters building did nothing to lift our spirits. It was dirty white, drab, and depressing, with large chunks of surface plaster peeling off the sides. A broken window shutter hung at an acute angle, held on by a single rusty hinge. Steel bars covered the windows. Privacy wouldn't be a problem, since it was impossible to see through the dirt covering the window glass.

We tied Tom and Jerry to a hitching post outside the main entrance to the building. "Well, here goes," Bill said.

We steeled ourselves as he pushed open the faded green door, which opened into a small plain room where a serious, heavyset man with well-oiled hair, probably in his thirties, sat behind a bare desk. Unsmiling, he motioned us to enter and silently waved a chubby hand holding a cigarette toward two high-backed wooden chairs. "Sit down, we've been expecting you," he said in heavily accented English, frowning his disapproval. "You are the people who walked into illegal territory. Explain yourself."

Bill and I both realized that we had slammed into an un-yielding wall of leftover Soviet bureaucracy. Bill began in a voice that was remarkably calm, given how worried he was. He told the official of the trouble we'd had finding the right track through the mountains.

"Yes, I've heard your excuse from the border patrol," the official interrupted abruptly. Then, pointing an accusing finger at me, he demanded my explanation.

"We made a mistake and went too far south," I told him in a voice that I hoped didn't betray my nervousness. The official stood and, without explanation, left the room.

Bill and I looked at each other in dismay. As we restlessly waited on the hard chairs, I looked around the room. Its dreariness was the perfect complement to our interrogator's bad manners. The walls had been painted a dark green many years ago, judging by the flaked paint and the numerous brown stains.

An ancient steam radiator sat in the corner, presumably waiting to ward off the polar cold that would sweep across the desert in winter. The floor was uneven, and loose boards creaked with each step. An old typewriter whose keys were yellowed with age sat on a small gray metal table beside the official's brown wooden desk. The only worthwhile furniture in the entire room was the comfortable padded chair behind the desk.

Suddenly the first official, followed by a thin sullen man, entered the room. The official sat behind his desk, leaned on his elbows, and stared at us with obvious contempt, while the other man, who perched on the corner of the desk, silently contemplated us. Finally, the first official seemed to complete his assessment of us: two hapless beings who were nothing more than an inconvenience to his orderly life. He told us in English that it was five o'clock and time to close the office. We would have to return tomorrow at 7 AM

I asked where we could camp safely overnight.

"You are both our prisoners, and you will stay overnight behind the building in a fenced area with a soldier on guard," he said in a tone that suggested that talking to us was a boring exercise completely beneath his dignity.

Bill asked about the camels.

The official now spoke condescendingly, as if talking to a child who has no ability to understand anything. "A soldier will take them to the well for water, and they will stay in a safe enclosure and will be fed native hay overnight." We had never heard of native hay, but assumed Tom and Jerry would know what it was.

With the night's arrangements made, the first man summoned two soldiers and told them to show us where to put our tent. He ordered two others to take care of the camels after we had unloaded our camping gear. Then both officials promptly disappeared. We assumed their day at the office was over. To have to wait until the next day to learn our fate was a crushing blow, but there was nothing else we could do.

The dry patch of sand and dirt behind the building was at least shielded from prying eyes, but it was also littered with empty food cans, a worn-out gray tarpaulin, and no less than thirty-three empty vodka bottles. We set to work to clear a space for our tent, with help from the friendly soldiers, who seemed to enjoy the task. After setting up camp, we climbed into the tent and zipped the door flap, glad to get away from people. At that moment, the loneliness of the desert seemed very inviting. "When we get back to the desert and start complaining of being the only people within miles, let's remember this place, and we will be cured of loneliness forever," I said to Bill.

We had no water to wash with and didn't want to venture out to the well, so we stayed in the tent and ate a dinner of dried fruit, cookies, and beef jerky. In our sleeping bags, we cautiously peeked through a tiny slit we had left open in the door zipper. Twenty feet away, two guards were smoking cigarettes, sitting on a wooden bench alongside the fence that enclosed us. We felt a small measure of comfort. Although we were prisoners, at least the town drunks wouldn't bother us overnight. Judging by the number of vodka bottles we had had to move when clearing our campsite, there was no shortage of habitual drinkers nearby.

The night passed peacefully enough, although sleep didn't come easily. We heard guards coming and going throughout the night as each duo ended their shift. Now and then they walked close to the tent, as if checking to make sure we were still there. We cleared our throats to make a recognizable sound, seeking to assure them that they weren't guarding an empty tent.

In a whispered conversation, we went over the story of our misadventures along the border in case we were questioned separately in the morning. Although our innocence should have been obvious, we were worried about the two official characters who were in charge of our fate. Their contemptuous attitude toward us didn't seem to bode well.

But in the end, I decided to give up worrying. "We know we

arrived at the border by mistake. All we can do is tell our story and hope they can be reasonable," I said to Bill.

"A good sleep will get us ready for tomorrow," he wisely replied. And so ended our tenth day in the Gobi.

DAY 11 > As dawn prowled across the village, we ate a breakfast of dried fruit and cookies, then headed for the well so we could wash up before the whole town came to watch us. Our two guards nodded permission when I told them where we were going. We crossed the deserted town square and, after choosing the cleanest bucket among the many scattered about, pulled clean water from the well. In the early morning chill the cold water stung our faces, hands, and arms. After all of our visible skin looked clean, we brushed our teeth and combed our hair with my comb, which was the only one we had.

Our clothes were still dusty, but they would have to do. At least we didn't look as bad as the two vagrants we'd resembled when we arrived yesterday. Now it was close to eight o'clock, and the town was awakening. Three joyful women approached the well, deep in conversation, wearing bright blue *dels* and carrying water buckets. An inebriated young man, his eyes glazed, staggered and wove his way to the same destination.

It was time to head for the green door of the government building. My heart beat a wild tattoo, and the slight tremor of Bill's hand revealed his own nervousness as he gave the door an inquiring push. It opened, and in we went to face our future.

The two men, who never told us their names, were already waiting for us in the same positions we had last seen them. Apparently they were to be our judge and jury. Bill and I sat in the same two chairs as before, and the interrogation began. First one, then the other, asked the same questions with slight variations.

"How did you lose your way?"

"How did you get to the border?"

"Where are you going?"

91

"Do you have relatives in Mongolia?"

And of course, the usual "Why are you walking across the desert?"

At one stage, the chubby official rose from his chair, walked around his desk, pushed his fleshy face two inches from mine, and yelled as if I were totally deaf, "You are both smugglers and deserve to be shot!"

I stared straight ahead, despite a surge of irritation that I barely held in check.

Bill was his next victim. "Give me one good reason why we should not shoot you now," he demanded.

Bill, his jaw set in anger, said firmly, "Because we're not smugglers."

Unable to hold back any longer, I interjected. "We're not smugglers, and you know that, because we have nothing in our papers or belongings that could possibly prove that we're smugglers."

Taken by surprise, the chubby man stepped back. But in a moment he regained his composure and yelled at me, "Be quiet, woman!"

That did it! He wasn't getting away with a remark like that. I stood, and with my hands on my hips to further demonstrate my indignation, I yelled back at him, "We're not smugglers, and you know it! If you don't know it by now, then you're stupid. We're much older than you. Your disrespect to innocent elders brings shame to you and Mongolia."

The official's brown face flushed red with anger. Now I was unstoppable! "If you must speak at all, make sure you show manners and respect."

Completely taken off guard by my attack, the official retreated to safety behind his desk, stammering something I couldn't understand. The thinner man jumped to his feet and led his compatriot to a far corner, where they whispered in earnest conversation. Then the whispering stopped and the angry official returned to his desk, staring at us, his jaw set with contempt as he fought to regain control of his emotions. The thinner man, who seemed to be the boss, asked in a friendly voice, carefully choosing his words, "Tell us again how you reached the border."

"No," replied Bill. "You've already heard the story from both of us."

With a sigh, the man turned to me and repeated his question, apparently determined to find some incriminating evidence, no matter how trivial, to report to headquarters. His Soviet training had turned him into a relentless interrogator.

I firmly repeated Bill's answer and added, for good measure now that we seemed to be gaining ground, "Your countrymen would be ashamed if they knew of the rudeness in this office."

Embarrassed, he switched tactics and asked if we had seen any sign of smugglers. We told them about the two suspicious men we had met. With this news the arrogance of the man behind the desk evaporated, and he said in a measured, polite voice, as if trying to gain our good opinion of him, "We have too many smugglers crossing our border. They're dangerous if someone sees them. People get shot."

The thinner man emphatically nodded his agreement. They asked for a description of the men and their vehicle.

The change of subject took the heat off us. Both men, now friendly, continued to express concern about our safety should we encounter more smugglers. At least we were making progress.

Two hours after our interrogation began, the chubby man stepped to an inside door, opened it, and called to a woman. She timidly appeared with tea and a bowl of *aaruul*, or pieces of dried milk curd, and we were invited to eat and drink.

I asked if we were free to leave. The disquieting reply was "Your punishment hasn't been decided." Without another word, the two left the room.

The sad-faced tiny woman, dressed in a gray *del*, kept filling our tea bowls and urging us to eat a generous amount of the rock-hard *aaruul*. Considering our delicate predicament, we made a valiant effort to drink two bowls of tea just to please her. We did our best with the *aaruul*, which was old and sour and would have challenged a sharp ax.

When she determined that our little tea party was over, the woman sighed as if her day had been quite ruined by our lack of enthusiasm. She then silently gathered her utensils and glided from the room.

A half hour later, the men returned. They had reached a decision. I held my breath, praying that we wouldn't have to go to jail. After seating himself at his desk, the first man, with elaborate theatrical movements, lit a cigarette. He knew that the two foreigners seated before him were at his mercy, and he prolonged every enjoyable moment of the drama. Only after his cigarette was lit, and after he had taken several long draws and sat back to send a cloud of smoke all the way to the ceiling, did he give us his decision, carefully enunciating each word as if English were a foreign language to us.

"We have reached the conclusion that you innocently traveled to the border and meant no harm. There will be no jail and no fine. You are free to go."

He sat back to take in our reaction.

I was so relieved I could have kissed him. We were finally rid of the overwhelming worry that had shadowed us ever since we had first been detained.

We both thanked him profusely. He warned us again about smugglers and told us that if we were approached again, we should do as we had done here. "Be friendly and act like innocent tourists who know nothing of smuggling."

He summoned the soldiers, who promptly returned our camels, well fed and watered. We stuffed our overnight gear into the camel bags, and with polite good-byes and handshakes all around we headed resolutely out of town, barely resisting the urge to break into a run. The interrogation had lasted three harrowing hours.

Just before rounding the corner of one of the station's empty cement buildings, its bulk sagging and ready to crumble into the dust, we looked back and saw our two officials still standing where we had left them. They enthusiastically returned our waves.

Then we turned the corner, and our ordeal was over. Joyous freedom was ours! Our first reaction was to whoop in celebration, but our route led past the lookout tower. A soldier looked down from his five-hundred-foot perch, following us with binoculars. We were two bugs under a microscope. Self-consciously, I ducked under Tom's neck so that his body shielded me from prying eyes, while Bill did the same with Jerry.

The border patrol stations and their watchtowers had been built by the Soviets and were welcomed by the Mongolians, who, due to a history of Chinese repression and cruelty, still view China with uneasiness and suspicion. The looming towers lent an uncomfortable "Big Brother is watching you" feeling to the border, but ironically, if the massive armies of China ever choose to attack, Mongolia's scattered border stations and few soldiers will provide no significant defense.

CHAPTER 5 **WILDLIFE**

Our need to avoid as much of the summer heat as possible didn't allow for rest days. Our midmorning start from Bayan Ovoo on Day 11 forced us to push hard to maintain our daily mileage. To the north lay the towering Aj Bogd Range, its highest peak—the 12,470-foot Khuren Tovon—still capped with snow, a vivid contrast to the shimmering heat of the desert floor that reached 102 degrees by noon. The range's rocky spine rose from stark flanks that formed a barrier between the desert and the northern steppes.

Ahead lay an immense plain covered with tennis ball–sized gray and rust-red rocks, barren except for an occasional thirsty saxual bush struggling for life. Not a scrap of shade was in sight. The unbroken view stretched all the way to a range of mountains that appeared as mere bumps against the sky on an otherwise empty horizon. Numerous drainage chasms, now dry, wound their way down from the Aj Bogd peaks to cross our path. The washes were filled with boulders that had been carried there by violent torrents of spring snowmelt from the high peaks.

We scrambled along, leading our unhappy camels through narrow gaps between the boulders. Then Tom stopped abruptly at the edge of a thirty-foot-deep gully and refused to budge. Camels are afraid of steep downhill slopes, where their lack of agility can break a leg. I pulled his lead and urged him into the channel, but he braced his front legs and bellowed an indignant protest. He would not move ahead, and he would not change his mind. Bill, trying to lead an equally reluctant Jerry, whose bellows easily outdid Tom's, said, "We'd better try different tactics, or we'll stay here forever."

Changing strategy, we paralleled the ravine for half a mile before finding a place where Tom agreed to cross, followed by a nervous Jerry. The need to scramble through boulders increased the pain in my leg to agonizing levels. I gritted my teeth and leaned heavily on my two poles, knowing that somewhere ahead the terrain must level out.

Incredibly, we saw a lake shimmering invitingly in the distance, with a large square building to one side that reminded Bill of an airplane hangar; but we knew better than to get excited. It was a mirage, an optical illusion. On hot, calm days in the desert, when light waves descend to strike a thin layer of intensely heated air close to the ground, they then bend upward into the denser air above. The image we saw on the desert floor was really a reflection of the blue sky, the irregularities creating the appearance of the lake and the building. Later, distant mountains seemed to float above the horizon.

After hours of fighting through rocks, Bill stumbled and landed heavily on his right leg. He yelled out a description of our path in the most graphic of terms but eventually resumed his hike, limping along with a deeply bruised thigh. Our collective pain was accompanied by a weariness that demanded attention. To rest, however, would mean that we would eventually have to begin the agony of movement all over again. It seemed easier to simply continue. I offered a trekking pole to Bill, but he refused it: "You need it more than I do." We were walking wounded, with no place to stop until this appalling rocky plain lay behind us.

Midafternoon found us in a level area of black and gray pebbles. To describe our surroundings as grim would be an understatement. The route was parched and seemingly empty of life. As the blistering sun marched across the sky, heat waves pranced above the wasteland.

Supporting myself on one leg, I tried to imagine what it was going to take out of me to complete this expedition. Although I had a passionate resolve to finish, the pain in my hip and leg was intense, and it was becoming increasingly difficult to push the doubts away. My body was strong, but did I have the mental fortitude to fight the pain, which had been increasing by the hour all day? How much more could I take? Tears stung my eyes. I was close to the end of my physical and emotional tether.

But then I looked across at Bill. I knew he was struggling with his own injury, but he was not complaining. *Damn it*, I thought, *I'm not giving up.* And on I struggled, concentrating on each step and reminding myself of my fifty-year-old dream. Somehow I would finish this journey, one step at a time, tears and all.

Bill was concerned about the stress of my injury too. But his philosophy of "When it gets tough, you just go faster and get it over and done with" helped me, just as it had in past expeditions. At times I petitioned for a slightly more manageable speed; at five foot two, my short legs sometimes made it difficult to keep up. But Bill occasionally protested that "when you get cranked up, you never stop to rest." Then it was his turn to appeal for a rest stop.

As in our many past expeditions together, Bill's determined speed and my storehouse of stamina made a good match. We urged each other on, combining our separate strengths into a well-oiled trekking machine with rare complaints.

And so the sun crept toward the horizon. The prospect of a cool evening, dinner under the stars, and rest, especially rest, spurred us on. The craggy mountains to the north glowed a burnished copper in the setting sun. A rising wind stalked the desolation, driving sand at our ankles as we entered the Southern Altai Gobi Nature Reserve, more commonly known as Gobi A. The reserve unfolded like a wrinkled blanket all the way to the eastern horizon and south across the Chinese border and beyond, interrupted by a few mountains and valleys.

Finally the last rays of the sun were reduced to a subsiding flame. "Let's camp," said Bill, whose usual springy step was now an anguished limp. "We've walked far enough for today."

After the tent was up, we hobbled Tom and Jerry, fed them their grain and cookies, lit our stove and cooked dinner, and then tended to ourselves. What a treat it was to sit and nurse our injuries! We longed for ice to reduce the swelling, but that of course was only a dream. Instead, we took pain pills and massaged each other's legs until the muscles relaxed, then rubbed them with anti-inflammatory lotion.

Although our capacity for end-of-day revival would continue undiminished, the daily sweltering exertion gradually took its toll on our bodies' reserves, weakening our mental fortitude ever so slightly. Each day's start was a little more difficult, the miles ahead seemingly longer. Instead of an early start, we would muse, how luxurious it would be to dawdle over breakfast, or even to listen to the sly inner voice telling us to take a day of rest in camp, to do nothing except eat and sleep.

Whenever we felt our resolve waning, we would remind each other that the heat was increasing, that the only way to avoid the summer's furnace was to reach our still-distant destination as soon as possible. Our determination to keep on schedule early in the expedition would pay off later in our trek, when we expected temperatures to rise above 120 degrees; we would be forced to slow down then just to survive. At all costs, we had to avoid the mental trap of losing focus and taking extra and longer rest periods. Many potentially successful expeditions fail because stressed-out participants become emotionally paralyzed after they lose the discipline to stay on schedule.

In other aspects of the journey, we were doing well. The everyday chores of loading, unloading, and feeding camels, making camp, cooking, and walking had smoothed out into rituals. Minor glitches had been solved, and the camels had also grown used to the daily routine.

After dinner in the cool twilight, as we wrote in our journals, intuition urged me to turn around. I was just in time to see Jerry reaching into the cookie bag that Bill had left open. Treats were disappearing at an astonishing rate. I grabbed the bag and shooed Jerry away, but he merely stood there pursing his floppy lips, in expectation of another chance. Only after he watched me put the bag inside the tent did he turn away with a grunt of disappointment, joining Tom in searching the bleak surroundings for food.

By now, Tom and Jerry were like big pets to us. They enjoyed having their ears scratched; they would press their heads into our hands, close their eyes, and drift into camel bliss. If we stopped too soon, their ear-splitting bellow would compel us to restart the process. They stood patiently while we inspected their footpads twice a day for wear and tear.

We learned never to leave camp until their loads were balanced. At the slightest annoyance, they would sit on the ground with roars of protest and refuse to move for two hours or more, until everything passed the camel test of complete comfort. Tom was particularly fussy when he carried the water. The sloshing of a half-empty container made him jittery, so we always loaded it toward the back, far from his sensitive ears.

The daytime Gobi A is a fragile place where rainstorms can

be years apart, and it is so hot and windy that few dare to live there. The lingering dusk always brought relief, though, when the desert cooled and the light softened. On this night, the sky gradually darkened into shades of violet as the first stars twinkled. Our camp was suffused with a quiet, reflective peace as we finished our journal entries.

Darkness sent us to our sleeping bags to rest and heal for an early start. I snuggled deep into my bed, happy in the knowledge that all we had to do for the next few hours was sink into blissful sleep. The torment of heat and the need to put one foot in front of the other was gone. In the gentle quiet of a cool desert night, it felt good to be alone. As we fell asleep, the single melodious cry of a distant wolf cut through the silence of the night.

DAYS 12–13 > Over the first twelve days we had gradually become one with the desert. Although the sand, dust, heat, and storms would remain a threat to our existence, we felt the desert's innermost character growing on us. Under its tough exterior, we sensed fragility and complexity. The desert's wildlife—shy, endangered, and rare—has a will to live that is beyond human capability. As our understanding of the desert increased, we naturally surrendered ourselves to the environment. It wasn't a matter of losing our identities to the setting, but rather of unconsciously making the adjustments that would allow us to survive.

To maintain a course that would take us through the heart of the Gobi, we followed the border as it plunged south. Our view of China revealed stark, lonely plains that stretched to distant mountains.

It was now the first week of June, with temperatures consistently over 100 degrees. Nights were in the high 60s. A steady wind had blown most of the previous night, and by morning the air was thick with dust. Bill's bruised leg was less painful, with little swelling, and although I still hobbled, my leg had greatly improved with rest. We expected easier walking over flat and rolling terrain for the next few days.

Following our usual careful check for scorpions and snakes outside our door, we greeted another sunrise. At times we felt overrun by the crawling pests that were becoming an increasing problem. We dared not leave our boots or any clothing outside at night, and when we broke camp and took down our tent, we always inspected the underside of its floor. Scorpions could hide underneath, hang on, get packed up, and then strike us with their venomous tails when we erected the tent the next night. Although usually not deadly, their strike is often painful and causes serious swelling.

Just as I stuffed the tent into its bag, a quick strike to my left hand from an overlooked scorpion sent a hot pain shooting into my hand and wrist. I let out a shocked cry as I grabbed my upper arm and squeezed to stop the poison from traveling. The tissues of my lower arm swelled and throbbed as I stared in disbelief. How could this have happened? We had been so careful.

With my left arm useless, Bill finished loading while I figured out how I was going to hold a trekking pole. I tried to make my fingers cooperate, but it was no use; they wouldn't close around the pole handle, so I would have to use my right pole only. It was a challenging start to the day, but there was little else to do except set out and hope that my arm would soon recover. The pain and swelling increased with the day's temperature and subsided somewhat at sunset. The scorpions weren't finished with us yet, however.

That evening Bill put on his fleece jacket to guard against the night chill and took over the main job of setting up camp while I rested my throbbing arm. Suddenly, with a loud curse, he tore off his jacket and grabbed his shoulder as he doubled over in pain. Four scorpions fell to the ground and scurried away. After a quick inspection of his back for more creatures, I helped him into the tent. He collapsed, groaning, across his sleeping bag. Swelling traveled from four puncture wounds across his shoulder. Immediately, to stop the spread of poison, I kneaded the unaffected tissue with my good hand. He lay back in agony, propped against my rolled-up sleeping bag, but soon shivered with chills and complained of a severe headache. I helped him into his bag and spread mine over the top. Then, with my good hand, I fumbled to get the stove going to heat water for soup. Too nauseous to eat, he said in a tired voice, "I don't think it would stay down."

Even in Ulaan Baatar, we hadn't been able to get an educated answer to our question about whether Gobi scorpions were deadly or just poisonous enough to cause illness and swelling. In my research at home, however, I had discovered that only a few of the numerous scorpion species could kill or even cause complications. Most strikes lead to only localized pain, as I had experienced in my arm. But I had only one sting, while Bill had four.

Sitting beside him, holding his hand and offering words of encouragement, I was desperately worried. When I had inquired at the capital's hospital about procuring antivenin just in case of a bite, our inquiry had met with blank looks, and we were told that none was available. Now as I watched Bill suffer with no way to reach help, I felt a cold stab of fear for his safety. I silently prayed that his body would overcome the onslaught. In the dark desert night, our isolation was even more evident, and my worry deepened.

Helpless, I sat beside him, going over in my mind all the possibilities for rescue. Our situation looked grim. Chuluu was our only hope, but if Bill continued to worsen, Chuluu might be too late. Hoping that everything might look more optimistic in the daylight, I did my best to sleep, but it was useless. Instead, I sat at Bill's side until, three hours later around 11 PM, his chills slowly subsided. Later, in a stronger voice, he told me, "I think the worst has passed. I'm not as cold and shaky."

I lit the stove, and this time the offered soup was accepted. By 3 AM the chills were gone, leaving Bill with an aching shoulder and arm. When I was sure he was stable, I reclaimed my sleeping bag, and we both slept sporadically until daylight.

DAY 14 > In the early morning light Bill appeared pale, but apart from the lingering severe pain, he had shaken off most of the effects of his scorpion encounter. Support from an improvised arm sling helped reduce his discomfort somewhat. From then on, our inspection of the tent, our gear, and our clothing before packing each morning verged on the paranoid. At night nothing went into the tent until it had been thoroughly inspected for wildlife.

In the mornings we often found large spiders clinging to the outside tent fabric. We theorized that these long-legged creatures sought warmth in the cold desert nights, and found our little red haven perfect for their needs. Snakes were not as numerous, but now and then one slithered by. I, in particular, disliked these sorts of visitors. Facing 1,000-pound polar bears on my solo journey to the magnetic North Pole was one thing, but dealing with thick-bodied gray spiders, scorpions, and snakes was entirely too much.

Bill, on the other hand, claimed to get a kick out of chasing "the things" away. My response was a heavy sigh that spoke volumes about my opinion of his definition of fun. Early on we had learned that Mongolians believe it acceptable to scare off these unwanted visitors, but never to kill them. Their Buddhist beliefs allowed them to kill animals for meat, but not other creatures—including scorpions, even if they entered a *ger*.

We learned this one day when standing outside a *ger* talking to a herdsman. Feeling a scorpion bearing down on his bare ankle with its venomous tail raised to strike, Bill scraped it off with his pocketknife and dispatched it with a quick stamp of his heel. With a gasp of horror, the man covered his face with his callused hands. We stared, confused and puzzled as to which point of etiquette we had breached.

Finally regaining his composure, the man tearfully explained that the scorpion could have been a reincarnated relative, per-haps even his mother. Bill, thoroughly embarrassed, apologized profusely, after which we appeared to have been forgiven. But it was evident that a gap existed between our cultures. We vowed to never repeat our mistake. Thou shalt not kill even the tiny creatures of the desert.

Breaking camp and loading the camels was a challenge given the fact that we each had only one good arm to do the job. It was 9 AM, three hours later, before we set out, greeted by a moderate wind that kicked up dust to whirl around us. To the north stood the impressive, rugged flanks of 8,839-foot Atas Bogd; although we were at 4,000 feet, the day had already warmed to 101 degrees. The immense, pebble-strewn rolling plain was burned with a dark "desert tan" caused by the blister-ing sun beating down on exposed rock.

Since the 1980s, due to many drought-filled years, the Gobi Desert has become increasingly arid. We had already traveled through areas that had not seen rain in the last two or three years. In earlier days, summertime travelers in this region would have found some natural springs to quench their thirst, but our route contained no water points. The underground water is drying up, and springs now occur only in a few small oases, usually in the mountains.

With no likelihood of fresh water until we met up with Chu-luu again, we watered the camels from our supply. They turned away satisfied after five gallons each. Their weight was holding well and their humps were firm, which indicated sufficient water. Although the food available in the desert had at times been des-perately sparse, we had come upon enough vegetation here and there, combined with the grain Chuluu had brought for them, to keep them sufficiently well fed.

By 10 AM Bill called a halt to rest his throbbing shoulder. Rather than hunker down under our umbrellas, we put up the tent so we could have a more complete rest. Using one arm each, it was a clumsy but comical effort. We finally succeeded, although some of the anchors were barely driven into the ground.

It was too hot for sleeping bags, so we stretched out on the bare floor. In an effort to ignore the rising heat, my thoughts drifted back to when I had decided, at the age of thirteen, to walk across the Gobi. New Zealand has no hot, dry deserts; therefore, they existed only in my imagination. It wasn't until after Bill and I visited Needles, the small town on the edge of California's Mojave Desert where Bill had spent his childhood, that I understood the full meaning of a desert.

In spite of temperatures exceeding 100 degrees, I fell in love with the generous spaces and plant life. Cactus flowers were my favorite. Snakes did not enchant me, however; New Zealand has none, and when I first saw a rattlesnake, I decided that in spite of my intense love of animals, I would have to relegate snakes to my short list of creatures that I could never love.

Around 1 PM I stopped, speechless, shielding my eyes as I strained to see the improbable creature ahead.

"A Gobi bear?" whispered Bill, unbelieving.

Time stopped. We stared, rooted to the spot. The hunched brown form loped on all fours, nose close to the ground, only two hundred yards away. As it crossed our route, the bear suddenly stood on its hind legs to face us, his black nose raised to catch our scent. Standing, he was about three feet high; we guessed he weighed around two hundred pounds. We stared at each other, two species gathering information.

Then, having apparently determined that we were not bears, he dropped to the ground and in alarm ran with a peculiar, rolling gait down a dip in the plain. His chocolate brown coat rippled as he vanished into the haze in the direction of the Shar Khulst oasis, north of our route. Along with an oasis within the Tsaagan Bogd Mountains, it is the last known refuge of the Gobi bear.

The world's only desert bear and one of the earth's most endangered species, the Gobi bear lives in the Gobi A reserve. No one knows exactly how many remain, but most reports quote precariously low numbers, somewhere around thirty-five. Even so, poachers kill the Gobi bear, known locally as *mazaalai*, for its gallbladder.

The bear we saw was most likely traveling to the oasis to find water and its favorite food, wild rhubarb, which in addition to wild onions, grasses, and rodents make up its diet. Living a solitary life, Gobi bears hibernate in the winter. Because they are seldom studied, even the most basic information such as reproductive age, litter size, and denning habits remain a mystery. The bears' continued existence is tenuous due to sparse food sources, poaching, and the severe summer and winter climate.

Although we had read about these bears, they are so rare that we never thought we would see one. We watched long after the little animal disappeared, as if watching might bring him back. It was with the most incredible luck that we were in the right place just as he crossed our path.

We approached the spot where the bear had been. There on the ground sat a cup-sized pile of warm, dark-colored dung. Paw prints showed in a sandy space between the pebbles. Traveling upwind from us, the bear hadn't sensed our presence until he saw us. We touched the prints as if touching the bear. I traced their outline with my finger. Our daily mileage goal was forgotten. Reluctant to lose contact and knowing that the bear would not return, we lingered just in case.

Bill wondered if we could follow its tracks and perhaps see it again. But we realized that tracking animals in the baked landscape was best left to those reared in the desert. With more than a thousand miles still to travel, we forced ourselves to continue east. For the next hour we talked of nothing else, the heat and discomfort forgotten in the excitement of our unexpected encounter, one of the highlights of our journey.

By 2 PM the thermometer read 111 degrees. We pulled our umbrellas from the top of Tom's load, hoping their shade would take the edge off the sun's burning rays as we walked. Heat waves danced above the ground, teasing us with more mirage lakes. The changing shapes of mountains floated on the horizon.

The raw heat of the unmerciful sun reflected from the surrounding pebble plain. Our shirts were salt-encrusted, sweat dried instantly in the dry air, and our feet felt as though we walked on burning coals.

Although we spent much of our time in the desert just struggling to exist, the wide-open spaces with horizons sweeping to a vast sky gave us a sense of belonging. When we began the journey, the desert had seemed empty. Now we noticed little things that earlier would have passed unnoticed. An oddly shaped rock, a tiny sliver of struggling vegetation, a dancing distant mirage, and the deep blue of the sky all gained our attention. Details were no longer insignificant. They were what made the desert, and in our passage we had become part of it.

Our boots crunched in the gravel as we walked in silence. The dust-choked wind had died earlier, but we could see that another storm was tormenting the desert three miles ahead. Suddenly a dust devil developed in the midst of a four-hundred-foot-high wall of swirling brown dust, then broke away and whirled with incredible speed as it turned and traveled straight at us, gathering even more sand and dust. The spout was at least two hundred feet across, tapering to a few feet at its base, and looked like the tornado in *The Wizard of Oz*. Pebbles, sand, and dirt were being sucked straight up the tall column.

We grabbed the camels' leads to couch them. They sat obediently, and we closed our umbrellas just as the seething, twisting shaft abruptly swerved to rush past, its edge lashing us with flying grit. A half-mile away, the spout's power diminished and slowly sank to earth just as, to the east, the colossal wall of dust dissipated as quickly as it had formed.

Later, Bill called a halt and pointed to Tom's foot. Close inspection revealed a cut front pad. Camels are tough, but any injury in such a remote place was serious. If Tom became disabled, it would be impossible for Jerry to carry a double load.

Happily, the two-inch gash was shallow. I cleaned the wound with soapy antiseptic and then packed the cut with iodine-soaked gauze. I padded the entire foot with strong nylon bandages for protection against the sharp rocks, and we held our breath as Tom took a few steps. So far there was no sign of a limp.

By late afternoon a gale-force wind blasted us with shrapnel-like grit, forcing us to wear masks and goggles. Sand slowly filled our boots, turning our socks into sandpaper. With each step, we felt our sweaty skin rubbing raw. Still three hours from camp, we stopped to change into fresh socks to prevent blisters. On reenergized feet we walked on, determined not to cut the day short.

By 7 PM we had reached the limit of our pain tolerance and made camp. Bill's shoulder and my arm, although improving by the hour, were still uncomfortable, and my hip and leg pleaded for a halt. Over the last two hours my pace had slowed, even with a double dose of painkillers. In spite of the rough walking surfaces, our feet were surviving the abuse due to well-padded socks.

Several times we checked Tom's bandage, and still he showed no sign of a limp. We tied him to his stake, and after a double ration of grain and cookies, he had no need to forage. Jerry wandered a short distance looking for food, but kept looking back as though expecting Tom to follow. Rather than go too far from his leader, he returned to Tom's side and nudged the cookie sack expectantly. At first we resisted, but then gave in. After an extra helping of grain and cookies, he settled down for the night at Tom's side, both of them contentedly chewing their cuds.

We erected our red tent, which provided the only splash of bright color on the dark plain. Just as Bill shoved the last tent anchor into the ground, three camels approached from the south. Surprised to see them roaming free in such a desolate place, we noted that they seemed different from our camels. Their more slender bodies were topped by two humps that were more conical and much smaller than Tom's and Jerry's, and their shedding wool was gray-brown instead of the dark brown of the domestic Bactrian camel.

Still some distance off, the skittish animals veered away

when they noticed us. They galloped southeast into China and were soon dots on the horizon, moving more gracefully and faster than our camels. Then it dawned on us. These were wild Bactrian camels, or *khavtgai*, reputed to inhabit the Gobi A reserve and the adjacent northern Chinese desert.

The Gobi A reserve is the last haven for the Mongolian wild Bactrian camel. It is believed that no more than 350 exist in the reserve, which made our sighting all the more extraordinary. Poaching by both Chinese and Mongolians, as well as wolf predation and insufficient water and forage, have caused the rapid decline of this extraordinary mammal, which is the main reason Gobi A was created. Ever decreasing water supplies force wild camels to adjust to drinking salt water from occasional saline lakes by the time they reach two years old. Females mature at four to five years and normally calve only every other year, after a thirteen- to fourteen-month gestation period, which makes conservation even more difficult. The resiliency of these endangered camels, which enables them to survive against all odds, is one of the wonders of the animal kingdom.

First the Gobi bear, and now the rare and equally endangered wild Bactrian camel! We were ecstatic. In our new excitement, we forgot the day's torture to our bodies. Over bowls of rice, we celebrated our incredible luck to have encountered two endangered species in one day.

The day's heat silently passed as the sunset streaked the sky yellow and red. After dinner, we sat outside the tent to enjoy the cooler temperatures. Relaxing and allowing our thoughts to drift without the need to concentrate on navigation was a luxury. Surrounded as we were by a landscape that had remained unchanged for centuries, I tried to imagine what it must have been like when the first nomads saw this vast place. It most likely looked then just as it did to us, but with larger populations of camels and bears.

Later we noticed five camels, again approaching from the south. Bill figured they would run off just as the first three had, but I wasn't so sure. Bolder than the first group, they kept on toward us. Tom was already staked; just in case these wild camels meant trouble, we also staked Jerry.

Earlier we had asked Tom and Jerry's owners about what we should do if we met an aggressive wild bull. Batbaatar thought it doubtful that we would meet any, but if troubled by other camels, he advised us to yell, jump up and down, and wave our arms. If they didn't leave, we should run straight at them, throwing rocks and yelling. The spectacle of the two of us shouting and leaping in front of a large, angry camel almost overwhelmed our imaginations.

But this group meant business, particularly the bull in the lead. The bull trotted and roared ahead of his harem, bellowing his annoyance at our invasion of his territory. Tom and Jerry faced him, giving forth nervous grunts. Defenseless and without retreat as an option, we quickly gathered rocks into a pile beside the tent. The bull was now only two hundred feet away, still roaring through yellow teeth. Green slime dripped from his mouth. Gray wool trailed from his shaggy sides. He was a sight out of a horror movie.

Then Bill, remembering Batbaatar's advice, shouted and swung his one good arm. I followed suit, adding a few soprano shrieks as we threw rocks as fast as we could pick them up.

The bull paused. His harem caught up as he silently watched, probably amazed at our bizarre performance. A large specimen, he looked enormous to two anxious humans. Cautious now, he took a few more determined paces toward us. Now sheer desperation improved our aim, and a few rocks hit him with a whack. After one rock found its mark squarely between his eyes, he spun and, with his harem close behind, galloped away without a backward glance.

We kept up the racket for a few more minutes, but had to stop when our voices gave out. The wild camels faded into the deepening dusk, and our pounding hearts slowed. Tom and Jerry, who had been terrified, now stood quietly. Our throats were raw from shouting. Only a short time ago, we had been excited to see these rare animals. Now we hoped we could leave the area without having any more encounters with them.

The excitement of sighting rare species made sleep come slowly, but later we drifted off. The desert hush didn't stay long, however. We awoke to a deep gurgling sound coming from outside.

Bill woke and mumbled, "What in the world is that?"

Investigation found Tom and Jerry still regurgitating and chewing their cud. The astonishing noises came from within their large intestinal tracts, where all those complex digestive processes take place. We returned to our sleeping bags, but for the next two hours the sleep-depriving clamor reverberated around us. Even ducking our heads beneath our fleece jackets didn't diminish the racket.

Finally, out of desperation, we stuffed our ears with white cotton from the first aid kit. The tactic was only partially successful. The two culprits happily chewed on, completely oblivious to our tossing and turning.

CHAPTER 6 **SILENCE**

DAY 15 > Leaving Atas Bogd Mountain behind, we looked ahead to a flat, featureless expanse that stretched hypnotically onward. Although it was well within the Gobi A region, we found it to be even more sun-baked than Gobi B—hardly a place to lift the spirits.

Our camel Jerry was the only one who had escaped from our journey unscathed so far. Bill's shoulder and my arm had recovered from the bites, although our scorpion paranoia remained. Tom's cut, which was healing nicely, was protected by foam padding cut to the shape of his foot and bandaged securely. To help my leg, I used two trekking poles all the time now, even around camp. It was impossible to ignore the pain. To keep the light of optimism burning, I thought often of the sheer exhilaration I would experience on the last steps of the journey.

The tactics we pulled from our strategy bag to ease the miles included singing duets in our tuneless voices, counting steps, telling stories, and planning future adventures. Sometimes we walked side by side, discussing the route and making navigation decisions. At other times we followed one behind the other in silence, deep in our own thoughts, each taking a turn to lead. Other than a small New Testament each, as on all other expeditions we carried no music or reading material. The uninterrupted sounds of nature, even if that meant complete silence, were important to us. The absence of outside distractions caused us to immerse ourselves fully in our environment, which meant that we were ready to respond instantly to any emergency that might arise. Rather than reading books at night, we used the time to sleep.

Occasionally a photo opportunity arose—whenever we saw something we needed for Adventure Classroom. Often a stop was preceded by one of us saying, "The kids need to see this."

By ten o'clock the temperature had risen to a sweltering 106 degrees. At noon, a light breeze grew into a hot ferocious wind that by 2 PM propelled a monstrous brown wall of dust toward us, obscuring the route ahead. This signaled a fast-approaching dust storm that our wind meter registered at more than fifty miles per hour. We were quickly engulfed by the towering wall and a brownout, and had only our compass needle to show us the way. Leaning into the wind, which at times sent us staggering, we struggled through the flying sand. Soon battered and done in, we couched the camels and sheltered behind them.

Gradually the gusts lessened enough to begin the race to erect the tent before the next one hit. In windstorms we used a foolproof system to keep the tent from blowing away. Attached to one corner was a three-foot-long lightweight blue rope with an anchor on the other end. Even before the tent was out of its bag, we pulled the rope out and drove the anchor into the ground. If a gust were to rip the tent from our hands, the anchor would hold.

Although the wind had grown more manageable, the gusts were still strong enough that one of us had to hold down the flapping fabric while the other crawled on hands and knees to pound in the anchor pegs. A powerful gust dumped me on the ground, knocking my goggles askew. I scrambled up in time to see Bill grasping a knee that had been struck by a flying pebble. After we tied the camels to their ground stakes close to the tent, and without unpacking, we dove through the tent door, swept in by a liberal blast of sand.

The tent had been erected at a certain cost to our bodies. The flying pebbles left bruises on our arms and backs, and my eyes watered painfully from lacerations that, although minor, left me temporarily blinded in my right eye. Only when I squinted could I see at all. Bill hadn't fared any better. An ugly black bruise welled up on his right arm, and his sand-scratched eyes watered badly.

We worried about what we could not see. Out in the open with no protection whatsoever, we were trapped, barely sheltered in this huge expanse of empty desert. Was this to be another "black storm," and how long would it last? Even more troubling, how much more battering could the tent take? And if the tent tore away, what were our chances of survival? Trapped within the margins of a tiny cocoon about six feet in diameter, and separated from the elements by thin nylon, we were completely cut off from the world. In spite of our injuries, we had managed to stay on schedule, but now could we meet Chuluu on time? Looking at my watch every few minutes was no help either. Past storms had taught us that patience made waiting easier. Finally casting frustration aside, I settled back to wait.

Dejected by the delay, Bill agreed. "We might as well sleep while we wait," he suggested.

In some ways, desert storms are worse than snowstorms. Breathing can be limited or even nonexistent in the suffocating sand and dust. The lighter dust is often carried thousands of feet into the air to completely blot out the sun. In contrast, the heavier sand rises in a thick layer only a few feet off the ground and races across the surface. In storms, our heads were often engulfed in dust while our feet disappeared in a moving carpet of sand.

It was dark before the wind slowed enough for us to rouse the two still-loaded camels. Their loads had almost disappeared beneath sand that had drifted over the top of their bodies. As they lumbered awkwardly to their feet, we could barely detect our duffel bags and other equipment under the thick layer of coarse grit. Days ago we had reconciled ourselves to having our equipment and clothes impregnated with dust and sand, and we'd given up the fight to keep our food and gear grit-free as well. It proved easier to get along with the stuff than to fight it.

By the time everything was shaken out, it was 10 PM: too late to light a stove and cook the usual dinner. While the camels munched their maize and cookies, we slipped into our gritty sleeping bags and ate handfuls of dried fruit. Outside, the desert was quiet, as if nothing out of the ordinary had happened.

DAY 16 > After four hours of sleep, we loaded the camels in the dark and set out. We lengthened our strides and picked up our pace, aiming to make up as many miles as possible so we would be able to meet Chuluu in four days. Sleep had improved our eyes somewhat, but later in the white glare they watered even behind our darkest sunglasses.

We saw a border patrol station marked on our map and steered clear of it. Although our letter of permission allowed us to travel along the border, in light of Chuluu's warning we thought it best to avoid the stations and the inevitable questions of the military personnel there.

Close by lay the mud-brick ruins of one of the many Buddhist monasteries that were pillaged and destroyed during the Soviet occupation. It was hard to fathom why the Soviets' political machine would slaughter innocent monks in a place so remote. A cloak of sadness shrouded us as we imagined the terror and suffering of the monks' last days. The waste of human life and of buildings painstakingly created by devoted hands was impossible to comprehend.

At an altitude of around 4,000 feet, we walked on with Tom and Jerry calmly following, their loads swaying from side to side. Later, in the heated air, a "dust devil" rose from the ground and danced across our path to whirl away into the far distance, followed by others a hundred feet high that twisted, turned, and glided as they vanished silently into the sky or sank into the earth one by one. One momentarily engulfed us, as if to tease, then swept harmlessly by. Two twisted and turned together, perhaps dancing to unheard music. Throughout central Asia, legend has it that lost souls take up their home within the "dust devils" in their search for the rest and peace that never comes.

That evening, as the day's light waned and the breeze fell away, the lingering blue of the clear sky quietly faded into the approaching darkness, bringing welcome relief from the day's heat. To make up for lost time we continued into the night, our path illuminated by the moon, its light dimmed by dust. There were no reference points except for the dark outline of distant mountains sculpted into the horizon. Loneliness and the extreme inaccessibility of the place were exaggerated in the bottomless silence of the dark night. Home, family, and friends seemed impossibly far away, existing at the far edge of my imagination. In silence we walked onward through the stillness, our footsteps and those of Tom and Jerry the only sounds to break the hush.

We hadn't planned to walk at night until later in the expedition, when our route would take us farther from the border and the danger of meeting smugglers, and when rising daytime temperatures would force us to seek night's coolness. But tonight would serve as a dress rehearsal for times to come.

Bill tripped over an unseen object and looked back to see a camel skeleton. "Some poor creature didn't make it," he said. We stopped for a closer look to see if we could identify it as a wild Bactrian camel, but the lack of light made it impossible to tell. Stumbling over death in the dark intensified the uneasiness that we felt about the night. Even in daylight, we never got used to finding skeletons and could never pass one without wondering about the poor animal's final suffering.

The compass needle guiding our way was pointing to a distant lone peak that seemed to never get closer no matter how much we stepped up the pace. The more we aimed for the peak, the more it tormented us. I noted the slow passage of time by my watch. Earlier, we had set midnight as a time to stop and get a few hours of sleep before moving on at daylight. But as fatigue set in, our steps slowed. A few snakes slithered by, and the scorpions and lizards were out hunting in full force.

The long hours of walking induced higher levels of pain in my leg and especially my hip, forcing me to drop back a few paces. Bill stopped, waiting for me to catch up, and passed me some beef jerky. "A pick-me-up," he said as he chewed on a large piece. The salted beef tasted good. At home we never eat salt, but in the sweaty heat we craved it. Side by side we walked on, and still that lone peak seemed no closer.

Fatigue settled into every joint and muscle of our bodies. At ten o'clock we stopped. Should we go on, or should we camp here? Although weary, we agreed that we should walk until midnight if at all possible.

As time went on, we both arrived at a place somewhere beyond mere fatigue. To ignore the pain, I allowed my thoughts to wander without any particular direction. I leaned a little more heavily on my trekking poles and plodded on beside Bill. After what seemed like an endless amount of time, midnight finally arrived. Our lone peak was definitely closer.

Slowly, exhaustion dictating our pace, we erected the tent, hobbled and fed the camels, and gave them three cookies each instead of the usual one, to reward them for their outstanding stamina during the marathon of a twenty-hour day. Too tired to cook, we ate another quick meal of dried fruit. Our navigation calculations read thirty-seven miles for the day, which made up for most of the miles lost in the dust storm.

I wrote in my journal by the yellow light of a flashlight, "Although I can't walk at my usual pace, I'm fast enough so that I'm not dropping us behind schedule. The main thing is that I keep going. Bill's patience is a boost."

We slept as though dead until dawn inched its way over the horizon.

DAYS 17–20 > The next few days were a blur of walking through heat, wind, and dust. Sometimes the idea of crossing this desert seemed more like fantasy than reality as we fought to stay on schedule. To the far north, brick-red peaks glowed in the setting sun, their starkness accentuated by the deepening shadows of night.

At 5 AM on Day 20 the alarm clock, which had become our enemy many days before, rang with its usual noisy clatter. Obeying its jingle, we dragged ourselves out of our sleeping bags. Tom and Jerry's louder-than-usual vocal complaints during loading were no doubt protests of the unrelenting pace of these last few days. As for us, the mental image of the tomatoes Chuluu had promised to bring spurred us along.

At midmorning another windstorm blew in with incredible speed, dust blotting out the sky, but to our relief it disappeared just as fast as it had arrived. Nevertheless, we kept up a relentless pace until encountering an area of sandy mounds where in places we sank to our boot tops. The camels, with their specially adapted footpads, remained on the surface and weren't affected at all by the soft sand, while we floundered through the loose yellow patches.

A mile or two later, the route became easier when the sand gave way to firm gravel. A salty bog that was once a miniature lake, no more than fifty feet wide and only inches deep, lay along our path. The water had dried, leaving a sticky mud crusted with white salt crystals, a condition commonly found in severely dry deserts. Evaporation greatly exceeds the insignificant rainfall, allowing minerals to gather on the surface. Even more minerals move upward by capillary action through the rocks and soils to reach the surface, resulting in water too salty to drink and leaving the surrounding surface covered in salt crystals. In many areas, salt water is all that is available to animals such as wild Bactrian camels.

Throughout the day we took few breaks and enforced a swift pace, determined to meet Chuluu at seven o'clock at our prearranged GPS position. Aided by a welcome twenty-mile-per-hour tailwind and our navigation gear, we arrived with an hour to spare. We had covered 535 miles, for a daily average of almost 27 miles!

Choosing a landing strip long enough, with no protruding rocks, was our first job. We tossed aside a few baseball-sized rocks and, after determining that the strip was safe, marked the ends with six-foot-square pieces of orange-red fabric and anchored them to the ground with rocks.

On one side we set up our tent and spread our green sleeping bags on the ground to make the strip as visible as possible from the air. Smoking flares would indicate the wind direction, important to ensure a safe landing. We staked the camels a quarter mile away so they would not be frightened and try to run away from the noisy plane.

After one last check that everything was in order, we emptied our boots of sand and sat back to watch the horizon for the first sign of the plane. In our excitement and impatience for Chuluu to arrive, we could barely sit still.

I felt victorious. Our plans included the possibility that we could abandon the trek and fly out with Chuluu if my injury proved too much. But on Day 20 we had arrived on schedule, and I was confident that I could at least make the next leg of the journey to the next resupply. In his unselfish way Bill had left the decision entirely to me, even though if I had to quit early he would also leave the desert, and all the miles he had walked would be wasted. So this was my decision: Tomorrow we would trek on.

Just after 7 PM we heard a plane, then saw it coming straight at us out of the glare of a clear sky. We each held a flare high in the air to signal the ten-mile-per-hour wind and its direction. After circling twice to inspect the landing area, Chuluu descended and taxied close to the tent, sending a cloud of dust into the air with the propeller wash. As soon as possible, he shut down the engine to prevent the blowing dust from damaging it.

The camels took the sudden appearance of the plane calmly, with only a hint of anxiety. Chuluu jumped out and we met in a giant triple embrace, then all began to talk at once. Finally settling into a more organized conversation, we first of all established that Bill and I would trek onward tomorrow. Then we began the task of unloading.

First, the camel water in a sturdy plastic drum. As soon as Bill took the lid off, Jerry plunged his head in and drank, while Tom stood patiently to one side as if by prior arrangement. Because we had walked for days without any sign of water, we had given them the last of their supply two days ago.

After Jerry had filled himself to capacity, Tom stepped forward and, for some reason known only to him, dunked his head entirely into the water, completely submerging it. When he came up for air he shook his head, sending a great shower of water over us. Only after he had completed this strange ritual did he consent to drink his fill. Chuluu looked on, puzzled by this peculiar, uncamel-like behavior. "Perhaps he thinks he's a fish."

With the camels' water needs attended to, we unloaded our new supplies. In addition to our usual food rations, stove fuel, and full water containers, Chuluu took out two huge sacks of fresh-cut green steppe grass for the camels that he had cut himself. We lay half a sack in front of them, and with grunts and other assorted sounds of joy, they set to work to consume the lot. A new bag of camel cookies and another two bags of ground maize completed the resupply for the camels and us.

After we loaded the sealed bags of exposed film, garbage sacks, and empty water containers onto the plane, Chuluu handed us a large box. In it were tomatoes, a loaf of fresh bread, a special

123

dessert of pastries, and a large bottle of fruit juice. We barely resisted consuming the lot on the spot, so delighted were we to see
such delicacies, but we managed to hold on to our good manners. Chuluu also gave us the news of the outside world, which
reassured us that there was still a world out there. At times our
solitary walk through empty space left us wondering if the world
had disappeared and left us behind.

Finally, it was time for Chuluu to go. There were last farewell
hugs all around, and then he took off on a northerly bearing to
visit his family on the green northern plains. As we watched him
disappear into the distant blue sky, Bill remarked, "That's the way
to travel across a desert." But flying could never give us a sense of
belonging, the feel of the earth, or the experience of a nomadic
desert dweller's life.

The hour was late, so we camped overnight at the landing
strip. The camels happily munched their grass, and we ate what
felt like a dinner fit for royalty. On this special night, paying no
attention to the order in which the courses "should" be eaten, we
began with the tomatoes, followed by generous helpings of bread
and jam. Then, in total ecstasy, we devoured all the pastries—
because, we assured each other, they would have been ruined in
the heat of the next day. Unaccustomed to such rich food, our
stomachs became a little queasy, but the ten hours of sound sleep
that followed refreshed our sleep-deprived bodies.

DAYS 21–28 > Over the next few days, the shimmering heat rose
to 113 degrees. We crossed the border into an *aimag* called Om-
nogov, meaning "South Gobi." After assessing the risks, we decided to continue along the border rather than follow our original
plan of heading northeast to the Gurvansaikhan National Park
before swinging south to meet Chuluu for our second resupply.
The struggle to navigate through the park's mountains—more
than 7,000 feet high—and its 4,000-foot-high passes, combined
with the daily energy-sapping temperatures, would have placed
too much stress on Tom and Jerry.

The five-million-acre Gurvansaikhan National Park, established in 1994, is one of Mongolia's most recently established parks. A national treasure, the park contains dinosaur fossils, mountains, and spectacular sand dunes, and its valleys and mountains make up the eastern end of the Altai Mountain Range. According to legend, Gurvansaikhan, which means "the Three Beauties," was so named because there was once a rich man with three beautiful daughters who were intent upon marrying three poor herdsmen. The girls' father forbade them to marry the men of their choice, and in their terrible sadness they ran away into the desert, where they remain to this day as the three ridges called the Three Beauties.

The park was created to protect the endangered wild animals that live there, but competition for food from domestic herds has made the preservation of the wild animals a tenuous proposition. Snow leopards live in the park's remote mountains, where they and their fellow predators the wolves hunt mountain sheep. But as in all of Mongolia's reserves and parks, there are no marked boundaries and no money to pay people to patrol the vast areas to prevent poaching and overgrazing.

Bill and I reminisced about our previous year's journey throughout Mongolia, when we had driven our jeep into the park's interior. There, mountains surround a green, fertile plateau as high as 8,000 feet, and spectacular sand dunes tower five hundred feet above herds of sheep and goats. About sixty miles long and fifteen miles wide, these dunes are known as the Khongoryn Els, or the Singing Sands. After driving the length of the dunes, we had doubled back to find a little-known primitive trail that cut north to south to connect with another track that would lead us west. Although tourists never travel this route, a local herdsman assured us that he often took the shortcut.

The dunes' shifting sands are unpredictable, however; that year the way was blocked by deep, soft sand, and we were soon mired in it up to the axles. Leaving the jeep surrounded by advancing large black dung beetles, we walked two miles back to find a herdsman who, we had earlier noticed, owned a tractor. He eagerly agreed to pull our jeep to safety. Two hours and one mile later, after a lot of heavy pulling by the grumbling tractor and a lot of energetic pushing by several locals who enthusiastically joined in, the soft sand released us to a firmer surface.

Of course, success meant the traditional vodka ceremony. Bill and I were invited to join the circle of Mongolians sitting on the ground in the tractor's meager shade to share vodka from the silver cup owned by the tractor driver. It was a casual affair, with no one expressing any need to hurry. Finally, an hour later, with slaps on the back and handshakes from these delightful people, we rattled and bounced away on a firm track that was far more suitable for camels than for a jeep.

Now, as we reminisced deep in the southern Gobi, we spoke with fondness of our cheerful tractor friend and his helpers. Our memories of the park's green plateau and fat animals contrasted sharply with the ocean of aridity and wretched deprivation that we now trekked through.

Ahead lay a short sandy zone where the sun reflected back to us in skin-scorching waves, even though we traveled with our shirtsleeves pulled down. A camel and three goats lay dead alongside a salt-encrusted bog, from which they had probably tried to drink salty water in desperation. Even a minor mistake in such a land can bring the torture of a lingering death from thirst.

Next we came to a dilapidated dry well and a round, packed-down area—ghostly evidence that a ger had once stood there amid the scattered bones of butchered animals. The dead animals we had seen earlier had probably belonged to the ger's owners, who might not have moved to a new water supply soon enough to prevent some of their animals from dying of thirst. It seemed unimaginable that people could live in such deserted surroundings, where all life forms seemed to have fled the dreadful heat and the only sound was the forlorn murmuring of a low wind.

As we entered some low hills, I suggested that we climb to the top so that we could see the route ahead. From the summit, we gazed upon another astounding void—an endless brown smudge that stretched eastward in utmost desolation for a discouraging distance that I dared not contemplate. The enormity of the task that faced us staggered belief and was almost too much to take in all at once.

Bill apparently felt the same. After a silence heavy with disbelief, he spoke tactfully. "I think it's best that we stay low and see the route a bit at a time. This huge chunk is too much." As we descended, I silently thanked him for not telling me what he really thought of my idea.

In the later hours of the afternoon, we took a meandering route through the southern foothills of the Tsagaan Bogd Mountains, their imposing dark rock summits reaching over 8,000 feet. To follow the flattest terrain, we traveled as far south as possible without crossing into China. Although the mountains are reputed to be another Gobi bear refuge, we saw no sign of any.

On Day 27, we took a half day of rest. My leg had taken a brutal beating in a sandy area and needed rest before we tackled the many miles of washes descending from the Gurvansaikhan Mountains. Although our southerly route along the border would enable us to avoid the worst, we were somewhat apprehensive after our experience negotiating the mountain washes east of Bayan Ovoo, where we had been detained for interrogation.

The luxury of relaxation would not be wasted. After eating our dinner at noon, we lay across our sleeping bags and slept soundly until the night-chilled air crept across our tiny home at 8 PM Wrapped in our fleece jackets, we sat outside enjoying the lingering 57-degree twilight, a drop of fifty-six degrees from the afternoon high of 113. The wildly fluctuating temperatures, although rejuvenating at night, were an additional test to our bodies. In the coolness, we caught up on our journal notes and ate another meal as darkness filled the sky.

After another eight hours of sleep, we awakened at 5 AM for an early start, more rested than we had felt in days. It was a nov-

127

elty to set out in the crisp, early air feeling wide awake rather than groggy, the state in which we had often begun our other days when traveling long hours on little sleep.

Day 28 brought searing winds that blew throughout the morning. By afternoon, rising dust clouds had transformed the sun into a fiery red disk that was barely visible behind a screen of dust. Finally, the sun gave up and disappeared behind a thickening brown barrier. The poor visibility, no more than a few yards, forced us to once more follow the compass needle. Suddenly, we saw a welcome refuge: the white shape of a *ger*, with a horse tied to a rail outside, stood twenty yards ahead.

We hitched our camels alongside the horse and, in observance of the Mongolian custom of never knocking on a door, opened it and walked in. The occupants casually looked up as we entered, but their facial expressions changed to open-mouthed surprise when they realized we weren't Mongolian. Quickly regaining her composure, the lady of the *ger*, a slender, elegant woman, sprang to her feet and went into instant action to make her guests feel at home. Several pieces of dried, odorless camel dung went into the stove to replenish the fading flame, while the teenage daughter hurried to make tea.

Camel dung is used as fuel by many nomads. With no trees in sight in the desert, saxual twigs have long been the fuel of choice, but these slow-growing shrubs are increasingly scarce due to decreasing precipitation and overuse of the shrubs as forage and fuel. Saxual twigs burn hot like coal, and as a natural stabilizer, the shrub prevents the erosion of soil and the spread of sand. But in places where saxual is scarce or doesn't grow, camel dung is gathered and stacked into neat piles in the spring. It dries all summer and is ready for use when the family returns in the autumn—an odorless, readily available source of fuel for winter warmth and cooking.

The husband, a tall, willowy man with deep-set eyes and three fingers missing from his right hand, lounged on a bed pushed against a wall. He invited us to sit down on tiny blue wooden stools. Obviously wondering how two foreigners had arrived at his door in a dust storm, he openly stared at us. I told him of our journey and how we had stumbled onto his *ger*. At the news that we were walking to the east, he immediately gave us his undivided attention. He poked his head out the door to see with his own eyes the two loaded camels. Only then was he convinced.

As his wife and daughter served us the customary salty tea, he launched into a dissertation concerning the hazards of desert travel and the extreme shortage of water, his face taut with concern. He repeated the information that we had already heard from other nomads: that summer temperatures were rising faster and were unusually high compared to previous years.

To gently change the subject, I asked about his animals and his family. In speaking with other Mongolians, I had found that "How are your animals?" usually stimulated an interesting conversation. This man, with tears in his eyes, told us of the loss of more than 300 sheep and goats during the deeply cold *zuds*, or winter storms, of the past two years. He had only 125 animals left, including sheep, goats, camels, and the horses they used for herding.

"But," he said with the unquenchable desert optimism that we would often hear throughout our trek, "next winter will be warmer, and our herd will increase." The frown on his furrowed, leathery face turned into a gap-toothed smile as he thought ahead to better days.

The serious-faced daughter set a plate of pleasantly sweet, jaw-cracking hard curds on the low table beside the stove, along with some camel's-milk yogurt. She was fourteen years old, with the peeling sunburned cheeks commonly seen on Mongolians in summer. Her black hair was pulled back into a neat braid and tied with a yellow bow.

Girls of the desert work hard and are trained early on to take care of the *ger*, cook, and serve the male members of the family. They are also expected to help herd and milk the animals. The girl's mother, though elegant, had the look of a woman who had worked hard all her life.

I pointed to an ugly red swelling on the girl's hand and asked

129

what had happened. In understandable English, she replied that a thorn had gone into her hand and she couldn't get it out. After I offered to help her, Bill ventured out into the storm and retrieved our first aid kit from the handy side pocket of a duffel bag, where it was kept in case of emergency. With a sharp pull of tweezers, I extracted the half-inch thorn. A liberal swathing with iodine and a large Band-Aid finished the job.

The girl, who had studied English at a winter boarding school in Dalanzadgad, was eager to practice her language skills and launched into a long series of questions about my childhood in New Zealand and our lives in America. She had watched television at school and particularly wanted to know if Americans lived the way she saw them on the screen.

In the pre-Soviet era, education was provided entirely by monasteries scattered throughout Mongolia, but under Soviet rule, monks were banned from teaching. The Soviets provided free compulsory education, however, including boarding schools, resulting in a high literacy rate—more than 80 percent.

Since independence, sadly, educational standards have plunged and literacy rates are dropping. Economic hardship and minimal teaching standards have resulted in decreasing attendance. But with help from the Dalai Lama, monastic schools have reopened after seventy years of repression, with training teachers as a primary goal.

Although many nomad families believe "book learning" is not necessary to master the art of caring for and herding animals, some families in remote areas do send their children to boarding schools in *aimag* capitals during the winter. There, although their education is minimal, they often learn a little English. More often it is the boys who attend school, but an increasing number of girls receive a basic education. They return home in the spring to help with herding and milking.

In the twenty-first-century age of satellite television, naïve students are exposed to programs showing what they interpret as realistic views of life elsewhere. This sometimes results in young adults leaving their herding families to live in Ulaan Baatar and seek, without success, the life depicted on the screen. So I tried as best I could to explain that the people on the screen were actors, and that real people went to school and worked at jobs. Meanwhile, the parents beamed with pride as they listened to their daughter speak English, a language of which they knew not a word.

Because their well was almost dry, the family intended to load everything onto their camels in four days' time and travel north to a place close to the mountains, where there was spring water and summer grazing. They spoke of their austere, hardworking life with total acceptance. After all, the man explained, his father and generations before him had lived the same life in the same place. His older daughter and a son, who were still out in the storm with the herd, and the fourteen-year-old would continue the family herding tradition, just as he had followed his father.

After learning that his other children were still outside herding, I asked, "How do they protect themselves from the storm?"

"We desert people are used to it," he explained with a shrug and a smile.

Three hours later the wind died down to an acceptable breeze. Before leaving, I gave a vial of iodine and several Band-Aids to the girl, and a one-pound bag of salt and five pairs of warm winter socks to the family.

Before we untied the camels, the husband beckoned us to a place a hundred feet away from the ger, where a bleached camel skull lay. As he placed a small rock on the skull, he explained that this was a mark of respect to the dead camel, and in return the camel's spirit would follow and protect us. The wife thrust more hard curds into our hands for the journey ahead. Thanking them for the unexpected pleasure of their hospitality on our long journey, we left, once again wearing our masks and goggles and breathing in the dusty air.

DAYS 29–30 > One day passed another in the wilting heat. Bill and I tried reminiscing about the temperatures of 70 degrees below zero that we had experienced on an earlier adventure in the far north, when we had walked across part of the frozen Arctic Ocean, but even that didn't cool us. The desert nomads' reports of the summer's unusually high and faster-rising temperatures worried us.

At times I wondered why I had clung to a fifty-year-old dream and subjected my injured body to the torture of walking in these hellacious temperatures. What am I doing here? my mind would whisper. Bill and I sought ways, in private thoughts and in words, to lift each other past the punishing heat, dust, sand, mind-numbing sameness, and exhaustion.

We had reached a stage in our expedition when emotional stamina was even more important than physical endurance, as we fought for every mile. It was becoming increasingly difficult to cast aside doubt, that devourer of motivation, as we forced our bodies to respond to the rigors of daily abuse and deprivation.

We could always count on one form of release from the day's struggle, though: the magic of the chilly night, serene under the sky's umbrella of glittering diamonds. At night the stars reigned, and in their splendor all the difficulties of the journey melted away.

DAY 31 > We were still in the midst of washes and shallow gullies, but we could see relief ahead as the terrain began to flatten out somewhat.

In camp I looked down at my dusty, salt-encrusted shirt and pants. The compass mirror showed uncombed, tousled hair that looked like something out of a comic strip. Suddenly it all seemed laughable: a sixty-three-year-old woman sitting in the middle of the Gobi, looking like a water-deprived hermit. No scented baths, hairdressers, or manicures here. My ragged fingernails held enough dirt to grow a crop. And most interesting of all, here this seemed normal, and I had not the slightest twinge of longing for the aesthetic bounties of the Western world. Perhaps there is a wild, or just an untamed, streak in all of us.

As a practical matter, time that might be spent grooming

and bathing on a trek, even if the extra water were available, was better spent resting for the next day's inevitable onslaught of exertion. And so I simply laughed at the dust-streaked face in the tiny mirror.

At the sound of my laughter, Bill looked up from his journal. I showed him his own image in the mirror. He declared that he looked a stage or two tidier than I, a notion I strongly disputed. Unshaven, his comb left on purpose in Ulaan Baatar, clothes disheveled, he was just as much a sight to behold. In the end, we declared it a toss-up as to who looked the worst and who cared the least.

According to our mileage calculations, we still had at least eight hundred miles to go. We had no illusions about what we faced, but in the cool of the evening, optimism prevailed as our bodies and minds responded to kinder temperatures. We had no idea that soon we would face the very real possibility of losing our lives.

CHAPTER 7 **THIRST**

DAY 32 > In the meager light of dawn, the camels were following us placidly when Jerry suddenly uttered a series of aggrieved bellows and stopped in his tracks. He seemed to be protesting that his load of water containers was uncomfortable, as happened from time to time. We unloaded everything, adjusted his back pad, and then reloaded, finding nothing amiss. A handful of cookies seemed to pacify him, and we were again on our way. But we were soon to realize how terribly mistaken we were.

All went well for a mile or two. Then, without warning, Jerry dropped to the ground and rolled on his back from side to side, his long legs flailing the air as he grunted loudly. Shocked into instant action, both of us grabbed his lead and tugged hard, forcing him to his feet. But it was too late for the plastic water containers that had been on Jerry's back. They gushed water from the wide splits created when he had rolled over on them.

Desperately we raced to close the gaps, but they were too large. We watched in horror as our precious liquid was instantly absorbed into the thirsty earth. Shaking in disbelief, we unloaded all of the containers, only to find each one empty.

As a precaution against such accidents, we always loaded a four-gallon container onto the second camel. Thus we glumly calculated our total water supply for the next nine days, in temperatures regularly exceeding 120 degrees, to be a mere five gallons, including the water in our bottles.

Numb with shock, we grappled with our predicament. The emotions I had kept inside concerning the pain in my leg and hip suddenly exploded. I was overwhelmed by the physical agony, the endless miles, the futility of traveling farther without enough water, and the risk of a horrible death from thirst.

I pulled on Jerry's rope and yelled at the top of my voice, my face inches from his, telling him in vivid terms exactly what I thought of him, the desert, and the whole idea of walking across this piece of hell. His huge brown eyes unblinkingly stared back at me, most likely thinking that I had lost my mind.

A despondent Bill sat with his head in his hands. "It's one thing to put up with the heat and everything else this blasted desert has in store for us, but we can't risk dying of thirst." He shot Jerry a killer look.

I fought to get myself under control. "We have to think our way through this mess somehow," I said in a flat tone that lacked confidence.

"Damn it," Bill said, determinedly rising to his feet. "We'll make it work!"

Although I wasn't sure how we could, I agreed. Our initial emotional reaction over, we struggled with what to do next. First we had to make peace with Jerry, who had no idea why we had been so angry. Embarrassed by my outburst, I offered him a cookie and stroked his favorite place, just below his ear, while Bill patted his neck. He seemed to have forgiven us, and we did the same. Something in the load had bothered him, and his reaction to get rid of it was natural.

Now to figure a way out of our predicament. Including today, we were nine days from resupply. Because our chosen route took us close to the Chinese border, government regulations forbade us from carrying a two-way radio for emergencies, lest we communicate with the Chinese. (We considered this reasoning absurd, since neither of us spoke a word of Chinese.)

Our two-pound compact saltwater converter could turn even filthy sludge into drinkable liquid, but where was the sludge? The last well we had passed was a day behind us, and the camels had drunk the last of anything there that resembled water. We could keep a close watch for wells along our route, of course, and we could also watch for any sign of salt crystals, a sign that water lay below the ground and had been forced upward by capillary action, then evaporated on the surface to form a white crust. With our shovel, we could dig and hope that the water was only a few feet down. We could also travel during the cooler night hours to conserve energy, but we might not see a well or salt crystal clues in the darkness.

Another option was to remain where we were, with no shade except our umbrellas, and hope that Chuluu would find us. Even after drastically reducing our daily ration, though, we would still run out of water before he arrived. No, we decided, our best hope was to travel onward and hope to find water along our route.

We decided that for the first four days, we would reduce our ration to two quarts each per day, including cooking, less than one-third of our body's requirement. For the following two days we would reduce our daily ration even further, to one quart each. This would leave us with no water at all for the last three days. Given the rising temperatures and fickle moods of this treacherous desert, our situation was desperate. The camels, still in excellent condition, could make do until our resupply arrived.

"There's water out there somewhere waiting for us," I said with feigned cheerfulness, my stomach in knots. "We'll find it."

Bill, his smile forced, nodded his agreement.

Having traversed a shallow gully, we started across a gravel plain, its mammoth dimensions emphasized by isolated peaks that sat low on distant horizons. "At least the search for water takes my mind off the pain of every step," I said.

We scanned the route for any unusual undulation or pile of dirt that might signal a dug well. The long day of walking, although filled with hope, was tempered by uncertainty. We kept reminding each other that this was only the first day on reduced rations. Although our situation was critical, we believed, based on past expeditions, that we would find water in time. Our maps, however, showed no particular reason for hope—no village or anything else that might lead us to water.

Although the desert herdsmen had probably already moved away from their dry wells, we thought we might find a *ger* with a well that had lasted longer than most. But the day went by with no sign of water. That night we barely moistened our dehydrated rice, making it almost too dry to swallow. As we slowly sipped the last of our day's measured ration, savoring each mouthful, we spoke of tomorrow and the water we would surely find.

Before falling into a restless sleep, I read aloud a few comforting verses from the New Testament and prayed that tomorrow would bring relief.

DAYS 33–35 > The next several days passed in a confusion of intermittent hope and despair. Enduring temperatures of more than 120 degrees, omnipresent dust, and headaches of increasing intensity, we felt our desperation growing in spite of our best efforts to keep it at bay. Our bodies wilted under the onslaught of a sun that burned to the core. Once, in an unguarded moment, I grabbed the water bottle, determined to drink the lot. But before I had unscrewed the lid, the thought of nothing to drink in camp that night stopped me. As I replaced the bottle, I sheepishly looked across to Bill, who merely shrugged his shoulders and confessed that he'd had the same urge a dozen times.

Conversation grew scanty as the days passed, our mouths dried, and our strength dwindled. Even when we rested under umbrellas, the air was almost too hot to breathe. One day sand dunes sculpted into ocean-like waves with sharp-edged ridges curved across our path, forcing us to travel extra miles to avoid having to climb the soft sand.

We used mental games to relieve the staggering tedium of the passing hours. We delved deep into memories of our hikes to waterfalls and along rivers in the Cascade Range at home. Then we dragged out all of our old and already overused jokes, and laughed eagerly as if they were brand-new.

As our cracked lips bled, our weary minds fought to stay focused. After four days, an increasing desire to lie down, give up, and let the world go by began to weaken our resolve. After each rest period, it became an increasing struggle to lurch to our feet and walk onward.

During the day we drank most of our ration of water, leaving just two mouthfuls each for dinner, which we drank one tiny sip at a time with our soup, a thick paste. Each night, as darkness spread its cooling arms to soothe us, glittering stars twinkled hope that helped distract us from our plight. Once a shooting star jetted across the heavens, leaving a long white trail which, in my imagination, was stardust that gently sprinkled our campsite.

We spoke of Leigh Beg, considered the most important observational astronomer of the fifteenth century. In 1449 he studied the stars along the same latitude and in the same approximate geographic area as we stood. Beg cataloged 1,018 stars and was the first to build a land-based observatory. As we watched the constellations of Scorpio and Pegasus climb higher in the heavens, we marveled that a patron of astronomy seven hundred years earlier had studied the same dramatic sky we now admired.

One night, just before settling into our sleeping bags, we set up a system to catch the evening dew. We knew that a shallow depression lined with plastic, under the right conditions, forms moisture on the plastic's surface, which if produced in sufficient quantities provides at least a small amount of water. The night air in the Gobi is especially dry due to the altitude and lack of humidity, but it was worth a try.

Bill made a V-shaped hollow in the earth. I split open a clean plastic garbage bag to line the hole, and then anchored the edges with rocks. But despite our painstaking preparations, the next morning we found only a few droplets.

DAY 36 > On our fifth day of thirst, we awoke well before dawn with pounding headaches. It was July 1, our fortieth wedding anniversary. We gave each other the anniversary cards we had carried in our bags for just this moment. Our dire situation made the day even more sentimental. Determined to celebrate, we read our cards and, after hugs of thanks for so many good years together, opened our gifts. Bill's was a belt buckle with a helicopter in the center; mine was an elegant red porcelain rose.

It seemed strange to reminisce over our first meeting in faraway New Zealand and the ensuing forty years of marriage as we now traveled the Gobi fighting for our lives, but we couldn't help ourselves. Bill had been transferred to New Zealand by his company in 1959, and two weeks later we met. My father had called for a helicopter to spray in order to kill a poisonous weed that was a danger to the cattle that roamed the lush green hills of our farm. I was detailed to show the pilot where to go.

From the first minute, we became friends. Bill's easy manner and love of sports and mountains were a perfect match for my outdoor interests. We kept in touch and were married two years later, in 1961. Afterward Bill was transferred to Guatemala and Honduras, and we lived there until 1965. Reflecting on our forty years together, we agreed that they had been remarkable years. But now we had to survive our predicament.

Following our plan, we halved our water again. One quart each was all we would allow ourselves for the day, which would leave one more quart each for the next day. After that, there would be no liquid. While we choked down a small breakfast of dry oatmeal, we discussed our dilemma. Our bodies were steadily losing the battle against dehydration. Adding to our worry were muscle cramps in our legs, backs, and abdomens that grabbed unexpectedly, forcing us to stop and massage the knots. We no longer sweated and were well into the heat exhaustion stage, which signaled a severe electrolyte imbalance. Heatstroke wasn't far away, but there was nothing we could do to prevent its deadly advance.

Survival was all that mattered now, and our most important weapon was optimism. Without it, this crisis would soon overwhelm us. To bolster each other, we talked of the pond or well we would find that day. I extravagantly proclaimed that we would find so much water that we would drink all we needed, then take a swim and wash all the caked dust off our bodies. After a moment's silence, Bill slowly nodded his head. "That's a good thought." As always, he was the master of understatement.

In the crisp early light, we walked across another pebbled plain and spoke of the food we looked forward to when we returned home. I craved a spinach salad. Even a single green leaf would do. Bill's choice was bacon and eggs. That sounded mouthwatering, but I still opted for the salad. The discussion of food took us all the way to midmorning, when increasing cramps forced more frequent stops to massage each other's legs. We stopped at a sand dune with foot-high saxual bushes thinly scattered over the low slopes, an excellent place for the camels to browse while we rested.

Afterward we walked onward over firm, barren earth, sometimes covered in gravel or pebbles. Sandy patches slowed us but were few and far between. As we bypassed more low dunes, we watched for glistening white salt crystals but saw none. Later we found an area of moist earth that had been a tiny two-foot-deep lake. Snowmelt had gathered here in the spring but by now had all evaporated in the summer sun. We squeezed handfuls of the thick mud, letting it ooze through our fingers. To feel something besides dust, sand, and gravel was new. But the frustration of again finding no water sent tears coursing down my cheeks as I pressed the soothing mud to my cracked, bleeding lips.

Bill turned away without a word, but his strained expression revealed his emotions. I followed him and took his hand, and silently we gathered strength from each other to persevere in the overpowering 126-degree heat, as we traversed a plain with no end in sight. In a weak moment I caught myself wondering if we would suffer a lonely demise, joining the many dead animals we had passed. I angrily shoved such thoughts away. Dwelling on death might make it a reality.

At day's end, two quarts of priceless fluid were left. For tomorrow, instead of one quart each as we had planned, we decided to cut down to half a quart, to leave a half-quart each for the following day. Resupply wouldn't be for another four days. We were on schedule to meet Chuluu, but at temperatures of 120 degrees or more in the shade, could we make it? Although unwilling to admit it to ourselves, much less to each other, we both knew that with our bodies already in a dehydrated state, a single day in the relentless heat without water would be fatal.

Our ability to handle the heat had been severely diminished. With each passing hour, our internal heat regulators were shutting down, causing our body temperatures to rise. As dehydration advances, the body draws water from the circulating blood, which thickens and eventually no longer fulfills its task of transporting heat generated by the body's core to the surface for cooling. This trapped heat eventually kills when the body's temperature rises to intolerable levels.

Dehydration is a peculiar thing. It's as if a slow paralysis creeps through the limbs, slowing the pace. Even the mind slows as concentration wanes and the body weakens. Erecting the tent now took twice as long, for instance. To save time and energy, we were tempted to sleep in the open—that is, until we remembered our neighbors, the snakes and scorpions, and their nighttime hunting forays.

We were also tempted to slow down to conserve energy, but instead we resolved to keep as fast a pace as we could manage. Even so, on Day 36 we covered only eleven hard-won miles. After consulting maps and the GPS, our overall mileage total came to 943. We were approaching the 1,000-mile mark—a milestone we had eagerly anticipated, though now, in our abysmal state, it seemed to us only a number.

That night we were exhausted, and the star-filled sky went unnoticed. How nice it would have been to have had a special anniversary dinner. But there was no extra water for cooking, and the effort would have been too great. With my journal resting in my lap, I tried to concentrate on the day's events. Writing in the evenings was something I normally looked forward to, but now I was too drained to finish a sentence. Bill took his journal out but leaned back against the tent, his eyes closed, unable to think of a thing to write. Later we tried to sleep, but our overheated bodies made it impossible.

DAYS 37–38 > As much as we tried to jerk some vitality into our debilitated bodies, our steps slowed. Bill wondered aloud how long we could keep going. I admitted to the same thoughts. But we both knew we had no alternative but to stay on our feet and follow our compass bearing.

My boots felt like fifty-pound lead weights. Even though we wore sunglasses, our eyes stung as we strained to see ahead. There seemed no end to the awful heat.

Noon arrived, but we chose not to rest. It seemed easier to continue. At least the wind had died, taking with it the blowing sand and dust. Exhausted, our energy almost gone, and our pace drastically reduced, we labored through the afternoon. My mind was blank and refused to concentrate. When I gathered enough energy to ask Bill what he was thinking, he just shook his head. Our gait was a stagger, with frequent stops to allow dizzy spells and muscle spasms to pass. Barely able to put one foot in front of the other, we grasped the camels' ropes to keep ourselves from falling. We were afraid that if we fell, we would never get up again.

In this painful way we stumbled side by side and talked, finally, about how it all might end. We spoke of those at home, our family and friends, whom we would leave behind. Our journal notes would tell them the story when Chuluu backtracked to find us. My calmness surprised me. Bill too was quite matter-of-fact, with no hint of panic. There was no fear, only acceptance that we had fought hard and might not win. But soon our talk of death jolted us into a new determination. We had reached the nadir of our despondency, and now the only way out was to fight back with our collective stubborn streak in one final assault. We resolved to walk until we dropped or found water. We staggered onward, our desire to live renewed.

The hours crawled by. Bill's face was ashen, his eyes sunken into dark wells, his pounding headache unbearable. My eyes were so deep in their sockets that I had trouble blinking, and my head felt as though it were on fire. Pain engulfed my entire body. A sensation of profound isolation swamped my spirit. We seldom urinated, and when we did it brought sharp pains. The meager fluid was dark. Even as the sun drifted toward the horizon to tease us with its last shafts of heat for the day, we took no notice, so intent were we on our struggle.

By now the pain in my leg and hip was almost beyond endurance. To take my mind off it, I counted steps out loud. After I reached two hundred, Bill joined in and we walked in step. One step at a time was all it would take. How ridiculous we would seem to anyone watching our march across the blazing, empty wasteland, counting steps at the top of our raspy voices.

At last, unable to wring more than eight miles from the long day, we camped, exhausted and worried over our lack of progress. Over dinner, determined to lift our spirits, we sang to the camels and the wilderness with as much gusto as our dry throats allowed. We dusted off our childhood memories and sang songs we hadn't heard in many years. Judging from all outward signs, the camels were not impressed by "You Are My Sunshine." In fact, they appeared not to notice us, which was just as well because, as I remarked to Bill, "We really do sound terrible."

Again that night, sleep wouldn't come. We could hardly stand the feeling of clothing on our hot skin. By the yellow light of a flashlight, I wrote in my journal, "Is this desert our hated prison? Is there no way out?"

The next day we were almost too sick to walk at all. Constant stops to hang onto the camel ropes and rest our heads against their sides became the norm. We dared not sit to rest. We stopped talking. Our throats could no longer tolerate conversation.

By the end of the day we had staggered only three miles, but in the last of the sun's rays I caught sight of a brief sparkle. Bill saw it too. It took a minute or two before our numbed minds registered what it might be.

"Water," I rasped through bleeding lips. Then I watched with suspicion, expecting it to transform into yet another cruel mirage.

"It's got to be water this time," Bill mumbled. We stumbled forward, clutching the camels. They too seemed to sense water, and were making a beeline for it.

Yes! It was water—wonderful, precious, life-giving water! A shallow salt lake, forty feet wide and perhaps six inches at its deepest, filled a stony depression in the earth.

We whooped with uncontrollable joy and unashamed tears and walked straight in, boots and all. We scooped up handfuls to drink, but immediately spat out the foul-tasting, salty stuff. The camels did the same.

After our first moments of celebration, we got serious. First we staked the camels away from the brackish pond. Then, fumbling in our hurry, we pulled the saltwater converter out of its bag. After making sure that it was working, we finished the last drops left in our bottles, then took turns slowly pumping the black handle up and down.

At first we drank in great gulps, but our stomachs rebelled and we vomited. Then we sipped slowly, and the precious liquid stayed down. As it trickled into our dry mouths and down our throats, it felt velvety soft. It tasted stale, but we hardly noticed.

Three hours later, it was dark as we finished filling our bottles and the four-gallon plastic container. Then we pumped an extra two gallons and, with triumphant shouts and howls of joy, poured the water over each other's heads to wash off the salt and dust. Our wilted, exhausted bodies returned to life, just as an unwatered plant finds renewed energy from a deluge of long-anticipated rain.

We filled the camels' water bucket twice by flashlight. In contrast to our undignified haste, the camels drank slowly, almost daintily, not having gone without fluid long enough to crave it as we did. It was now after midnight, so instead of cooking dinner, we drank more and slid into our sleeping bags. Although we were still weak, our headaches and other symptoms were improving. Muscle cramps were still a problem, but our skin felt cooler. For the first hours, our bodies' tissues absorbed water like sponges, and very little emerged as urine.

146

It was exhilarating to feel alive again, without fear of the future. Our pump, a recent addition to the desalinization units on the market, had saved our lives.

While we rested, we spoke of the stories we had read of people who had allegedly gone days without water. One such tale was of a small group of prisoners who traveled from Siberia during World War II without maps or compasses and thought they might have traveled about 250 miles across the narrowest width of the Mongolian Gobi from the north. According to the story, the prisoners traveled weeks with little water and then, in an already severely dehydrated, starving state, walked eight days more in the sweltering summer heat with no water at all. We now knew the story was an exaggeration, if not an outright invention. We had experienced seven days of insufficient water rations in extreme temperatures and could not have survived the next two without any water at all, so we knew it would be impossible to survive eight waterless days.

That night we slept soundly, and in the morning we allowed ourselves the luxury of two extra hours of sleep past daybreak. I

used my wet boots as my pillow; just lying my head on that dampness brought me joy.

DAY 39 > After a breakfast of water-soaked oatmeal that made up
for the dry stuff we had choked down over the last few days, we
topped off our water container and filled our bottles. As a precaution against further disaster, we wore our small yellow backpacks,
each loaded with two bottles of water. With our compass bearing
fixed and feeling unbelievably energized, we set out. Bill's springy
step had returned, and although my hip and leg weren't improving, I had not a care in the world. A hundred feet away, we stopped
for one last look at the tiny lake that had saved us. By the end of
July it would be dry, leaving only a white crust of salt crystals.

CHAPTER 8 **ICE**

DAY 40 > Emerging from the quagmire of weariness, we sustained a ruthless pace. About midmorning a cluster of buildings, not shown on our maps, materialized in the distance. Searching for a well, we entered an abysmally poor village. Small concrete one-story buildings in various stages of disrepair lined sand-filled streets. But it was the astonishing quantity of multihued glass from broken vodka bottles, scattered over the sandy surface of the entire village, that gripped our attention.

A young boy, the only human in sight, pointed the way to the town's well, but it was impossible to find a glass-free path. Concerned for Tom and Jerry's safe passage, we doubled back to find a safer route to the clean well, which sat on the outskirts of town. It was the perfect place to replenish our water supply and allow the camels a long drink.

If we hadn't found the salty lake, this well would have been our first water source. Quietly contemplative, knowing that we would never have reached the well in time, we filled our containers.

After dumping a few buckets of the heavenly coolness over each other, we dunked our filthy second set of clothes into a bucket of water that instantly turned dark brown. With our laundry tied to the camel loads to dry, and water draining from our clothes and sloshing in our boots, we left the village, unable to resist one last look at all that glass. With the exception of a few scattered, barely producing gold mines in the surrounding ridges, there appeared to be no available work. Apparently what money that could be earned was spent on vodka, with the empty bottles thrown asunder.

We forged ahead to make up for the lost miles of the last few days. Allowing only a ten-minute noon break, we set off as the thermometer rose to 119 degrees. The prospect of resupply and Chuluu's company drew us like a magnet to the coordinate numbers of our prearranged meeting place. As 7 PM arrived, we anxiously watched the sky, and even as our legs protested the brutal pace and long hours of walking, we reached for more speed. We arrived at 7:30 PM, after a punishing eighteen-hour day and thirty-nine miles. After some quick landing-strip preparations, we heard the familiar hum of the approaching airplane.

We had traveled 1,007 miles, overcoming delays by sheer resolve to average more than twenty-five miles per day. We were thankful that Chuluu was bringing us new boots, which would replace the worn shells that had taken a fierce beating on the sharp rock and gravel plains. These, fresh socks, and new trekking poles would provide a boost.

Chuluu was clearly shocked as he listened to our story of lost water and our search for more. He fingered the split water containers, his usual jovial expression serious, and said in a worried tone, "You could have died."

Deeply concerned about the rest of the trek, he warned us, just as the nomads had, about higher than normal temperatures, and told us that most families along our route had already left. The area hadn't seen rain in three years, and wells had gone dry early. Although the desert had already proved its murderous reputation, we were determined to continue.

After unloading our supplies, including full, clean water containers, we changed into new boots and gave Chuluu the worn ones to take back. Incredulously, he held them aloft. "You walked them to death!"

He had found a dozen tomatoes, six apples, and two apple pies for us. There was jam of yet another mysterious Mongolian fruit, and a loaf of fresh bread. In return, we handed him three full journals, many rolls of exposed film, our dust-caked clothes, and of course the split water containers, which we were especially happy to see disappear.

At dusk Chuluu reluctantly prepared to leave. Our friendship had cemented into an easygoing relationship of trust and caring. His cheerful attitude and bright smile were a tonic to our desert-worn bodies and minds.

The engine chugged to a powerful roar. Gathering speed down the dusty runway, Chuluu's plane gracefully lifted off into the broad sky, leaving us momentarily shrouded in a fog of isolation. But the prospect of a fine dinner soon switched our attention to food, and any concerns about the future were temporarily forgotten.

That night we ate a special meal, with an emphasis on the tomatoes and apples. Bill gave Tom and Jerry an apple each. Later, while we ate dinner, both camels sidled quietly up to the tent, stretching their long necks to nudge our backs with soft noses, making calf-like mewling sounds. Determined to resist this shameless begging, we did our best to ignore them. The nudging grew more urgent. Finally we gave each begging camel a tomato. Then, for good measure, we spread jam on two pieces of bread and fed it to them. So much for discipline. Like children, they had figured out how to get their own way. To conserve what was left of our delicacies, we tied the camels to their stakes and fed them more steppe grass.

Our gluttonous meal left us unable to eat the pies, so with reluctance we left them for breakfast and retired to bed. But in the middle of the night, Bill awoke and suggested a snack. The pies made a luxurious midnight feast.

DAY 41 > Our route took us north to the cheerless, dusty capital of the *aimag*, Dalanzadgad, the town where the teenage girl we'd met had attended school. Its tantalizing but misplaced name meant "Seventy Springs," but in fact it was a collection of dilapidated, Soviet-made concrete buildings. Apartment buildings with flaking exteriors and broken windows added to the atmosphere of disrepair and despair. *Ger* compounds, surrounded by stockade-like wooden fences, skirted the town.

An airplane service, loosely described as reliable, flies from Ulaan Baatar south to Dalanzadgad to give tourists the opportunity to experience a glimpse of the Gobi. Occasionally along the twisted, potholed streets we encountered a tourist taking photos, presumably to take home as a souvenir of their visit.

Beyond that, activity was minimal. A few groups of listless, uninspired youths hung about with nothing to do, since work is almost nonexistent here. A drunk staggered our way and, with a lopsided smile of generosity, offered us a drink from his partially empty vodka bottle. Another bleary-eyed man, gaunt and filthy, slurred his words and begged for money to buy another bottle of the potent liquid. Two more inebriated souls, arm in arm, wove an uncertain path in our direction, each holding aloft empty bottles and mumbling incoherently.

Desert city life, unemployment, and the resulting despondency presented a sad contrast to the hardworking, smiling, fresh-faced herding people we had met in the desert.

The wind whirled in eddies between buildings, hurling paper and other garbage into the air in clouds of blinding dust. Our decision to enter the town to see the sights, most of which appeared both dispirited and drunk, had not been a good one.

Ever since the Soviets left, Dalanzadgad, like most other Mongolian towns, has been in a state of steady decay. The few towns in the Gobi suffer due to their extreme isolation. Electricity is frequently cut off, for instance, and today was one of those days. Our inquiry as to when it might be available again was met with "When someone repairs the problem."

Essential goods are scarce and there are no real roads, which makes even the delivery of gas in ancient, leftover Soviet trucks unreliable. The drivers must cross vast roadless expanses, necessitating sometimes desperate measures to keep their reluctant engines going through the heat and dust. Soviet engines have a well-earned reputation for reliability, but they also have a serious limitation, as we quickly discovered on last year's jeep journey. As we drove along steep, winding roads over mountain passes in the jagged mountains of the north, the jeep's engine overheated with maddening frequency. The only solution was to turn the vehicle into the wind, raise the hood, and wait a half hour for the engine to cool enough to continue. We often found ourselves part of a collection of overheated trucks with the same problem, parked on the brow of windy hills.

Dalanzadgad was surrounded by open gravel plains that in the west run right up to the flanks of the most easterly of the Altai Mountains. Here the plains merge with the vast, flat eastern Gobi Desert, which stretches like a rumpled, dusty blanket hundreds of miles all the way to its eastern boundary. Hidden deep in the mountains is a unique ice-choked gorge, while farther north the Flaming Cliffs, the scene of historically significant dinosaur-fossil discoveries, rise above the plains. We could travel an extra hundred miles, which at our present pace would take four days, to see these places of interest, or head directly east along the main route of our journey.

Discussing our choices over dinner that night, I was at first adamant that we continue east without traveling any extra miles. I

153

was reluctant to add more stress to my injured side. But Bill pointed out that we might regret not visiting these uncommon desert features. Intensely interested in dinosaur history, we knew that the scientific information and photographs of the region would be a valuable addition to our Adventure Classroom program. This last argument won me over. We agreed to take the extra time and miles and travel north. Then we would continue our trek east.

While cooking rice and dried vegetables we noticed a river of sheep and goats approaching. Soon the white, bleating river parted to flow around our tent and continue north, followed by a gangly young man, perhaps no more than a teenager, riding a camel and singing at the top of his robust voice. He gave a cheery wave as he passed, as if it were an everyday occurrence in his nomadic life to herd his animals around a bright red tent in the middle of the enormous reaches of the Gobi. Even the two accompanying dogs that skirted the flock passed by as if we were of no importance in their busy herding lives.

Fascinated by the nonchalance with which the camel rider had accepted us, we watched as he became a speck on the plain, completely forgetting our dinner. Soon the distinctive odor of a burned saucepan reminded us, though. The pan survived well enough for us to add water and start the cooking process again. As darkness fell, we slid into our comfortable beds to ready ourselves for the next day's adventure.

DAY 42 > As daylight spilled across the undulating plains, we trekked north. Twenty uneventful miles later, as the plains gave way to foothills leading to precipitous mountains, we arrived at a rusted rail connected to a post at each end. This was the makeshift gate and entrance to Yolyn Am ("The Vulture's Mouth"), which guarded the snowfield: a deep, sunless gully with high, steep sides. In the absence of a gatekeeper, we led Tom and Jerry around the well-trodden path that bypassed the gate and continued into a wide valley approaching the icy canyon. A dozen yaks grazed on ground-hugging green plants, looking up as we passed. The docile beasts, closely related to cattle, sported long shaggy coats and impressive horns.

The inner mountains and valleys were a remarkable contrast to the dry desert plains that lay only a few miles away. Here, scattered green broom-grass clumps grew, surrounded by low juniper bushes whose sweet alpine scent floated on the breeze as we followed a gentle stream that twisted its way through the gradually narrowing valley. Ground squirrels darted almost at our feet, scurrying into burrows at the last minute. Though somewhat idyllic, the entire area had been severely overgrazed by domestic herds of sheep, goats, yaks, and horses, which had eaten the green plants right down to the ground.

About eight miles from the gate, we staked the camels close to the stream so they could eat and drink. Bill and I walked another twenty minutes into a steep-sided, narrow gorge where five-foot-thick ice was squeezed between almost vertical walls of reddish brown rock several hundred feet high, standing only about seventy-five feet apart. The snow had avalanched off the mountainsides and accumulated over the winter along the six-mile sunless gorge, which wound its way ever deeper into the mountains. In the dark shadows, ice melt was slow, even though high above the gorge the mountaintops sweltered in hot sun. We had seen this phenomenon many times in other mountainous regions where the winter's snow, trapped beyond the reach of the sun, remained intact throughout the summer in the depths of valleys and narrow gorges.

Cool ice was a novelty. Gleefully we rubbed handfuls on our faces and felt the cold sting on our cheeks. With the excitement of prospectors searching for gold, we dug beneath the surface with our pocketknives, chopped out clean, bite-sized chunks, and chewed them like candy. The cold, velvety smooth liquid trickled down our dust-ravaged throats.

Eager to explore the depths of the canyon, we walked across the ice between the sculpted rock walls, which provide nesting sites for the abundant birds that dart in and out of the high rocky crevasses. As many as two hundred bird species inhabit the park, including the cinereous vulture, the desert warbler, and the Mongolian desert finch. The musical song of the cuckoo bird, which inspired Beethoven's Pastoral Symphony, echoed off the canyon walls above us. According to Mongolian legend, if travelers hear the cuckoo's sound at least twelve times in a row, they will have good luck for the rest of their journey. This cuckoo trilled well past twelve times. The wild beauty of the gorge, its cool peacefulness, and the romantic song of the cuckoo made it difficult to leave.

With the sun dipping to the west, deepening the shadows within the gorge, we grabbed a few pieces of ice to chew as we returned to the camels. Just before dark we walked around the makeshift gate and made camp for the night on the open plain.

DAY 43 > The next day, an hour before daybreak, we broke camp and headed to the Flaming Cliffs, which, according to our map, were only thirty-two miles to the north. The name was bestowed upon the place by foreigners and is never used by Mongolians, who call the area Bayanzag, meaning "rich in saxuals." In the 1920s the cliffs became famous as a dinosaur graveyard when an expedition, led by American paleontologist Roy Chapman Andrews, excavated the red sandstone cliffs and discovered the first dinosaur eggs and skeletons in central Asia. The eroding sandstone exposed numerous skeletons of such importance that several more expeditions led by Andrews were launched over the next several years. The cliffs proved to be a treasure trove of dinosaur eggs, some with fossilized embryos still intact. An extremely rare *Oviraptor* was discovered crouched protectively over a nest of twenty-two eggs. After the Soviets gained control of Mongolia and realized the value of the American finds, they halted all further foreign expeditions. Since the installation of the new government, however, expeditions of many nationalities have resumed and discoveries continue to be made.

In the early evening, after traversing easy sloping plains, we arrived at the Flaming Cliffs, a dramatic place where tall cliffs of crumbling red sandstone have been sculpted by wind and erosion into caves, crevasses, and twisted columns. Thousands of years ago the Gobi was a much wetter place; a river flowed across the plateau, cutting through softer sandstone to form canyons where grass and plants grew in abundance. As the climate grew hotter and drier, the vegetation gradually disappeared, exposing the soft sandstone base of the cliffs and valley floors. The plains people and their animals were forced to leave an increasingly severe climate. The remains of the ancient animals, which lived there long before the plains people arrived, were gradually uncovered by the sandblasting of the changing climate. Sandstone columns two or three hundred feet high lean outward, then crash and disintegrate into sand and dust.

Dr. Angela Milner, one of the world's leading dinosaur experts, believes that the Gobi Desert is still an important dinosaur locality. Many of the dinosaur fossils found there are more primitive than those found elsewhere, she says, suggesting that the species evolved in Asia and later traveled to North America, crossing a land bridge that once joined the great land masses. Experts believe that numerous ancient secrets lie hidden in the Gobi, waiting to be unraveled.

Green, woody saxual bushes that take a century to grow to three or four feet dotted the flats and slopes around the cliffs, which glowed red as the setting sun played across their surfaces. Not far away was a saxual "forest" of gnarled and ancient shrubs that stretched many miles to the northern edge of the Gobi. The roots served to prevent the erosion of sand, although the lack of water had reduced the tortured shrubs to bonsais. That night, absorbed in the pastel glow of the evening, we camped among the silent red cliffs and watched their ghostly splendor melt into darkness. The dust-free night produced yet another sensational display of stars across the dark expanse of sky.

Relaxing under the twinkling stars, we talked of the life that had once thrived here. In the silence of a desert now empty of ancient creatures, it saddened us that not only in the Gobi, but also all over the world, valuable animal species struggle to survive the onslaught of humans' relentless advance.

That night I wrote in my journal:

The desert's changeable moods and even its challenges are tempered by a nighttime peace and tranquility that gives us the zest to look forward to our journey's next challenge, which we know is just around the corner. Even when there is no sound and no visible life, in the moonlit darkness we sense, just beyond our vision, the nocturnal life that emerges in search of food.

Bill wrote in his journal, "I guess it's the lack of human demands and artificial society and all its plastic veneer that draws us to these lonely places. By day we struggle, but in the cooler nights we live."

DAY 44 > By 5 AM the red cliffs and their ancient secrets were behind us. We set a compass course southeast to return to the core of the desert and the hottest part of our journey, more than seven hundred miles of shimmering heat that stretched far beyond sight.

We were traversing a coarse gravel plain at an altitude of 5,000 feet when we spied a lone figure in the distance. We hurried to catch the thin, slowly moving man dressed in a dusty, deep maroon *del* with a bright yellow sash.

When he saw us, the stranger stopped to allow us to catch up. After the usual polite greetings, he asked in flawless English where we were going. We told him, expecting the usual incredulous response. But he merely smiled and said, "It's farther than I'm going, but can I join you as far as my family's *ger*, just a few miles from here?" We were delighted to walk with this soft-spoken, gentle man, who told us that he was a Buddhist lama. From below his long *del*, which covered thin, rounded shoulders, peeked worn brown leather sandals. His gray socks were so full of holes that they were beyond mending and barely protected his tough-skinned feet from the sharp gravel. A hood draped loosely about his shaven head framed his face, which was deeply lined. In a small black canvas bag he carried several Buddhist books and a string of lama's beads, and he leaned heavily on a twisted wooden cane that had seen many miles of travel.

We tied his bag on top of Tom's load, and as we walked side by side he told us his story, traversing the corridors of distant memories. His name was Bayarsaikhan, or Bayar ("Joyful") for short, and he was a monastery teacher. He had set out from Dalanzadgad at daylight, planning to spend a few days with his family before they packed their belongings onto camels to travel north with their goat and sheep herd.

Bayar was an old man. He didn't know exactly how old he was, but he had taken his training in secret under senior Buddhist lamas as a teenager during the harsh rule of the Communist regime. Until the Communists fell from power in 1990, he had lived secretly in a series of mountain caves with other monks, not far from the shattered remains of a monastery.

Buddhism in Mongolia embraced the ancient faith of shamanism and its belief in the spirits of the boundless sky, the sun, the water, and the earth. The sixteenth-century Mongolian ruler Altan Khan, the country's first Buddhist ruler, made Buddhism the national religion and ordered the construction of the majestic Erdene Zuu monastery in the historical capital of Karakorum.

The monasteries gathered enormous wealth. Their vast riches bought influence and power in an underpopulated land racked by poverty. By the first decades of the twentieth century, the number of monks had swelled to a staggering one-third of the adult male population. The all-powerful monasteries owned a quarter of the country's land, ruled over most of the population, and tightly controlled the educational system. Eventually there were 140 Living Buddhas, a term used to describe a reincarnated Buddha. The Bogd Khan, who was Mongolia's holy king, led a depraved lifestyle of self-indulgence and waste. When Chinese rule collapsed, the Bogd Khan became Mongolia's secular and religious leader.

159

After the Communists took power in 1921, it wasn't long before the Soviet regime realized that the power and wealth of the monasteries were a deterrent to their own rule. Even when the Bogd Khan died three years later, the monasteries still retained their riches and powerful influence over the people. Under Stalin's cruel policies, Soviet persecution of Buddhism began by stripping all power from the monasteries, sending monks into military service, and forbidding them to teach children. But Buddhist power persisted even in the face of unprecedented persecution. In 1934 the Buddhist religion's annual income was still quite large—almost equal to that of the state—and more than 3,000 temples remained throughout the country.

Then, in 1937, just when the Japanese were poised to invade Mongolia, the Soviets stepped up their persecution. Some 2,000 of the highest-ranking lamas were rounded up and executed, while many others were sent to work camps in Siberia and never seen again. Monasteries were looted and demolished, and valuable artifacts stolen or shattered. Golden Buddha statues were taken to Russia and melted down. The number of people said to have been killed, imprisoned, or sent to Siberia between 1937 and 1950 varies. Some authorities estimate 40,000, while others believe that more than 100,000 perished.

Only one temple, the Gandan Monastery in Ulaan Baatar, was permitted to remain open, as a showcase to the outside world of Communism's so-called tolerance of religion. Fewer than a hundred monks were allowed to remain in the temple, and they became state-controlled puppets, with execution being the penalty for disobedience to the Communist state.

Under Soviet rule, Mongolians could no longer attend their temples or practice their religion. Instead, the Soviets gradually installed their own educational and governmental systems. Those who desired to continue practicing their religion did so in secret.

In 1990, when Communism crumbled and the Soviets left Mongolia, people were free once more to attend those few monasteries that had escaped destruction. Monks in their maroon and gold robes began appearing on the streets and in the temples. The teaching of novices began, and a slow revival of the Buddhist religion gradually extended across the country. Although there is little money in Mongolia for the reconstruction of ruined temples, they are slowly reopening in a less ornate and lavish way.

In a sad, quiet voice, Bayar told us that one summer Russian soldiers had attacked his remote mountain monastery. The monks were warned of the soldiers' approach and ran to hide in their well-concealed caves. A few older monks, unable to escape, were caught by the soldiers and beaten to death on the spot, their bodies left where they dropped. Statues and other religious vestiges were stolen, and then the monastery was systematically demolished, until all that was left standing were the remnants of the outside clay-brick walls.

After the attack, the frightened monks remained hidden deep within the caves for weeks. Before they emerged, they concealed their robes in wall crevasses, then walked across the countryside, avoiding villages. They returned to their families, who were nomadic herdsmen in the Gobi Desert or in the northern steppe grasslands, and integrated with them as herdsmen. Within months several monks, including Bayar, returned to the mountainous area close to the destroyed monastery. They retrieved their robes and a few simple belongings and lived a secret life of worship and teaching in hidden caves until the Soviets left Mongolia.

At last free of the Communists, Bayar and his fellow monks were now worshipping Buddha openly once more. Bayar was leading the restoration of the ruined monastery and hoped to have the building ready for the new generation of young monks being trained to follow in his footsteps.

"It was a sad time, but in the end we triumphed," said Bayar as he finished his story. "We have many students who will continue our work, and our brave elders who lost their lives to barbaric savagery live on in our prayers and thoughts. The pure of heart and deed can never be destroyed, and we must forgive those who sought to eliminate us."

We continued on together in silence, Bill and I each lost in thought about the reflections of this gentle, dignified man. Although there was no adequate response to such savage cruelty, Bayar's calm and forgiving attitude affected me deeply. His difficult path through life was more of an inner journey than an outward, physical one. He exuded a quiet stillness and an emotional strength that seemed more powerful than any demonstration of physical prowess could be. Could I ever achieve such internal strength, I wondered, strength that would enable me to not only survive merciless barbarity but to forgive those who practiced it?

I stole a sideways look at Bayar. As his feet touched the stony earth, they seemed to caress its surface; as he moved his hands, they gently moved the air. His eyes looked ahead into a desert that was his friend. My own problems of pain and the constant need to keep a steady pace were suddenly reduced in importance. At that moment I fully understood that our walk across the Gobi wasn't about conquering this vast desert. Rather, it was an inner journey that we were taking, passing through the Gobi in friendship, caressing and understanding our surroundings as we walked.

After about five miles, we reached a white *ger* in a shallow hollow surrounded by the gray gravel plain. Sheep and goats were scattered across the barren landscape, seeking the last dried wisps of grass. We marveled that they could find anything at all. An almost dry, hand-dug well sat close by. We tied Tom and Jerry to a rope stretched at head height between two posts twenty feet apart, where two horses were already tied. The ubiquitous Gobi wind pelted our unprotected faces with fine grit and whipped the horses' long tails and manes to curve upward over their backs. Mongolians usually allow horses' tails and manes to grow so long that the tails brush the earth and the thick manes sometimes reach the horses' knees.

Bayar led us into the *ger*, observing the traditional Mongolian custom of entering unannounced. Even after weeks in the desert, we still felt a timid, even guilty twinge when opening a *ger* door without first knocking. The family immediately rose to greet Bayar, paid him homage with deep bows, then took his hand and led him to the place of honor at the rear of the *ger*, while we sat in the customary visitors' place to the left.

The sturdily built husband, Bayar's son, held his father's hand and bowed deeply many times, while his wife hurried to prepare tea and his three grandchildren gathered around him. The girl, a slender ten-year-old, sat at his feet with her cheek lovingly placed on his knee, while two rugged boys, ages six and eight, squatted at his side, doing their best to look manly.

After serving Bayar, our hostess served Bill and me and then her husband. Bayar explained to them how we had met. The entire family smiled and nodded their heads in approval. Bayar was clearly a god in his family, and anyone who was a friend of Bayar's was a friend of theirs.

We drank our salty tea obediently, but when the *aaruul* arrived, Bill had to get creative because he couldn't stand the pungent smell of the curd. Pretending to put some in his mouth, he instead cleverly held them in his hand, and when no one was looking he slipped them into his pocket. It was a delicate way of disposing of the inedibles, since in Mongolia as in many cultures, it is the height of rudeness to refuse anything offered by your hostess.

The hard curds were not wasted, however. We kept them for the future, when we arrived at other *gers*. Every *ger* has at least one dependable guard dog, we had discovered. These dogs sometimes take their duty too seriously and will attack an innocent traveler. But with curds in hand, we had no trouble buying off the guard dogs we met.

Next it was time for the snuff ritual. The husband passed around a brightly colored, tiny container. Each man raised the lid, took a minute bit of tobacco between his thumb and index finger, sniffed with each nostril, and passed the container along. Women don't take part in this ritual, and I gave a silent prayer of thanks that I could allow at least one custom to go untried.

But worse was to come. Bayar's visit was such a grand occasion that it warranted a drink of vodka. Tiny glasses of the clear liquid were handed to us. At the first glassful in a ceremony to appease the gods, one must take the ring finger, dip it into the vodka, and flick a drop between finger and thumb toward the sky. A second drop is flicked into the air, a third goes toward the earth, a fourth is touched to the forehead, and then a sip is taken from the glass. We managed the first part of the ritual, and because we had already tasted the antiseptic liquid on a previous occasion, this time we chose to just barely wet our lips while pretending we had drunk a little. Only if it appears that a foreign guest has taken some is it acceptable to pass the glass on, and we certainly didn't want to hold up the proceedings.

Then it was time for the most grievous challenge to our Western stomachs: the revered national drink of *airag*, or fermented horses' milk. Horses' milk is quite drinkable when it is fresh, but when it has sat in the heat for days, it turns sour. Without knowing what it was, I took a large mouthful and swallowed. The entire family watched me with smiles of anticipation, ready to share in my enjoyment of such a pleasurable drink.

As the liquid hit my stomach, my entire body puckered. Even my eyes watered, and it was only with the most determined of efforts that I held the stuff down. In order to please our hosts, I managed—with an effort that required my total concentration—a smile that I thought might be my last. Once satisfied that I was enjoying my drink, they turned to Bill. But he said later that he could tell that all was not well with me and was forewarned to be careful. He wet his lips, swallowed, and smiled his approval, at which point our hosts were overjoyed at having pleased us.

Horses' milk is poured into an animal skin container, hung inside the *ger*, and stirred periodically until it ferments, and is drunk in large quantities all summer long when horses' milk is available. There is an *airag* finger game played by two people in which custom demands that the loser must drink a full bowl of *airag*. We often watched these games and could only stare in awe as the loser drank his bowl almost without taking a breath. Our admiration for the quality and thickness of the Mongolian stomach lining grew by the day. Later, we learned that an ancient Mongolian cure for tuberculosis called for the patient to drink copious quantities of *airag* from a white mare.

Our hostess next passed bowls of newly made sweet yogurt to us. In an attempt to offset the effects of the *airag*, I ate the entire contents of the bowl in record time. My stomach thanked me. Next came a bowl of typical Mongolian soup, made of noodles, diced potatoes, carrots, and onions, with chunks of mutton and even larger chunks of fat floating on top of the hot liquid. Although the basic soup was delicious, our appetites quickly disappeared at the sight of the floating blobs of fat and the powerful mutton smell that filled the air. Being raised in New Zealand, where mutton is almost a national dish, I was somewhat prepared for Mongolian mutton. Its fatty, gamey flavor, however, was still a challenge to our taste buds. Bill, American born and unused to mutton, worked hard, with only partial success, to get the strong-smelling meat past his nose.

Mongolians eat a bland, simple diet compared to Westerners. They don't use spices at all; onions and especially garlic, used sparingly, are the only seasonings in a desert Mongol's diet. The American dish called Mongolian beef is far too spicy and is unheard of among herdsmen. And because nomads move constantly, following the supply of food and water, they have no opportunity to grow vegetables or other crops. Instead, they rely on the food their herds provide. The meat and milk products of various animals are their dietary staples. They love mutton and eat it almost daily, and they add fat to food in large quantities.

Indeed, their sheep are of a breed that not only withstand the extreme climate and limited vegetation but also have enormous tails of pure white fat weighing four to eight pounds. The tails function as a source of nourishment in times of starvation, similar to the camel's hump, and their white wool is sought after by the carpet industry. Milk from camels, horses, goats, and cattle gives

165

nomad families a wide variety of dairy products, such as cheese, rancid butter, yogurt, dried curds, sour cream, and, of course, salty tea, which they consume in abundant quantities.

In addition to making mutton soup, they use meat in many ways. They cook it, dry it, and cut strips off a sheep carcass hanging inside a *ger* and barely fry it. In the summer they eat what they call a "white food" diet, which consists almost exclusively of dairy products available in the summer milk-producing months. In the winter the easily stored dairy foods, such as cheese and hard curds, are added to a cold-weather diet that consists mostly of meat.

To a Mongolian herdsman, a vegetarian would be a demented soul who could be made well only with a heaping bowl of steaming, fatty mutton. A diet without a generous daily infusion of meat is simply unheard of.

Although reluctant to leave the gentle family, we finally rose from our wooden stools to travel a few more miles before nightfall. Before leaving, we presented our gifts to Bayar, according to nomad custom, since he was the most senior family member. There were two pair of winter socks for each person, and a one-pound bag of salt. The grateful wife hurried to her cupboard, took out two large handfuls of hard curds, and, with tears in her dark eyes, pressed them into my hands. The father sent the boys to water our camels at the well. Bayar told us that in three days, the entire family and their herd would move to a valley in the northern mountains close to his monastery, where they always found food and water for the summer. In the autumn, just before snow fell, they would return here for the winter, when their well would be full again.

As we left, the wife ran back into the *ger* and returned with a pan of milk. With an expert flick of her wrist, she threw it into the air behind us. As the white droplets fell to the ground, the whole family raised their hands in the air and shouted, "*Sain yavaarai!*"—safe journey—in farewell. We replied, "*Bayarlaa*" (thanks). Just before disappearing down an incline, we looked back to see them still watching our departure. With a final wave, we disappeared from view. We would never forget these kind, sincere people, and we hoped Bayar would live long enough to see his monastery rebuilt.

It took the rest of the day for us to recover from the fatty food. We agreed not to mention eating to each other; the mere thought of it made our stomachs churn. All we wanted was plain water. The hard curds we had received as a gift were placed in the pouch where we kept the bribes for the *ger* guard dogs we would meet along the way.

As darkness settled over the slumbering gravel plain lit only by a yellow slice of moon, we stopped walking and set up camp. After we fed the camels and ate a small bowl of plain rice to appease our still-upset stomachs, we sat outside the tent, basking in the soft light, allowing the coolness of the night to wash away the day's fatigue.

DAY 45 > Lately we had noticed that our sweat no longer tasted salty, which signaled that our bodies were experiencing salt depletion. Since then, every morning with breakfast, we had each been taking two salt tablets with a pint of water. Today we increased the dose to four tablets.

It was Bill's turn to empty the tent so that it would be ready for loading onto the camels, while I gathered the garbage lying on the ground outside to take with us. Just as I grabbed a food wrapper, a snake's head whipped up from the other end. I dropped it and jumped back in fright. Along with the wrapper, I had snatched the tail of a snake that had coiled up underneath overnight. The surprised three-foot-long reptile wriggled away to a hole close by, while I stood there dumbfounded at my stupidity. Normally, before picking anything up from the ground, we flipped it over with a trekking pole. As my racing heart slowed I resolved not to make that mistake again. What if I had grabbed the snake's head instead of its tail?

By now my leg and hip had become so painful that I was forced to increase the daily dose of pain pills to relieve the sharp edge of each step. On Day 45 I took my two trekking poles, looped Jerry's lead around my wrist, took a deep breath, and set out with Bill to conquer another day.

We struggled through blistering 115-degree temperatures in the shade of our umbrellas. The air dried our throats and nasal passages, leaving our lips cracked and bleeding again in spite of liberal applications of lip balm. Although we were constantly sweating, the sweat instantly dried, leaving a salty crust on our shirts. Even though we were traversing a 5,000-foot plateau, it was a challenge to breathe in the afternoon's hot dry air, which came in vibrating heat waves that rose from the sweltering earth.

Scorpions were still a problem. Relief came as the sun rose and they dashed to the shelter of cooler burrows. Our painful run-in with them twenty-three days ago was still indelibly imprinted on our minds.

Hot winds barraged us as we plodded along, following a careful compass course. The emptiness of the desert and the loneliness of our journey were underscored each time we encountered a nomad family moving away, leaving dry wells and intolerable heat behind as they sought refuge near food and water, usually in the less severe northern desert. Meanwhile, we traveled ever deeper into the hot summer Gobi.

That morning we were surprised and pleased to hear singing ahead. It was a herdsman on horseback singing a Mongolian Long Song, or *urtyn duu*, to his sheep and goats as they foraged the last few wisps of grass. Long Songs can go on for hours, and they usually tell stories of the steppes, the desert, and love. This one provided us with much-appreciated relief from the day's discomforts.

The herder's rich voice reached us long before he saw us. We envied him his obvious comfort in his uncomplicated world of desert and animals and in his proud heritage. With a shouted welcome he galloped his horse to meet us, standing in the stirrups, a necessity when using the unforgiving wooden Mongolian saddle at speed. Carrying a long *uurga*, a traditional wooden lasso, he was at one with his horse as both flowed across the uneven ground.

With a flourish of showmanship, he reined the horse in and asked with a puzzled tilt of his head why we were walking. We told him of our journey and braced ourselves for his reply.

"You should ride the camels," he said, as he looked them over with an experienced eye. I explained that my injured leg made that impossible. He slowly looked me up and down, then turned his inspection to Bill, and in the totally innocent way we liked so much in Mongolians, simply said, "It's crazy. It's too far." Then, as an afterthought, he added, "Foreigners are all crazy."

Having established our mental condition, he looked with admiration at Tom and Jerry. He dismounted his horse, dropping the reins and trusting the horse to not move an inch, and opened Tom's mouth to inspect his teeth. Then he poked Jerry in his well-fleshed ribs. Stepping back, he nodded his head in approval. "You know how to choose camels. They must be from the north; there aren't any camels that look this good around here." We were pleased that in spite of his negative assessment of our mental state, he approved of our camels. To avoid bursting his bubble of admiration, we did not tell him that the camels had been chosen for us and that we really were not the camel experts he thought we were. Then, in the hospitable way of the desert people, he invited us to his *ger*.

Just as we arrived, two look-alike teenage girls galloped up, grinning from ear to ear, and leapt to the ground even before the horses were completely stopped. It was an acrobatic display for our benefit and approval. We clapped our hands, smiled, and nodded our admiration of their riding prowess and their horses. Thoroughly pleased with our reaction, they tied the horses to the nearby rail and ran giggling into the *ger* ahead of us.

These animals were superior specimens of the little Mongolian horses whose ancestors had helped conquer half the world in the days of Genghis Khan and his successors. To this day, Mongolians' horses are one of their greatest assets. These horses, not much bigger than large ponies, carried whole armies to victory on their powerful, thick-necked bodies. The modern-day

169

horse carries nomadic herdsmen across the desert and steppes with graceful strides and incredible stamina. Their riders stand in the stirrups for mile after mile, exhibiting the balance and confidence that comes from learning to ride almost before they can walk.

Mongolians use two types of saddle. One is a padded Russian leather model, while the other is the brightly colored, traditional Mongolian wooden saddle with a high back and front, which looks to Western eyes like an instrument of torture. The design is perfect for lassoing horses in the wide-open steppe and desert, and it holds riders in position so they will not be unceremoniously dragged to the ground by a runaway lassoed animal.

Serjee, our host, ushered us into the *ger* to meet his smiling wife, Daasha. Dressed in a pale blue *del*, she immediately impressed us with her ability to keep a clean and well-organized home despite the dearth of water and the inevitability of dust. Rainbow-colored hand-embroidered panels circled the base of the round ceiling, and embroidered covers adorned dressers and beds. Her pots and pans could have been used for mirrors.

The two look-alike girls, with almond-shaped eyes and fresh friendly smiles, were impeccably clean, as if they had stayed inside all day instead of working outside herding animals. Glowing with pride, Daasha told us that the girls were fifteen-year-old twins. Both wore dark blue pants and bright flowered blouses. Serjee told Daasha about our camels. After a quick inspection, she nodded her agreement. "They are fine animals," she said, as she placed dried camel dung in the stove. As we'd observed before, the dung burned hot, clean, and odorless.

As we sipped the salty tea, Serjee told us they had lost two hundred sheep and goats from their herd of four hundred during the past winter's deep snows, cold winds, and temperatures that dropped to 50 degrees below zero. To make matters worse, they were able to save only four camels and six horses—essential animals used for transportation during the summer moves.

Dejected, he described the family's dual agony: watching their animals die in the cold, and feeling helpless because they could do nothing to save them. One of the girls cried as she told how she had lost her favorite horse, a five-year-old black mare. The only way they had saved any animals at all was by feeding them the hay they had carried back from the northern steppes for winter feed. But there wasn't enough to go around.

A few yards from the *ger* was a round shelter pen without a roof, where the animals would have stayed in winter. It was thirty feet in diameter, with three-foot-high walls made of hundreds of rocks that had been painstakingly gathered one by one from the surrounding desert. Under normal winter conditions the rock walls would provide a windbreak, and the availability of a small amount of food from the surrounding desert, together with hay, would be enough to keep animals alive until spring. Then moisture from the spring snowmelt would enable plants to grow before the summer heat arrived. But the conditions producing a full-scale *zud* were too much for most animals to take. Only the hardiest would survive in a meager shelter like this one.

Their herds are desert families' only source of food and income. The families sell wool and cashmere to buy hay and food staples that help make life bearable in the desert. They stuff the wool and cashmere into bags and take it to the nearest village, where buyers representing large companies gather. Since the fall of Communism and its collective farming, herders are at the mercy of the market. The herders have little bargaining power and take whatever is offered.

Mongolia produces some of the world's highest-quality cashmere, which is used to create beautiful high-fashion sweaters. Cashmere, or *nooluur* in Mongolian, comes from the small cashmere goat, usually brown or white, which originated in the mountainous area of Kashmir in the Himalayas. Due to the cold Mongolian winters, these goats grow a thick, downy undercoat for warmth. It is these fine fibers, particularly those of the white goat, that the herding families rake out each spring using a

171

long-toothed comb. The animals' four legs are tied and, sometimes with considerable protesting, the goats are combed one at a time. It takes the labor of the entire family, as well as immeasurable patience, to comb two or three hundred goats, each producing about six ounces of cashmere. (Sheep and camels are easier to handle; they are shorn of their wool using long-bladed scissors.)

Cashmere is Mongolia's most valuable crop, yet the fragile ecosystem that these animals depend on for sustenance has become threatened by the overgrazing of increasingly larger flocks of sheep and goats in the Gobi. This is having a serious impact on the Mongolian economy, and on individual Mongolians.

Which animal is his most valuable, we asked Serjee. His brow wrinkling in deep thought, he finally answered that the goats are the most valuable for food and cashmere, but they need the camels and horses for transportation and to carry the *ger* and possessions as they move about the desert.

When I asked him if times were easier now that Mongolia had achieved freedom from Soviet rule, he shrugged his shoulders in resignation. For the desert herdsmen, far from the capital in a country with few roads, he said, the collective society of the Soviets was easier because the government made all the decisions and provided desert towns with hospitals, doctors, and schools free of charge. Herdsmen belonged to large collectives with strictly enforced quotas. The government bought cashmere and wool at a set price.

"Now, under the free market system," he told us, "we never know what we will be paid." A pensive mood settled over him as he reflected on the past. "Political change arrived too fast, and jobs in the towns were replaced with empty shops and famine. Second-generation city families were forced to return to the countryside and their traditional herding ways just to survive.

"At least," he said, "a herdsman is now independent and owns his own food supply and can feed his family. But markets are uncertain, and most herders have no money to pay for schools and doctors. Perhaps when Mongolia is financially stable again, the independent system will work." With a deep sigh, his voice trailed off, leaving a substantial question mark in the air.

After the family graciously accepted our farewell gifts, we gathered the camels' leads and resumed our journey as the smiling family waved good-bye and invited us to visit again. But as with our other new desert friends, it seemed unlikely that we would be able to find them during the summer months as they moved from place to place. Already bags of wool, cashmere, and various household possessions were stacked in readiness for the move north. With an almost dry well, it was time to leave and not return until the arrival of the first winter snowfall.

CHAPTER 9 **HOSPITALITY**

DAYS 46–48 > Just before dawn, a two-foot-long gray snake darted down a nearby hole as I stepped from the tent. An even longer specimen slid silently into its home as we ate breakfast. With the discovery of more holes, we chose a hurried retreat to avoid additional encounters.

Jerboas scurried across our path. These tiny, mouse-like nocturnal animals with long tails and large eyes and ears can cover ten feet in one leap. In the absence of humans, for days at a time jerboas, geckoes, and scorpions had often been our only company in the cooler evenings and early-morning hours.

As we traveled across a vast reddish plain, an insidious

weariness that edged toward exhaustion dogged our steps. We were still in the first half of July, and although the plain stood consistently at 5,000 feet, the midmorning's temperature rose to 122 degrees. It was impossible to continue without shade. Under our umbrellas we lay on the hard-packed earth, and after a long drink we made a futile attempt to doze away the fatigue, but the July heat was too much.

The faint sounds of camels reached us from the south. Soon twelve plodded past, one behind the other, carrying ponderous loads of family possessions: chests of drawers, a stove, the folded latticework of *gers* and their felt linings. Nine glum-looking adults and four children rode horses, some ahead of the camel train and others bringing up the rear, just as silent as their camels.

I raised my hand in greeting to the closest rider, a young man who slumped wearily in his saddle, and sensed in the tone of his response that something was seriously amiss. He mumbled that they had gone without water since the night before and asked if we had any to spare. Holding out my water bottle, I offered him a drink. With eager hands, he grabbed the bottle and swallowed in great gulps. After conferring with Bill, I told the man that he could take five gallons.

Without further conversation, he spurred his horse forward to his family, who in their thirsty weariness had ridden on with no energy for talk. As he went he yelled "*Us, us*"—water, water. Without delay, an older man with a plastic container galloped back on a black horse, and we filled it. In gratitude, he took from his saddlebag a sack made of a sheep stomach filled with sweet yogurt and presented it to Bill with profuse thanks. Before leaving at daylight, the man said, they had given their last well water to the herd, which left the family with no water. Even as adapted as they were to the desert, the raw effects of thirst had crept up on them through a waterless day. Turning to his family, who had by now ridden back upon hearing that we would share our water, he urged them all to drink two full bowls.

His tiny wife, whose round face beamed as she took her share, told us they were one day away from a mountain spring, where their sheep and goats would already have arrived, herded by two brothers. She raised her bowl high with both hands, as if offering it to the gods. "*Us,*" she exclaimed, then drank. Afterward she kissed first my hand, then Bill's, then shyly hugged me and said "*Nuudelchin,*" nomad. To be called a nomad by one of the desert's own was the ultimate compliment.

The young man lashed the now partly full container to the back of his saddle, and everyone set off on their way. Just before crossing a ridge that would put them out of our sight, the older man turned his horse at the summit to face us, stood in the stirrups, and extended his right arm skyward in a final salute. We waved in return, and later, as we ate the delicious yogurt, we talked of the dedication these people had displayed toward their herd. Apparently having left their move north until almost too late, they had chosen to give their last water to their animals.

A short time later, in the hot breath of a gentle breeze, we set out across a particularly monotonous area of sand and rust-colored gravel. There was no sign of life anywhere, not even a gecko. My frequent checks of my watch to count the hours made time crawl by. Bill put his own watch in his pocket to avoid the temptation.

North of our route, about twenty miles away, lay the enormous Tavan Tolgoi coal mine, which contains one of the largest coal deposits in Mongolia. Lignite, a soft coal, is used for most of the country's energy needs, especially city power plants and the stoves of urban dwellers. This results in severe air pollution in Ulaan Baatar and other cities.

A major part of Mongolia's foreign earnings comes from mining. The country includes one of the world's largest copper mines; a variety of gem and marble mines; and hundreds of small, family-run gold mines as well as those operated by large companies. Oil exploration is also on the rise in areas of the Gobi. Several nomads we met felt that the Gobi's increasingly dry climate is caused by the major disturbances of the soil and rocks due to mining. An ancient custom decreed that the soil should never be dug and the rocks never disturbed, so that the gods would remain in peace. These nomads believed that their mother, the god of the earth, and their father, the god of the sky, are angered by modern excavation and are punishing the people by keeping the rain away. In a country struggling to find its way in a fast-paced world, the old ways will continue to compete with the new.

The days had merged into a blur of heat, mirages, and pain. I was now using my second set of fiberglass trekking poles, the first valiant pair having given out on Day 44. The wrist straps, which resembled cross-country ski pole handles, had worn through, and a fiberglass shaft had split. Our second pair of boots already showed the effects of abuse.

With about 650 miles to go, our steps slowed as we forced ourselves across the impoverished land. It was impossible to imagine anything that could live here. We passed the dead bodies of a camel and a sheep. As always, with sadness, we wondered about their end.

We skirted a hollow that had held a miniature lake but was now dry and crusted with salt crystals. In the ruthless July heat, the water had long since disappeared. In the afternoon we retreated under our umbrellas in air so hot even the shade was overpowering.

As we sought relief from the sun, we tried to visualize the expanse before us in winter: below-zero temperatures, snowstorms, killer winds that sweep south from Siberia to blanket the desert in snow and ice from October to March. In the unrelenting heat, it was beyond our ability to grasp the full impact of living in a place with such a dramatic shift in climate—a place where winter is divided into nine periods of nine days, the Buddhist lucky number, which makes the season officially eighty-one days long. The Buddhists have named each period, the first being "Lambs Must Be Covered." Winter's end becomes "Not Cold Enough to Freeze Soup," and spring, "Brings Back Life to Normal."

After the eighty-first day, Tsagaan Sar, White Month, is celebrated. It begins the Lunar New Year and is one of the two most important holidays in Mongolia (the other being summer's

Naadam Festival). After consulting the stars, the lamas decide when in January or February the three-day celebration will start. Every home lays out a lavish supply of food and drink to welcome the continuous stream of visitors. Bright-colored candies and cookies, specially prepared bread, mutton, and the mainstay of all celebrations—a sort of small mutton dumpling called *buuz*, and of course vodka—are consumed in abundant quantities.

After dinner on Day 48, in the light of the moon, I gathered a few rocks and stacked them into a two-foot-high cairn. I wanted to leave something behind that would mark our passage across a land that, although harsh and demanding, had become our life. Bill placed a few larger rocks around the base and a tiny one on top, and then I wrote a short note on a page torn from Bill's journal:

> *Although the harshness of this desert sometimes climbs
> beyond human endurance, a deep feeling of tranquility
> floods our senses as we allow ourselves to become part of
> the earth, wind, sand, and dust that surrounds us. We can
> never conquer the elements; we can only experience them as
> a visitor, knowing that after we have passed, the desert will
> continue its ways both gentle and violent long after we are
> gone. It takes time to understand the special freedom that
> comes when we join hands with Mother Nature and follow
> her lead. The increasing weariness and outward struggle is
> made easier when we are at peace with our surroundings and
> at one with our Creator.*

179

Sealing the note in a small plastic bag, Bill placed it in the center of the cairn. Perhaps some weary traveler would read it one day and find comfort in it.

DAY 49 > The new day began with no sign of humans or their herds in a landscape that fell away to distant horizons, seemingly barren of life.

Toward evening we saw a *ger* a mile away, slightly to our north.

As we approached, we felt as though we had encountered a hectic desert intersection. Two large black-and-brown dogs barked their displeasure as we approached the few young goats they guarded so loyally. We tossed them a handful of *aaruul*. Their guard duties immediately forgotten, the dogs bolted down the cement-hard curds and looked up, expecting more. Dropping pieces now and then to keep them happy, we approached the *ger*.

The door burst open, and a man with legs bowed by a lifetime on horseback stepped out to greet us. Dressed in worn dark pants and an often-mended gray shirt with ragged sleeves, he had a welcoming smile that revealed teeth in urgent need of attention. He beckoned us inside and chuckled when he saw the two dogs alongside us, wagging their tails. When we showed him the pouch of *aaruul* dog bribes, he laughed.

Our dirty, disheveled appearance appeared to go unnoticed as he ushered us to the visitors' stools. It was immediately obvious that this family was critically poor. A woman whose deeply lined, leathery face revealed years of hard work washed a butchered goat's head at the side of the stove. She looked fifty, but she could have been only in her thirties. Her ragged blue *del* was held together in places by safety pins, and her boots were so worn that the soles were almost gone.

Her husband told her about the dog bribes and their effect. In that moment, the years fell from her worn face as she laughed and clapped her hands together. She explained, in broken English that she had learned as a worker at a girls' boarding school years ago, that a cousin had brought the two dogs to them because they were the most vicious dogs in their small village. The cousin had told them, "Nothing will get near your herd." It was hilarious to them that two strangers had walked right in.

The Mongolian steppe and desert is a land of magnificent dogs. Usually brown and black and very large, most descend from the Tibetan mastiffs that Tibetan monks brought with them to Mongolia in the pre-Soviet era.

Two children—a boy and girl aged eight and ten, both of

whom looked tired and underfed—rolled dough on a low wooden table, ready to slice into noodles. As my eyes adjusted to the dim light of the *ger*, I realized that a teenage girl was lying on a bed on the opposite side of the room, with a newborn baby suckling at her breast. A young man, who was later introduced as her husband, sat at the bedside beaming with pride. He proudly told us, in Mongolian seasoned with a little English, that the baby was only two hours old. They believed that the arrival of strangers so soon after the birth was a good omen for the baby's future. The young mother, whose name was Surenjav, appeared to be in poor health caused by malnutrition, which left her with little energy after a long period of labor.

The *ger* lacked the usual embroidery and brightly colored dressers. A white ceramic Buddha sat on a plain box at the back of the *ger*, but there were no wall coverings and no carpet to cover the packed-dirt floor. The older woman, now a grandmother, immediately served us salty tea from a pan already heating on the stove. Her husband, a new grandfather, brought more dung patties in from the pile outside as she stoked the fire, then set out a battered tin plate of *aaruul*. To please her, we each nibbled a piece and were pleased to find that it was the best hard curd we had eaten so far.

We followed the now familiar polite custom of inquiring about the health of their herd. "Are the animals fattening over the summer?" I asked the grandfather. His was yet another sad story of losing almost all their animals in the *zuds* of the last two winters. All they had left were twenty sheep, eleven goats, four camels, and six horses. They would stay for two more weeks, waiting for his brother, his wife, and their two children, who had also lost most of their animals to the winters' cold. The two families would join the remnants of their herds and travel north to find more food and water. He explained that when members of the same family lose animals, they often combine their herds for an improved chance to rebuild and survive. In spite of their great loss, his attitude was optimistic. He was sure their lot would improve next winter.

181

When the grandfather, Batbayar, asked how many animals we owned, we told him of our goat herd. He politely asked if they were fattening as we hoped, ready for winter. "Yes," I replied, "they are doing well." As soon as the formalities were over, we moved on to other popular conversation topics of the desert, such as water. He expressed the same concern we had already heard many times from herdsmen, that the water level of the desert was dropping, affecting water wells and drying up areas where animals traditionally found water. They hadn't seen rain for three years, and like others we had met, they spoke of earlier and higher summer temperatures. Rather than use their water, we used our own water supply for Tom and Jerry, and gave the family three gallons.

As we sat drinking tea, quite unexpectedly, the young girl stepped forward to softly touch my lips with her fingers. She had noticed that they were cracked and bleeding. Her mother nodded her head, "Too much sun and wind. In the winter it is too much cold." The young boy showed me a deep, infected cut that ran all the way across the back of his hand. The grandfather displayed an angry abscess, full of pus, on his left elbow. Suffering terribly along with their animals, the family had lacked sufficient nutrition over the winter to fight off these infections.

While Grandmother—whose name was Erveekhei, or Butterfly—cooked dinner, I treated the wounds. As I drained the abscesses, she mumbled some incoherent sounds as she sprinkled two drops of milk on each wound in a shamanistic ritual, then lit a candle and knelt before the Buddha statue to pray for healing for her family. After the wounds were dressed, they admired each other's bandages. Grandmother tied a strip of blue silk, the same type used on *ovoos*, around each bandage, explaining that the silk would stop evil spirits from entering the wounds. A devout Buddhist, she also clearly believed strongly in the shamanist spirit world.

I left a large supply of ointment, bandages, various-sized rolls of adhesive tape, and an unopened bottle of iodine on top of a cabinet. I gave a tube of anti-rash cream to Surenjav for her baby, then gave her all of our remaining vitamin and mineral tablets, explaining that these would help her regain energy and health. At first she was skeptical, but when I explained that a healthy mother makes good milk for her baby, she agreed to take the supplements.

The grandfather and grandmother invited us to stay the night, but they were so poor we felt guilty eating the food that they, as good hosts, were bound by tradition to serve us. I told them we would stay only if they would honor us by sharing our rice. In silence they looked at each other, puzzled by the offer, unsure what they should do.

I suggested that Butterfly cook the rice on her stove. The idea of the hostess doing the cooking won them over. Before they had second thoughts about the arrangement, which we knew was a totally new concept to them, we made a speedy retreat to get the rice from our pile of gear and food, which lay stacked on the ground outside.

From our large supply, Bill untied a ten-pound sack and gave it to Butterfly. She clasped her hands to her face and gasped at the sight of so much rice. Even after we assured her that we had plenty, she shook her head and worried that we might run short. To reassure her, I took her outside to show her another full sack. Satisfied, she returned to the *ger* and began cooking.

183

We were deeply touched to see her anxiety over our food rations when she and her family were so poor that they had not eaten well all winter and faced a bleak future. When the rice was half cooked she took a sheep's fat tail, cut it into bite-sized chunks, and mixed them with the rice and more water. It had been added as a special treat in honor of our arrival close to the birth of their grandchild. The result was the greasiest meal we had ever seen. She filled bowls and handed one to each person. The family immediately dug in with extraordinary zeal, noisily slurping each mouthful in the best Mongolian tradition.

Later, it was time to perform the evening milking. After we helped them milk their few goats, we retreated to our tent. Earlier we had explained that we would feel guilty if we crowded them, especially with the new baby, and we really wouldn't mind sleeping in our tent. Only after Butterfly and Batbayar had made a thorough inspection of our tent and sleeping bags did they agree to allow us to sleep there. As a last precaution, Butterfly tied a tiny piece of blue silk to the tent "to keep away evil spirits."

Just as we were about to slide into our sleeping bags, Butterfly ran to tell us that the family wanted to demonstrate throat singing in our honor. Back in the candlelit *ger*, Batbayar demonstrated the *khoomi*, or throat singing of Mongolia. From deep within his throat, he produced a beautiful harmony of varied musical notes. Butterfly proudly told us that he had been trained as a boy to sing the *khoomi*, and when she first met him as a sixteen-year-old, he sang a love song to her.

Throat-singing tones are deep and rich, usually performed by men. The nomads' life, so closely interwoven with their animals and the environment, is strongly reflected in their songs. For an hour we listened to one enchanting song after another. Finally Batbayar put the accompanying fiddle away, and with the melodious singing still ringing in our ears, we returned to our tent.

In a whispered conversation, we discussed the new baby. The family was so poor that I worried about the mother and her meager diet, and what this might mean for her nursing infant. Our extra food supplies wouldn't be enough to sustain them through the next winter. The baby had no clothes and was wrapped only in a thin cotton cloth. They had told us their relatives, who were due to arrive at any time, were also poor due to their own herd losses.

"There must be something we can do," I told Bill.

We tossed ideas back and forth until Bill said, "I wonder if Chuluu could find them in the desert and deliver a supply of food and clothes?"

I replied, "It'll only work if we can pinpoint the place they'll move to for the rest of the summer."

Our bank account in the capital held $3,000 for emergencies. We agreed that this was an emergency.

DAY 50 > Soon after we awoke, we were summoned to the *ger* to drink a bowl of salty tea before the morning milking. We took the opportunity to have Batbayar and Butterfly describe exactly where they were moving. We explained that a friend would fly in with extra supplies, and clothes for the baby, if he could find them. At first they found it incomprehensible that anyone would fly into the desert to deliver anything to them, and they were adamant in their refusal of that much help.

To preserve their sense of independence and pride, we reminded them that they had told us that as the first strangers to see the new baby in its first hours, our arrival was considered a good omen for the child's future. "This," I explained, "would be the expected good omen, and you can accept help on behalf of the baby."

This last comment persuaded these proud people to agree to our offer. They described their intended route and the number of days they expected to travel. Because they don't use maps, they instead described ridges, hollows, and mountains. An hour and several pages of notes later, we were confident that we had a route description that desert-savvy Chuluu could follow in his plane.

Morning milking-time had arrived. Men and boys almost never perform milking chores, because it is considered woman's work, but Bill broke this tradition, as he explained to them, "just for the experience." While the girl and her mother milked six goats, we laboriously milked four.

Next, with rapidly improving technique, we milked the four camels, which all stood still, except for one that slapped me in the face with her short, whip-like tail, perhaps in protest at my less than experienced hands. Then, for good measure, just as I was extracting the last few squirts of milk, she gave me another mighty whack across my face.

Under Butterfly's watchful gaze, I tried my best to look as if nothing out of the ordinary had happened, but for several minutes I could barely see through the stinging pain. It reminded me somewhat of milking Holsteins on our own farm.

Explaining that we needed to move on before the main heat of the day descended, we passed up the family's offer of breakfast. They understood and helped us take down the tent, although the tent poles, with elastic joining each section, were a complete puzzle to them. The grandparents and two children grabbed a pole each and pulled each end at the same time, watching the lengthening elastic in consternation. I reached over and showed them how to pull and fold each section of pole. There was a collective "ah" of understanding. Thirty minutes later the tent was still a heap of red fabric on the ground, but at least the poles were folded and put away.

In the meantime, while everyone was distracted by the tent and its strange ways, Bill sneaked over and emptied more of our remaining rice into an empty bag. He then quietly placed it inside the *ger* alongside the first bag, giving the family sixteen pounds all together. It would be a surprise for them after we left.

After we gathered the tent and the other gear, we loaded the camels. We gave the family two pairs of socks each, several cakes of soap, and three pounds of salt. I pressed our spare sleeping bag into the new mother's hands, telling her it was for her baby. Their smiles of delight were a sight to behold.

Then I had an idea. I asked Batbayar if he would be kind enough to take our extra *togrogs*, which is the Mongolian currency. I explained that we were almost ready to go home, and if he would take the money for his grandchild, it would save us the trouble of exchanging it. He beamed from ear to ear.

We were well versed enough in the ways of nomads to know that if we had offered money to him directly, he would have been insulted and would have refused it to save face. But saying the money was for his grandchild made it acceptable. Only a man could give Batbayar money, so Bill gave him enough *togrogs* to equal fifty American dollars, which was a fortune to a desert herdsman.

Butterfly ran to the *ger* roof, reached up, and took down two saucer-sized pieces of precious dried goat meat from a large pile spread out to dry on the roof in the sun. It was our turn to smile and nod our profuse thanks. As a favor, Batbayar asked us to herd his four camels for about one mile along our route to a dip in the desert and leave them there to graze for the day. "You will know the dip because there is a dead goat on one side," he told us. After assuring him that we would be glad to escort the camels, the family set about bringing them to us, which gave me the opportunity to place the disks of meat back on the *ger* roof, alongside the rest of the meat they were drying for winter, without anyone noticing.

We were given the sort of good-bye that is normally reserved for highly respected elders. Butterfly performed the traditional ceremonial tossing of milk into the air and then held me tight, tears streaming down her lined face, not wanting me to leave. Surenjav appeared with the baby still wrapped in her pitiful cotton cloth and pressed the girl's tiny hands into mine. As I looked into the innocent new face through my own tears, I silently prayed that the baby and her family would be protected from harm. Batbayar shook Bill's hand and then, with a deep bow, briefly took both of Bill's hands in his.

Finally, with waves and wishes for our continued good health and, as custom demands, the good health of our animals at home, we departed for the open desert. Before dropping down in a dip in the plain, though, we turned for one last wave. Butterfly waved a blue silk banner, and the baby was held aloft in a final salutation. I could barely see through my tears as we descended out of sight.

DAY 51 > Still far from our journey's end, we forced a brisk pace hour after hour through air that made breathing a stifling affair. At noon on Day 51, with the temperature over 123 degrees, we rested in the shade of our umbrellas and, over the next three hours, drank four quarts of water each. Our seven-day bout with thirst had made us even more aware of the severe consequences of dehydration.

My leg and hip were in a pathetic state, with pain well beyond anything I had previously known. But I knew that to stop anywhere along our march would make all the miles I had so far fought for, a waste. I didn't want to look back on this journey and wonder if I might have made it if I had tried harder. And our struggles felt even more worthwhile because we were gathering more photography and information to add to Adventure Class-room than we had ever dreamed possible.

Just before three o'clock we saw what we thought must be a mirage of camels, sheep, goats, and horses approaching. But soon our sun-blasted eyes made out the forms of people riding horses. In a half hour they were upon us, surprised to see people walking and leading two camels.

The man was dressed in a dark, worn *del* with an orange sash at his waist. He wore the traditional high leather boots with up-turned toes, which we had been told earlier would prevent the wearer from disturbing the spirits of the soil. (It is believed that if the spirits are disturbed, they might not allow plants to grow.)

He told us they were traveling to meet his brother and his family. Then, together, both families would drive their herds north to food and water. We soon discovered that, by an amazing coincidence, he was the brother whom Batbayar and Butterfly were waiting for. This man also spoke of a winter with little to eat and of helplessly watching his animals die.

Although the entire family wore clothes that were well past worn out, and they all had the same pinched, unhealthy look as their relatives, we were impressed by the physical and emotional strength of the husband, who we were sure would be responsible for the survival and well-being of both families. After we wished each other safe traveling, he reached down to shake our hands and profusely thanked us for our friendship to his brother and his family. They rode away, driving their animals slowly before them, while we continued east, determined that Chuluu must find them before winter.

CHAPTER 10

BRIDE

DAYS 52–54 > With the Khan Bogd Mountain in the background, we walked through the sand-strewn streets of a small remote village of the same name at an elevation of 3,608 feet. The town's well was the most sophisticated setup we had so far seen. It was surrounded by a locked cement blockhouse attended by a matronly, business-like woman who was selling water to a line of women who patiently waited their turn with a variety of containers.

While I held the two camels to one side, Bill stepped into line with his container. We immediately became the object of attention. I smiled, trying to look as if I fit in, while Bill looked as if he wished he were somewhere else. After looking us over, everyone resumed the conversations that our arrival had interrupted. It was an hour before Bill, who was tenth in line, reached the front, where he paid the equivalent of five cents for ten gallons.

Outside the village, we wound our way for several miles through mounds of sand and gnarled shrubs, which offered little sustenance to the few camels and goats that wandered listlessly about. Bill named the place Desperation Valley.

That night, to our astonishment, we came upon five twenty-foot-high ancient trees, called *tooroi*, in a shallow, rocky valley. They had thick, deeply grooved bark, and roots that reached down to water not far beneath the surface. It was a delightful novelty to finger their dark green leaves, which were smooth to the touch. We gleefully set up camp beneath the grove, amid sand berms bordering washouts formed by melting spring snow. Our joy was short-lived, though, when we met our neighbors—snakes and scorpions—which also found the trees to be an agreeable refuge.

The next day we arrived at the Janchivdechlen Monastery, set at the base of stark mountains a few hundred feet high. A monk told us that the monastery had been looted and destroyed by the Russians in 1938 and now was being rebuilt. Desolate and austere, it housed 530 monks, far short of the 1,000 who had lived there before the Russians killed most of them and reduced the buildings to rubble.

The area was so remote and deep in the desert, we wondered how the Russians ever found the place. Except for a few *tooroi* trees, which we were told were two or three hundred years old, the bleak and deserted surroundings would have been depressing but for the inspiration of meeting people with the strength of character and passion to rebuild a place of worship from the dust and rubble, without any trace of malice for the forces that had destroyed it.

As we left the area, two *khulan* spent a startled few moments determining whether we were friend or enemy, then galloped away into the nearby barren hills.

DAYS 55–58 > The next four days were one of the worst stretches of the entire journey. It was unbearably hot, and our path took us over sand mounds and hills where broom grass grew, its spiny two-foot-high stalks ready to scratch and pull at us as we fought our way through it. Sand clumped our hair, permeated our clothes, and crept into our boots. Taking each step on the soft surface was a trial. And the daily struggle increased the pain radiating throughout my left side; I ate pain pills like candy.

Tom and Jerry fared much better. Their taller stature enabled them to avoid the more unpleasant aspects of broom grass, and their well-designed feet helped them glide over the sand. During a grazing break they snatched mouthfuls of the green blades at the base of each clump of dried stalks, while Bill and I seized the meager shade that a four-foot-high thicket provided, vowing that we never again wanted to see this plant, or any other like it, as long as we lived.

DAYS 59–60 > On Day 59 it became apparent that we would have to travel forty-six miles in two days in order to meet Chuluu on time on Day 60. Although this would not have posed a problem earlier in the journey, now it seemed a monumental task, given all of the energy we had expended in the last week or so to make progress over the exhausting terrain. Happily, the sand mounds, hills, and broom grass were behind us, and ahead lay the kinder open plains.

Anticipating the need for a lengthy rest at noon, we set out with the first light. Around midday we stopped, and as we rested beneath our umbrellas, we figured out a way to navigate an easier route through some wicked-looking rough ridges ahead, without running the risk of backtracking if we chose the wrong approach. We headed toward what appeared to be the line of least resistance and were pleasantly surprised to find a wheel track that, although churned and rutted, led us through the ridges.

After the track turned north toward a village several miles away, where people worked copper and gold mines in the mountains, we made our own way east. We stopped to cook dinner, fed Tom and Jerry, then continued on into the night across a flat barren plain. We camped at midnight, only to start all over again at 5 AM A short noon break kept us on schedule and, still surrounded by a level, horizontal world, we arrived at the resupply coordinates with two hours to spare. The entire area resembled a landing field, it was so flat and rock free. We were ready for Chuluu's arrival in no time, and took the opportunity to take our boots off our tired feet and rest.

Promptly at 7 PM Chuluu arrived, churning up the usual dust cloud as he taxied toward us. We unloaded everything, including a surprise box of goodies that Chuluu told us not to open until dinner. After confirming arrangements and coordinates for our next meeting, which would be our last day if all went according to plan, he left for the capital to attend his sister's wedding. Although he was with us only briefly, his visit and upbeat, jolly attitude was a breath of fresh air, particularly after the tiresome struggle to navigate through many miles of sand and washouts.

Eager to open our surprise rations, we ate early, and to our delight discovered the largest apple pie we had ever seen—made especially for us by a lady in Ulaan Baatar, who included a note wishing us well and sending her love. Our unanimous verdict was that it was the best pie we had ever eaten, and most likely the best pie in the entire world. That dear lady and her kindness brought our drained bodies back to life.

DAYS 61–62 > For once we didn't set the alarm clock; we'd let our bodies tell us when to awaken. Fourteen hours later, at the decadent of hour of 10 AM, we awoke as the sun's heat warmed the tent to an uncomfortable level.

After feeding grain and the newly delivered grass to Tom and Jerry, we ate a breakfast of fresh bread and peanut butter, then headed in the direction of Zuunbayan, a town notable for increasing oil exploration in the adjacent desert. To our north lay the 2,500-foot Dadiyn Khar Ovoo, amid a sand and gravel plain. Later we encountered more rugged, shallow valleys surrounded by rocky ridges. In one, a ten-foot-deep well nestled among the trees still held an ample supply of clear water. Tom and Jerry happily drank the sweet liquid, which we pulled up in a bucket we found beside the well.

Desert custom dictates that when a traveler finds water, they are welcome to take all they need but must fill the trough for any passing animals. No sooner had we poured the first bucket into the trough than we were stopped by the sound of galloping hooves. It was a herd of around twenty horses that, sensing water, were racing to get their fill. We sloshed water into the trough as fast as we could pull it up, but were no match for the thirsty beasts. Finally, for safety's sake, Bill, with a lot of arm-waving, kept the horses at bay while I hurried to fill the trough. Once we stepped back, both sides of the twenty-foot-long trough were lined with horses bent on quenching their thirst. After the last horse left, we refilled the trough. Very likely the animals belonged to a family whose *ger* lay some distance away, out of sight across the rocky ridges.

We continued to trek steadily through furrowed valleys of rough, rocky volcanic ridges and numerous sand hills. Close to Zuunbayan, we broke out onto a blank expanse that was empty space on the map. It was so flat that we could have played billiards on its surface. Plant life had disappeared, and so had people and animals. Mirages danced, teasing us with vast lakes of nonexistent water. To the south stood Burdene Bulag, some of the largest sand dunes in the Gobi. As we swung north on our way to Sainshand, we left the Chinese border 120 miles behind us.

The next morning, the 60-degree night air quickly fired up as the sun burst above the horizon to burn across the tabletop. Our route took us directly into the sun's glare. Even sunglasses couldn't adequately protect our protesting eyes, which watered in the intense light.

Skirting Zuunbayan around noon, we found a well three miles north of the village, where the camels happily drank. Unlike their human companions, they didn't seem to mind the garbage that floated on the surface of the chocolate-colored water, or even notice that the surrounding area was covered in animal dung and human feces. Unwilling to linger, we guided the camels' feet around dozens of broken, scattered vodka bottles.

Zuunbayan and other small desert villages are a crumbling legacy to the Soviet regime—places of neglect, poverty, and drunkenness. The new Mongolia has no programs or money to provide jobs and support for the people left stranded by political change. Most of the once productive Soviet factories here, which produced goods ranging from clothing to heavy steel beams, have been shut down and stripped of anything worthwhile. Schools cater to the basic educational needs of village children and to a few nearby nomadic families who agree to send their children to school in the winter. A tall black smokestack signals a coal-driven electric plant—often no longer working, or at best working intermittently. The lack of work and future opportunities leaves the inhabitants hopeless, and it is vodka, usually the cheap home-brewed variety, that often relieves their misery.

Medical facilities, if they exist at all, have only the most basic supplies and structures. Hospitals are often dilapidated and poorly constructed. Undertrained staff and doctors with little medical training do their best with their limited knowledge and facilities. Their job is made impossible by the lack of antibiotics or diagnostic equipment.

We heard horror stories of mistreatment for routine medical problems. An attractive young woman suffered a simple fracture of the lower leg and was confined to bed in a half-body cast for a year. By that time, the leg had wasted away and the joints and muscles were stiff and useless. A ten-year-old girl suffered recurring abdominal pains. In the hospital they "bled her," after which she died of appendicitis and lack of blood. Although the open desert was brutally harsh, it was easy for us to leave these dismal places and move on.

DAY 63 > After a morning of crossing a level, stony sea of pebbles, we were surprised to see a group of five *gers*, with a gleaming white one in the center, sitting on a low ridge a mile away. A man in his midtwenties, who had herded about five hundred sheep and goats close to the *ger*, was tying his horse to a rail. He looked up as we approached and enthusiastically beckoned us into the new *ger*. This was not the usual well-established family *ger*; it was the home of a new bride and of the groom who had just ushered us inside. Married only one week, they were still in the midst of festivities, which last two weeks for well-to-do families.

Mongolians welcome a visit by strangers during celebrations, regarding it as an omen for a future full of children and happiness. Consequently, we found ourselves to be the guests of honor. In the best Mongolian newlywed tradition, everything was brand-new, from the *ger* to the smallest pots and pans. Gleaming kettles sat on a shiny iron stove, and the walls were festooned in bright woven mats. Our feet sank into the soft green carpet as we sat on freshly painted blue stools. The smiling bride, radiant in her golden *del*, which she had hurriedly put on as we entered, passed heaping plates of special wedding candy and cookies along with sweet bread baked in long twisted rolls. Her mother-in-law piled more plates high with chunks of mutton fat and a hard white cheese. The bride's sister made tea and passed it to us in new china bowls.

Separating myself from the vast array of food being placed on my plate, I went outside to find suitable gifts. I gathered a one-pound bag of salt, six bars of white scented soap, and four pairs of winter socks. I racked my brain for something romantic, but there was no such thing in our practical supplies. Back inside, I presented the gifts to the bride. She declared that she had never seen socks so warm or soap so white.

Bill, observing an important tradition when visiting newlyweds, placed a few *togrog* notes on the foot-high pile on the altar at the back of the *ger*. The money was to help provide a generous start to the marriage. The bride urged us to take more food, especially the chunks of mutton fat, which are considered a special delicacy. A bowl of the sweetest yogurt was thrust into our hands. We were awash in food!

195

I glanced at Bill, who eagerly attacked a foot-long bread roll as if it might be his last. Avoiding the chunks of fat, I unabashedly dug into the goodies, chewing cookies and candy between spoonfuls of yogurt. Just as I was about to reach for the bread, I suddenly became aware of the picture we must be presenting, of two mannerless foreigners. With a discreet cough, I tried to hint to Bill that we should slow down. But he was so engrossed in the flow of delicious food that he seemed not to notice. Feeling a little self-conscious, I glanced at the family.

I need not have worried. The young couple and their extended family, ten people in all, were watching us with intense satisfaction. Taking my pause in eating as a signal that I needed more, they thrust delectables into my hand. Inevitably, we reached the threshold of queasiness. Praising the thoroughly commendable meal, I explained that we could eat no more. Now we were in trouble. It seemed an ungraspable fact that we had already eaten well beyond our normal capacity. I feared their goal was to never allow us to stop eating. These were undeniably the most obliging of hosts, with an intense aim to please. After struggling to force another cookie down, we gave up, much to our hosts' consternation. The tension was relieved, however, when I changed the subject from food to marriage traditions.

Eagerly, the bride, in a soft voice and exceptional English, explained that only after festivities were over could they settle down to married life. The wife, who normally moves away from her own family, sets up a home with her groom alongside the *gers* of his parents, his brothers, and their wives. In a successful marriage, the bride is accepted into her husband's family and soon becomes pregnant. With the birth of her first child, her new role as a mother elevates her status, even more so if the firstborn is a boy.

At an early age girls are trained to work hard, wait on the men, and remain obedient to their wishes. Desert marriages are still sometimes arranged, but are often the result of a young man falling in love with the girl from the next herding camp, several miles away.

The wedding is an agreement between two families and is accompanied by the transfer of a negotiable number of livestock to the bride's family, who in turn present a dowry of jewelry, household furnishings, and clothing to the groom's family. Glancing at her husband, who nodded in agreement, the bride went on to explain that wives are influential in family decisions and are well protected.

The bride's mother, who raised her children during the Soviet occupation, added that the Soviets had decreed that motherhood was a woman's patriotic duty and offered maternal incentives. Women with five or more living children received the Order of Maternal Glory second class, while those with more than eight children received the Order of Maternal Glory first class. Lucrative monetary rewards and other social privileges accompanied the medals. After the Soviets left the country, both awards were abandoned. We had observed that the families we had met so far had between two and four children.

The kind family's hospitality was nearly overwhelming, and finally we rose to leave, but it was not to be. Expressing the need to resume our journey produced a flurry of activity in which plates of candy, cookies, and bread were placed in a sack for our future sustenance. The groom's mother thanked us for all the good luck our presence would bring. Now, she was certain, the bride would bear many healthy sons. I wondered what would happen if the poor girl produced only daughters. At least we would be far away by then.

The newlyweds smiled their thanks. A brother thrust the camel leads into our hands, and the groom's mother tossed the traditional shower of milk into the air. Everyone waved good-bye, the bride's golden *del* gleaming in the sun.

We approached Sainshand across a plain that was quite flat in all directions. The glare from its pale gravel surface strained our eyes in the insufferable heat. Fuel trucks—great rumbling monsters, some quite ancient—rattled by, the drivers' faces set in grim determination to reach their destination.

Eventually we closed in on the sprawling city of Sainshand. But to our dismay, as we reached the outskirts we entered an area of abandonment and destruction the likes of which we had never seen before. Several acres of concrete buildings and the walls of a former Soviet military base that had housed hundreds of soldiers confronted us. When they left, the Russians had reduced to unusable rubble everything that could not be carried away, so that nothing would remain intact for the Mongolians to use. The waste was beyond belief.

The Soviets had created Sainshand in the 1950s when they opened the military base and a nearby oil field. The low-grade oil found here had a high wax content—good only for lubricants. In the extreme winter cold of the Gobi, however, the oil thickened, making extraction difficult. To compound the problem, the Soviets' archaic equipment and crude methods severely contaminated the surrounding desert. After discovering immense deposits of oil in Siberia, the Soviets abandoned the Gobi oil well and concentrated on extracting the higher grade found in Siberia. When the Gobi refinery was mostly destroyed in an explosion in 1965, the Soviets capped the well and left without repairing the damage and contamination.

We turned east to parallel the Trans-Gobi Railway, also called the Trans-Siberian Railway. It begins in Moscow, continues across Siberia to Ulaan Baatar, then crosses a narrow stretch of the Gobi Desert north to south and ends in China's Beijing. To prevent trains from colliding with animals, especially gazelle, a fence was built in the mid-1970s along both sides of the tracks. By some estimates, between 300,000 and one million gazelle inhabit the eastern steppes, providing one of Asia's premier wildlife spectacles. But due to habitat loss and barriers that interfere with migration, such as the railroad fences, population numbers have dropped drastically. Wilderness seems to have become irrelevant to humans in their rush to commercialize and control all that they touch, without regard for the needs of animals.

Two miles farther on, we found the crossing we were seeking.

Two boys, probably ten years old, were standing there with bicycles. Rather than take Tom and Jerry into the city, we asked the boys if they would watch over the camels until we returned. After settling on an inflated price equal to five American dollars, we left our two friends in the boys' care.

We followed a partly sealed road that, as Bill remarked, looked as if the thin black tar had been plastered on with a paintbrush. After about a half-mile we turned left and walked into town. Unlike the desert towns we had so far encountered, Sainshand, meaning "good spring," was a busy government center of about 20,000 people, most of whom were government employees. The town was clean, although dusty—not surprising, considering the desert that sat on its front and back doorstep, poised to sweep in during every sandstorm. Well-dressed people hurried about with an air of prosperity. Meaningful employment resulted in fewer drunks, and the despair we had observed in the desperately poor smaller towns was noticeably absent.

Gobi poplar and wicker trees lined many streets, and the mostly one- and two-story buildings were in reasonable condition. In the town center we found several well-stocked shops, no doubt a result of the town's being located on the railway line. Just to remind us that we were still in the Gobi, two cows wandered across the supermarket parking lot as if it were an everyday occurrence. Our desert-worn appearance drew polite stares of curiosity. Due to its southern position close to the Chinese border, almost three hundred miles south of Ulaan Baatar and surrounded by formidable desert, tourists seldom visit Sainshand. The town has only one or two basic hotels, which primarily accommodate train travelers on their way to Beijing.

In the well-stocked supermarket, we found fruit juice, sodas, fruit, and vegetables. Restraining myself from grabbing everything within reach, I gathered orange and mango juice, several cans of soda, a dozen apples, and tomatoes, while Bill, with a much more exotic diet in mind, headed for the bakery. When I joined him, he was contemplating a large chocolate cake covered with thick, creamy icing. As mouthwatering as it was, we decided that it would never survive the heat we were still to encounter. He finally settled on six doughnuts and several chocolate bars. "We'll eat it all as fast as we can, and what melts we'll give to Tom and Jerry."

At the mention of the camels, I picked up a bunch of carrots. Sheba, our donkey at home, loved carrots; perhaps camels would also enjoy them. Loaded to capacity, we paid for everything and then walked back to the crossing, where the two boys were feeding hay to Tom and Jerry. Their cousin had stopped by and returned with the sweet-smelling dry grass.

Such good care deserved a reward. To their pay we added two chocolate bars, a bottle of juice, and two doughnuts. Delighted, they offered to lead us to a good well and show us the way east out of town.

Our city visit had given us some relief from the endless plodding, but now we were once more back in the desert. We faced another four hundred miles of trekking to the eastern town of Ovoo, where we planned to end our trek.

CHAPTER 11 **FRIENDS**

DAY 64 > We headed southeast, toward the border, to avoid a particularly wicked barrier of sand hills and broom grass interspersed with rocky washes, which descended from the surrounding ridges.

Even though we still slung our water bottles on the camels' shady sides, keeping the water cool was futile. By ten o'clock the sun had warmed the water to an uncomfortable level, and by noon it was almost too hot to drink. In the far distance, heat waves produced tantalizing illusions of trees and small lakes beyond the sandy mounds we struggled through.

The passage of time takes on a different quality in a desert without shade. We would drink enough water to prevent dehydration, and travel until the heat had sapped so much strength and fluid from our bodies that we had to stop before the onset of heatstroke. In our struggle to meet our daily mileage goals, the tendency was to step beyond the red line of safety. Sometimes, in the midst of our regimented schedule, we had to remind each other to call for a halt for safety's sake.

Later in the sweat-ridden day, a tiny white dot appeared in the distance. Hoping it was a *ger* and not a mirage, we changed course by two degrees. As we approached, a *ger* did indeed materialize out of the haze. The only obvious signs of life were two black guard dogs that rose from their shady spot beside the dwelling. With deep, intimidating barks, their neck ruffs raised in indignation, they ran full speed at us. But we were prepared with handfuls of rock-hard *aaruul*. Instantly, their guard duties forgotten, they braked to a stop to gobble our offerings. Then, with wagging tails, they looked up in happy expectation. Pleased to oblige, we tossed more treats to them and resumed our approach to their home, with the now friendly dogs following on our heels.

I called out, "*Nokhoikhor*," which roughly translates as "Can I come in" but literally means "Hold the dog." Because some dogs become overly enthusiastic in their guard duties at the approach of strangers, "Hold the dog" is a common greeting.

Still, no one appeared. We braced ourselves for the traditional Mongolian entrance, which we were still unaccustomed to. In approved fashion, I pushed open the yellow wooden door and stepped high over the threshold, careful not to touch it. Bill followed close behind. As our eyes adjusted to the dim interior and our noses took in the smell of decaying, overly aged meat, an unsurprised woman with a lined but regal face quietly looked up from her stove. A squarely built man with a steady gaze and powerful shoulders rested on a bed and casually waved his hand toward the now familiar tiny wooden guest stools. The traditional Mongolian hat, made of blue felt that rose to a point with a red tip, capped his head. Tobacco smoke curled to the ceiling from his intricately carved, foot-long pipe. They had heard the dogs announcing our arrival. Two young girls, only about five or six years old, dressed in bright, Western-style blouses and long pants, stared shyly at us. The youngest hurried to her mother, leaned on her, and peeked out from the folds of her gray *del*.

While we exchanged greetings, the wife handed us bowls of salty tea. Meanwhile, the husband swung the door wide open to let in more light and to allow the heat from the stove—and, we hoped, some of the smell of overripe meat—to escape. The canvas and felt roof had been rolled back, and the bottom of the *ger* wall was raised to encourage a constant flow of air to help cool the interior. Only half the earthen floor was carpeted for the summer.

We sat on our stools welcoming the shade, drinking tea and eating goat's-milk yogurt. Thankfully, we seemed to have skipped the sour curds.

We were invited to stay the night. Delighted, we agreed and tied Tom and Jerry alongside the two horses, which were already secured to a rope that stretched like a clothesline between two tall wooden poles dug solidly into the baked earth.

Soon a fifteen-year-old girl, dressed in a dusty gray *del* and bright orange scarf, rode up on a white horse, driving a bleating herd of sheep and goats that bedded down beside the *ger*. Her older sister, a tall, slender, serious young woman who arrived with fifteen adult camels, along with their calves mewling at their sides, soon followed her. Upon the arrival of the herds, everyone went outside to start the evening chores, which began with tying the calves by their halters to a long rope anchored to the ground. Their mothers wandered off to browse on wisps of coarse broom grass, which grew in sparse clumps all around the area.

We offered to help. After a short, whispered conversation, they consented with smiles of approval and, I suspected, a little amusement. Our first job was to gather thirty sheep and goats from where they grazed, a half-mile away. At our approach the animals, used to being assembled in a country without fences, gathered into a tight bunch, ready to be herded back to the *ger*, where guard dogs would protect them from wolves throughout the night. Out of habit, the throng headed for the *ger*, moving as one, while we did little more than wave them along.

Meanwhile, the maternal grandmother and grandfather, who lived a mile away, had arrived on horses. The elderly couple had never met any foreigners, and their stares displayed curiosity peppered with wonderment at our strange practice of crossing a vast space on foot for no apparent reason.

One of their first questions concerned our age. When told that I was sixty-three and Bill was seventy-four, the grandmother gently ran her fingers over my cheeks and said, "There are no lines in your faces." I suppose that compared to the older nomads, whose faces were deeply lined from the extreme heat, wind, and winter cold, we looked young.

After introductions were made with the appropriate nodding of heads and smiling, everyone began dinner. We started with the customary bowl of tea, whose salty taste we had by now grown used to and enjoyed. Next, our hostess handed us fresh, delicious hard squares of goat's-milk *aaruul*, which we enthusiastically chewed. Then pieces of bread, covered with sweet cream that had been scraped off the top of boiled milk, were thrust into our hands. In other visits with nomads we had enjoyed sweet cream that was fresh, but once the cream sits in a dish for a few days in the summer heat, as this cream had, it turns rancid and sticky. Everyone else enthusiastically dipped their bread into the sour-smelling stuff. Appreciative slurping and loud burps complimented the hostess.

The wife, whose name was Suren, had made *buuz*, which resembles small boiled dumplings and is a favorite centerpiece of a Mongolian meal. First she mixed boiled mutton, which had been cut into fine pieces, with chopped onion and a small amount of garlic and flour. Then she placed the ingredients on a small circle of dough and, with a twist of the wrist, formed plump little balls. The dough edges were pinched together to ready them for steaming. A large plateful was ready in minutes.

Eagerly, unwashed hands reached for the *buuz* and, judging by the grunts and sighs of appreciation, it was a big hit. The little dumplings tasted good to us, so we dug in too. The first plateful disappeared with astonishing speed and was immediately followed by a second and third, but after eating a dozen of the tasty morsels, the fatty taste and smell of the gamey mutton caught up with us. Then it was on to the next delicacy served in our honor. We watched in horror as Suren went to a large leg of extremely ripe mutton hanging from the ceiling just inside the door. She cut off small pieces, laid them in a pan, and warmed them. Everyone watched in eager anticipation. That is, everyone except Bill and me.

As each person was served the still raw, stale meat, a few pieces dropped on the floor but were quickly returned to the plate. This was going to be a gastronomical test beyond compare. Desperately, I racked my brain for an excuse that would allow me to avoid eating my portion while still not violating the tight boundaries of nomadic etiquette, but there was none. With a smile that I hoped disguised my dread of food poisoning from the putrid meat, I took the smallest piece and placed it in my mouth.

Shock paralyzed my taste buds. I chewed, but could not swallow. Announcing that I had left something I needed in our pile of gear, I rushed out and spat the fetid meat onto the ground. After I returned, I made a futile attempt to drown the taste in salty tea, but hours later the taste still lingered.

Bill was served after me and had more time to consider his course of action. With the deftness of a magician he appeared to place a piece in his mouth, but instead palmed it. At a convenient moment he slipped it into his pocket, just as we had done previously with pieces of *aaruul*. His theatrical chewing convinced everyone of his pretended enjoyment. Next we were offered the delicious leftover *buuz*, which we accepted gratefully.

At meal's end the husband, whose name was Batbold ("Strong Steel"), passed a tiny red snuff bottle to the men, who took a pinch, raised it to each nostril, and then passed the container on. When Bill's turn came, he went through the approved motions.

Batbold reached into a space between the clothes dresser and bed for his *morin khuur*, or horse-head fiddle, a common Mongolian musical instrument. Distantly related to a Western cello, it has a top that is a distinctive carving of an equine head. Two strings made of horsehair stretch about two feet from the head down to a square wooden body that is placed between the musician's knees and played with a bow. According to legend, the sound is similar to that of herd animals, and playing it within a *ger* drives out evil spirits. The *morin khuur* often accompanies the Mongolian Long Songs that herdsmen sing as they tend their flocks. The many verses of Long Songs relive traditional stories of nomad life, describing the beauty of the steppes and the desert.

As Batbold passed the bow over the strings, sweet, rich music filled the *ger*. Suren, in a soprano voice, sang a few verses of a song that told of a herdsman tending sheep and goats for many weeks, until he reached a paradise of rich grass in the north. But he wasn't happy there. He missed the desert's wide-open spaces, and soon returned with his animals to live happily, singing to the desert winds.

Later in the evening, I asked Batbold a question that had puzzled us. "Why haven't we seen any cemeteries or other places where the deceased might be buried?" An uncomfortable silence greeted the question, with the adults looking off into the far corners of the *ger*, obviously wishing to avoid eye contact in a most embarrassing moment. Finally, Batbold told us that Mongolians don't like to speak of death. "It's a subject we try never to discuss. It's an ill omen to speak of such things, and brings bad luck. Mongolians have a proverb that says, 'Life is arranged according to your luck. Death is the unluckiest subject of all and must be avoided, or disaster awaits those who speak of it.'"

He went on to explain, "Because you are my guests and foreigners, I will tell you just a little. In the old days Mongolians practiced a Tibetan sky burial, where the dead were laid on the ground in special places. After a short, holy ceremony, the body was left for animals to find. If the body disappeared quickly, it was because the person had led a good life. The custom was outlawed under the Soviets, when earth burial became the law."

I carefully asked, "What about now?"

His answer was barely audible. "We do what we have to do in the desert. Some believe the old ways are best. We can't talk about this anymore. It's disrespectful to our ancestors." With that, the subject was permanently dropped. Conversation immediately switched to the more comfortable topics of animals, droughts, *zuds*, and children.

Just before dark, we went out to milk the camels. The calves were allowed to suckle their mothers just long enough to let their milk down. Then Suren, with a wooden bucket placed on a raised knee propped up by the other leg, in a sort of one-legged stance, milked the first camel. To prevent the mothers from wandering far during the night, calves had been tethered close to the *ger*.

We were given four animals to milk. Aware of several pairs of eyes staring in judgment, we tucked our heads into the camels' sides, copying Suren's one-legged stance, and pulled on the teats. To our immense relief, the warm milk squirted into our buckets, and not a drop was spilled. Suren clucked her approval.

With the arrival of darkness the three guard dogs were already on duty, patrolling quietly among the various animals. Even Tom and Jerry were included in their protective rounds to keep the wolves away.

The grandparents had decided to stay the night. We couldn't imagine how ten people were going to sleep in such cramped quarters. However, we had forgotten that Mongolians do not have our sense of personal space; in their world of one-roomed *gers*, the concept does not exist. To see two Mongolians in conversation only an inch or two apart is common. They think nothing of standing tightly pressed together, shoulder to shoulder, in a crowded room. And we were to discover that in a *ger* there is always room for one more.

That night everyone bedded down on the floor, with the exception of the husband and wife, who had their own bed pushed against the wall. After each person had carefully examined our down, nylon-covered sleeping bags and marveled that anyone would actually sleep in such strange contraptions, we laid them on the floor. Everybody slept on inch-thick wool felt pads with a coarse, brightly colored wool blanket as the only cover. In their own time they went out to the bathroom, which was anywhere nearby in the wide-open space of the desert.

The youngest girl, only two years old but already boasting the round, sunburned cheeks characteristic of Mongolian children, was typically independent. On her way to relieve herself, she took her coat off a peg. I offered to button it but received a shrug of refusal as she went out alone.

I asked her mother, "Should she go by herself? What about scorpions and snakes?"

The very wise, very Mongolian reply was, "If we worry about danger, then it most likely will happen. She's safe." The toddler returned a short time later, hung her coat on a peg, and lay down to sleep.

However, sleep didn't come easily to Bill and me. "What should I do with my feet?" Bill whispered in my ear. "I'm hitting Grandfather."

I peeked out of my bag and could see that if we angled a little to our left, we might succeed in not touching anyone. We carefully moved a few inches in unison. It was the best we could do. However, it is doubtful that Grandfather cared where Bill's feet were, judging by the astonishing volume of snoring he gave forth for the next two hours. At last he ran out of steam, and then the only sound was the heavy breathing of a *ger* full of sleeping people. We finally joined them.

DAY 65 > As the first light filtered through the skylight, everyone stirred and then rose to begin another workday in the life of desert nomads. They folded their sleeping pads and blankets and stacked them neatly against the wall. Suren spread an elaborately embroidered, rainbow-colored cover over the whole pile. After pulling a bucket of water from the well, they all gathered outside to brush their teeth with well-worn toothbrushes, a concession to modern-day living, but without any toothpaste. The two teenagers and Bill and I were dispatched to milk the goats, while Suren and Grandmother lit the stove and cooked breakfast. The husband and Grandfather went out to saddle the horses for the day's herding, and the two youngest children held the goats while we milked.

Later, Bill and I herded the thirty sheep and goats to the area where they had been the night before. Meanwhile, the men on horseback drove the camels, their calves, and the rest of the four hundred goats and sheep to graze about a mile away. Our early morning chores finished, everyone returned for breakfast.

Tea accompanied our favorite noodle soup mixed with chopped potato, carrots, and onion. To make the homemade noodles, the two youngsters rolled dough into a thin, round slab two feet wide and cut the dough into perfect strips. A machine couldn't have sliced them more evenly. After the soup was cooked, a spoonful was tossed into the stove as an offering to the god of fire, so that he would agree to cook the next meal. Just as Suren was about to add chunks of a fatty sheep's tail as an additional delicacy to our bowls, I had an idea born of desperation to avoid having to survive another onslaught of blobs of fat. "Can we take the sheep's tail with us to add to our meal in our camp tonight? It would make dinner very special," I said, hoping I sounded convincing.

"Of course," came the reply. Suren scooped up the tail, added one more for good measure, and placed them in a bowl, ready to pack into our duffels. I could hear Bill's sigh of relief.

But there was one more test. Marmot meat. Strips of the greasy flesh, considered a delicacy, were placed on our plates. I remembered the cuddly-furry animals that whistle shrilly to each other throughout the Cascade Range at home. My next thought was of the bubonic plague that marmots sometimes carry, which is still endemic in Mongolia. I mentally ran through the list of

209

vaccinations we had endured before leaving home. The plague wasn't on it.

Bill, who had visibly paled, cleared his throat, stalling for time, while I stared at the meat, searching my mind for a graceful way to refuse. Suren hovered, smiling over us, proud to offer her guests such tasty morsels, making refusal impossible. I picked up the smallest piece, held my breath to avoid breathing the thick smell of oil, chewed the leathery meat twice, and swallowed the chunk almost whole.

"Can we add the rest to the sheeps' tails for dinner later?" I asked hopefully as I tried to ignore the oily taste that spoke severely to my stomach.

"It's better to eat marmot meat as soon as it's cooked," Suren replied.

Inspired by the need to survive, I said, "But think of how wonderful our evening meal will be, and we'll think of you as we eat."

Clearly impressed, she enthusiastically piled my plate high with the rest of the meat and poured the grease over the top. Without a word, Bill dropped the piece that was halfway to his mouth onto his plate and hastily added his plateful to mine. Then all was emptied into our spare plastic container and the lid snapped shut. Another catastrophe avoided.

After breakfast, we gathered our belongings and loaded the camels, with everyone eager to help. To say good-bye to our new friends was difficult. "Perhaps we will see you again one day?" I said. Heads nodded vigorously, but we all knew that was most unlikely. Nomads have no addresses, and the family, which had already moved twice this summer, would travel to another location in three weeks, when their well went dry.

Grandfather beamed with pleasure when we presented him with two pairs of winter socks for each member of the family, ten bars of soap, and two pounds of salt. Handfuls of *aaruul* were given in return. This *aaruul* was sweet and softer than any we had so far tried to eat, so this time only half went into the dog-bribe pouch, leaving the rest for us to chew along the way.

Then Suren asked if we would we take their pictures. We had already used several rolls of film to record their many activities, but they must have wanted something special. I agreed, and they rushed away to dress in their finest clothing, emerging with shining faces and smoothed hair. Two hours later, the various combinations of people and people with horses had been photographed to everyone's satisfaction.

Most Mongolians liked to have their photos taken, which set them apart from many of the other cultures we had traveled among. At first we were at a loss as how to send the photos to them. Then we inquired if they ever went to Ulaan Baatar. Yes, Grandfather had a brother in the capital. City dwellers have no home addresses, so on a page torn out of my journal, we wrote detailed directions to Chuluu's apartment and told Grandfather the photos would be waiting for him there.

It was time to go. The traditional shower of milk was tossed in our wake, to a chorus of *Sain yavaarai*, "Go well." Then the husband and the two oldest girls left to take care of the herds for the day, while Grandfather and Grandmother mounted their horses and rode home. Our visit was over and the day's work continued, as did our journey.

CHAPTER 12 **SMUGGLERS**

DAYS 66–67 > By the last day of July, a night's sleep wasn't sufficient to allow us to rise refreshed. Our bodies were gradually slipping into fatigue brought on by high temperatures, wind, and the physical need to keep moving. All morning we trudged across the folds of the land, through a hot wind that drove sand into our masked faces. Dirt covered our clothes in a gray film. The air was so dry that sweat dried even before it had a chance to soak our clothes. At snack time each mouthful was more grit than food, but the need for a constant resupply of energy compelled us to eat. Our immediate task was to keep walking.

Mongolia's southern border is strangely irregular given the

geography, with wide swinging curves that cut deeply north and south. By noon the wind had gone, but the still air was filled with choking dust that left our throats raw. When we held our thermometer in the shade of our bodies to obtain an accurate reading, it read 126 degrees. At noon, the scorching heat forced a stop. Bill, in spite of frequent swallows of water, had noticed a decrease in his sweating and his face was flushed, signaling the beginning of mild heatstroke. I was approaching the same stage.

Drained of energy, we sat under umbrellas, each drinking a gallon of water during the next three hours. Aware that heatstroke kills, we constantly watched for its insidious symptoms. A cooler environment was the best cure, but unable to change our circumstances, all we could do was sit beneath our umbrellas in what passed for shade and drink until satisfied. The merest hint of green would have uplifted our weary minds, but there was not a speck to be seen in our austere surroundings.

214

In the late afternoon, instead of the temperature dropping a few degrees, the heat stayed on, reducing us to a dragging, stumbling crawl. Pain in my hip and leg accompanied every step. As our pace slowed I called for an end to the day, and Bill immediately agreed.

After feeding the camels, we lay in the tent with all the doors wide open, hoping to catch a breeze that refused to come. Lying down was relief beyond imagination. As the pain subsided, our mental outlook improved. Even the heat was more tolerable. We ate very little dinner, but drank two quarts of water each. Our individual consumption of water for the day was eight quarts. In more temperate climates such a quantity would be considered excessive, but in the summertime Gobi it was barely enough.

The evening hours, as always, were a welcome contrast. The golden sunset gradually faded. The sky darkened as the desert's subdued mood wrapped us in a comforting blanket. After dinner we sat leaning against the tent, looking into infinity, with nothing to do but relax and enjoy the desert. The Gobi's many moods are never more apparent than in the quiet evening, when it is a perfect place to be, to reflect, and to enjoy. This desert had already humbled us in many ways. We could not defeat it with our Western ways and modern equipment, but if we observed its rules of survival, it would allow us to pass through safely.

DAY 68 > Daytime temperatures were consistently more than 115 degrees, draining our energy and destroying our appetites. All we craved was water. Judging by our clothes, which now hung in loose folds, we had both lost several pounds. Although we took painstaking care to consume adequate calories, the grinding day-after-day effort caused a gradual weight loss. Until now, due to the risk of meeting smugglers, we had traveled at night only sporadically, but our desperation to avoid the grilling heat forced us to toss caution to the winds. It became increasingly easier to convince each other that we most likely would never cross any smugglers' path.

At 10 PM, after an hour of sleep, we carefully navigated a route barely north of the border. The moon shone dimly from behind a thick veil of dust, reducing its light to a scant glimmer. The temperature, 84 degrees, was invigorating. We walked on through the vast silent darkness and wondered why we hadn't begun night travel much sooner in our walk. But our bubble of enthusiasm was about to burst.

A little after 1 AM, we froze at the sound of the low hum of engines just a few hundred yards away. Three jeeps without lights slowly crossed the border from China. The sound was unnaturally loud in the heavy silence of the night.

Bill whispered, "Smugglers! Who else would travel without lights?" Then, more urgently, "Get down!"

I needed no urging. We pulled on the leads to couch the camels and huddled motionless at their sides, hoping we hadn't been seen. One vehicle turned toward us. My heart thumped louder as I cringed, trying to disappear. But the jeep turned away, following the other two directly north.

As the vehicles crossed our route, two more, also without lights, arrived from the north to join the first three. If we had been a quarter mile farther on, they would have seen us. The vehicles met in a brief rendezvous while shadowy figures darted back and forth between the vehicles—to transfer smuggled goods, we guessed. Then the first three returned to China, still with no lights.

We remained stone still at the camels' sides, not daring to move or even make a sound. Even though as far as we could tell we were alone, the gaping silence of the dark desert seemed to magnify sound. Some time later, having seen no sign of more vehicles, we plucked up the courage to move on. But just in case we had stumbled onto a smugglers' regular rendezvous route, we increased our pace, praying for the fast approach of daylight, when smugglers most likely wouldn't risk detection.

"Nice to see people, but not that kind," Bill remarked wryly. That summed up my feelings as well. The episode energized our steps; we hastened through the dawn and into the blazing heat of midmorning before we dared take a rest stop. By unanimous vote, we decided to return to a daytime schedule while we were traveling close to the Chinese border.

The thought of spending another eight days in this fiendish place, combined with the pain racking my body, was close to overwhelming. But when I was reminded of our combined investment of sweat, mind-crushing effort, and sheer willpower, it was impossible to contemplate failure. It would all be worthwhile, I told myself. Besides, we were making good time in spite of my limp. Our pace had slowed, but we were still walking about twenty miles per day.

Although Bill was just as dog-tired as I, and the shoulder he had injured in the car accident nagged at him occasionally, he had no trouble agreeing that we could make it all the way. "We'll make it together, heat, limp, and all," he said, squeezing my hand encouragingly.

Another critical moment in the journey had lumbered by.

At 5 PM the lack of sleep hit us hard. We dragged ourselves through feeding and staking the camels. With the border so close, we couldn't allow Tom and Jerry to forage in their hobbles in case they wandered into China.

Our light sleeping bags had long ago become too hot. With the tent doors wide open, we lay on the half-inch foam pads that we normally slid underneath the sleeping bags. The thought of scorpions and spiders hardly entered our minds. The task of staying cool enough to survive was our only concern.

DAY 69 > China, just a hundred feet away, showed us the same monotonous landscape that we had been crossing in Mongolia. There was no sign of villages or, for that matter, any life at all on either side of the border.

Around ten o'clock a fast-moving vehicle approached us in a cloud of dust. If these were more smugglers, then we were in trouble, caught as we were in the open. The jeep swept to a standstill alongside us, and four soldiers jumped out with handguns drawn. Bill and I looked at each other in terror. The soldiers quickly lowered their guns, however, when they realized we were foreigners.

The captain in charge, who spoke good English, asked us with a puzzled tilt to his head, "Where are you going?" He almost lost his military composure as he absorbed our answer. Quickly gathering himself, he asked politely if we had seen any smugglers. We told him of the events we had witnessed the night before. He translated for the others, and they all nodded.

"Yes," the captain said, "they were Mongolian smugglers. We've known about this group. They transport drugs. It won't be long before we catch them."

We expected them to dash away in pursuit, but instead the officer turned his attention to us. In a stern voice, he told us we were too close to the border and could be arrested and jailed.

Oh boy, here we go again, I thought.

"Not again," Bill said as he handed the captain the letter giving us permission to travel along the border. I held my breath, waiting for the bad news that we were sure was coming. After a short pause to read the letter, the captain told us, "This is unusual, but this letter is official." He summoned a soldier to fetch paper and pen from the jeep. "I'll also write a letter telling of the information you have provided about the smugglers. No one will question you again about traveling close to the border on the Mongolian side. Just make sure you never cross the border."

We both breathed again. Of course we had no intention of crossing into China. Apparently we were in good standing with the authorities, and we intended to keep it that way. But in view of the fact that no one was in any hurry to go after the smugglers, I wondered just how our information could be of any help in their capture.

Then, to our complete amazement, the captain, a typical unhurried, patient Mongolian, told one of his men to bring the *airag* from the vehicle. The soldier returned with a five-gallon container and six bowls. The officer motioned us to sit with them to celebrate our journey with a drink. After we hobbled the camels, we relaxed on the stony ground there in the middle of the desert. The sun beat down on us with the captain and three soldiers all dressed in full military uniform, right down to their shiny black riding boots. Our companions' discreet beads of sweat contrasted to the rivulets that ran freely down Bill's face and mine and dripped from our chins.

One fellow poured the *airag* and, with a deep bow, handed us a full bowl. The very thought of drinking fermented horses' milk made my stomach cringe, but we thought it better to pretend enthusiasm until our precious second letter of permission was tucked safely in Bill's pocket. We weren't about to offend these people or lose the respect of the captain, who had the authority to arrest us.

After several toasts to our health, our journey, our future, and, as an afterthought, our camels, we all drank. Bill and I forced the first drink down just as the captain was inspired to toast Mongolia, the end of smuggling, and friendship between our two countries. More toasts meant more bowls of *airag*. Somehow I drank the second bowl. Bill struggled with his but drank it all.

After inquiring about my non-American accent, the captain

learned that New Zealand was the country of my birth. He rose to new heights of ardent toasts, this time to New Zealand, its people, and, of course, all the country's animals, which meant yet another bowl of sour liquid. It was impossible for us to keep up.

"Our Western stomachs are not as tough as yours," I admitted. "Three bowls are too much for us."

Bill looked at me with relief clearly stamped on his face. I could see that he had had an even greater struggle than I to force down his share. As each of our new friends absorbed what I had just said, they looked at each other and then burst into gales of laughter. The captain was beside himself with merriment. They were laughing so hard that they couldn't speak for several minutes. We couldn't help joining in the laughter, even though it was at our expense.

Eventually, all regained control. "We must go to America one day," the captain said, "and you can find a drink that will set our Mongolian stomachs on fire."

I assured him that there was nothing equal to *airag* that had sat for a few days in the heat.

Still beaming, he asked, "Please allow us to pour just a little *airag* into your bowls, because we can't possibly leave without a toast to New Zealand."

"Just a little," Bill said.

The captain motioned the soldier to pour enough to cover the bottom of our bowls. Naturally, theirs were filled to the brim. After the last round had been completed, we sat for a while longer, chatting about the desert and life in the military. They were a contented lot. We envied their relaxed, unhurried lifestyle and their joyous grasp of good humor.

"After all," the captain said, "we can patrol all day and celebrate whenever we want to." Then he suddenly remembered the smugglers. "We must go now and look for them. We might find them before dark." As they put the bowls and *airag* back into the jeep and prepared to leave, the captain had one last piece of advice. "Don't travel at night. Daytime is safer when you're close to the border. Smugglers stay away during the day."

I had to ask one last question. "Why do you carry so much *airag* with you on patrol?"

The captain laughed and explained that they never knew when they would have an occasion to celebrate; therefore, it was always a good idea to have plenty on hand.

"But five gallons?" I said.

They all looked at each other knowingly as he explained, with an amused twinkle in his dark eyes, "Sometimes we Mongolians have a lot of celebrating to do, even in the desert."

After two rounds of handshakes and several hearty backslaps from the captain, they drove off in a merry cloud of dust, leaving us standing alone once more in the middle of nowhere.

We unhobbled the camels and walked on, but the *airag* soon made itself felt. A short time later, Bill stepped aside and vomited. I soon followed.

A little before three o'clock, we were forced to stop because of heat and weakness. Vomiting had rapidly dehydrated us, causing us to lose precious fluids. We put up the tent and endured our knotted stomachs. If we were going to finish this journey on time, we had better avoid the drink at all costs in the future, especially if it wasn't fresh, we resolved—even if it meant breaking the rules of etiquette.

We rested until five o'clock. In the cooler temperatures we set out again, then stopped when darkness fell, heeding the captain's advice not to travel at night. Our fear of more smugglers left us feeling exposed and vulnerable in a place with nowhere to hide. All we could do was hope that we weren't camped near a contraband route.

We had traveled 1,370 miles so far, with a planned 130 miles to go. Despite the delays, soft sand, storms, and visiting, we were only a little behind schedule.

DAY 70 > At daylight we noticed Tom all by himself, still tied to his stake, but Jerry was nowhere in sight. Fearing the worst, Bill grabbed his binoculars. In the distance he saw our runaway camel, about a mile south of the border.

If we retrieved Jerry and were caught in China, we would be in more trouble than we wanted to imagine. But if we left him, he would eventually die of thirst and hunger. We had to take the risk.

Leaving Tom at his stake, we rushed across the border, keeping a nervous eye out for the border patrol, although in the absence of anywhere to hide, we had no idea what we would do if we were approached.

Bill ran ahead, stepping over what might have been the remnants of a border fence, while I hurried behind as fast as my leg allowed. The pounding pain went almost unnoticed amid my raw fear of being arrested. Well into China, Jerry, dragging his uprooted stake, placidly munched on a clump of dry grass. Bill grabbed his lead, and we dashed back into Mongolia with a surprised camel trotting behind us. But we weren't out of trouble yet. Our tracks in the soft, sandy earth clearly told the story of our foray into China. Without feeding the camels, we loaded them and left, taking a bearing due north to put the border well behind us as fast as possible. It was noon before our adrenaline-fed pace forced a stop.

Satisfied that we hadn't been spotted, we lounged under our umbrellas, drinking water, until we noticed a fast-approaching jeep traveling straight toward us. In a second we were on our feet, our hearts thumping in fear. Our bodies were frozen, our nerves paralyzed, as the vehicle closed to within three hundred yards of our position.

Then it abruptly turned east and disappeared into nearby sand hills. Expecting to see the dust kicked up by the vehicle as it continued onward, we watched. But the dust cloud stopped just beyond the first hill. We had feared that the vehicle might be a border patrol that had somehow found our tracks, but now it seemed more likely to be smugglers concealing themselves.

We grabbed the camel leads and fled north to the safety of a spine of barren rock that crossed our route. Dashing through a gap, we couched the animals to conceal them from anyone watching through binoculars and carefully eased our way up to the crest, staying low behind jagged rocks. From the top, still hidden, we scanned the sand hills, convinced that the jeep's occupants were waiting there until we moved away from their route north. We had almost given up when we saw dust rise and heard the hum of an approaching vehicle. Soon the jeep lurched into view, traveling at breakneck speed on a route that skirted the ridges, and disappeared ahead of a swirling cloud of dust.

Although shaken by the episode, we were reasonably confident that the danger had passed. Now twenty-six miles from the border, we took stock of our situation. Our dilemma was that our northern flight had taken us far from our original path and our prearranged resupply coordinates. Somehow, over the next five days, we had to make our way southeast to meet Chuluu. We had no way to contact him, and he would never guess that we had traveled so far north.

Worried that we might have stumbled onto a regularly used illegal trade route, we chose a campsite concealed from the plain beyond. Even before erecting the tent, we checked maps and air charts to figure our next course of action. It looked as if two hard days of traveling southeast would put us on course to meet Chuluu on time. Now that we had a workable plan, the tension of the day dissipated somewhat and we made camp.

As the light faded, and with our emotions calmed by the tranquility of the evening, we prepared for bed. Bill checked Tom and Jerry's tie-down stakes. Suddenly he shouted a "What the . . . ?" that trailed off in alarmed surprise. In a flash I was out of the tent and was horrified to see a man dressed in a dark gray *del* appear, ghost-like, out of a notch in the rocks. For a long moment he stood there and then approached, raising his hand in greeting. Suspicious, we didn't respond.

Noting our distress, the stranger said in clear English, "I'm sorry to have startled you. I come as a friend."

After the events of the day, we were still guarded. "Who are you?" I asked without bothering to observe the traditional custom of polite greetings.

Obviously wishing to put us at ease, he again apologized and explained that he and his family worked a gold mine close by. His son had seen our camp while out with the goat herd. We told him of the day's events and pressed him for information concerning smugglers. Suddenly apprehensive, he asked for details. "Can you describe them?"

We told him no, but we described the jeep.

His face revealed deep concern as he invited us to his *ger*, where he told us he would answer our questions.

Taking Tom and Jerry with us in case wolves might be lurking nearby, we followed the man, whose name was Baatar, to his *ger*, which lay over the next ridge. After securing the camels, we entered the candlelit house and were greeted by his smiling wife and, of course, the inevitable salty tea. A teenage boy and girl looked on.

To satisfy our curiosity, we asked Baatar where he had learned English. We were surprised to learn that he was a lama and had completed his education in the Soviet-approved monastery in the capital. Forced to endure years of Soviet interference in monastery affairs, he had returned to his family after the Communists left the country. Now he, his brothers, and their families mined gold in the nearby hills and ridges.

True to his word, Baatar returned to the subject of smuggling. He was certain that the jeep we had seen belonged to people smuggling gold ore from Mongolia to China.

We had stumbled onto their usual travel route to the mines they dealt with, and Baatar believed we were lucky that they hadn't confronted us. He described them as sometimes ruthless in their dealings with those who might interfere with their unlawful operations. His family and relatives sold their ore to a company in the capital and had no dealings with smugglers, he said, even though they offered a higher price.

Baatar described their family mining enterprise as very hard work, using hand tools and muscle to extract the ore containing the gold. The family mines we had seen in our earlier travels appeared to be places of unending toil with minimal returns.

223

Noting the late hour, and knowing the Mongolian custom of sometimes staying up until well past midnight, we thanked our host and prepared to leave. One more bowl of tea was thrust into our hands, and finally, at 1 AM, we said good night to our hosts, who warned us to travel due east a few miles onto the flat plains before turning south. Baatar was certain that we would be safer on the plains, away from the gold-mining area. As we left, he shook our hands and bestowed upon us a Buddhist blessing for good health and safe travels, after which his gracious wife gave us a piece of blue fabric as part of the short ceremony. Comforted by these delightful people, we returned to our tent and slept well.

DAY 71 > Next morning, taking Baatar's advice, we set a course due east, past the tunnel of a gold mine where an older man and his two sons were excavating a barren, rocky ridge with picks and shovels. After a few miles east, we were out of range of the gold-mining area and, presumably, any smugglers. But with the extra mileage we had logged to evade authorities and smugglers, we still had 157 miles and five-and-a-half days to go to reach our final GPS position.

Just as we changed to a southerly bearing, a maddening wind picked up. In scorching gusts, it steadily built into a blinding dust storm. Taking turns leading, we walked as long as possible following the compass needle. Everything was obliterated from our minds except the need to stay on course. We fixed an imaginary point in the blank brown wall ahead, walked to it, then set another point.

The sun had long since vanished in the dust and cast no shadows by which to tell direction. Visibility was only one hundred feet. Sand raced sideways across the ground, hiding our feet, while a lighter layer obliterated everything above one foot high. We fought on as the wind continued to increase, until it became a howling monster cutting visibility to arm's length. We hung on to the camels to stay on our feet, struggling to breathe as the wind did its best to snatch the air from us.

We couched the camels, tails to the wind, and hunkered down at their sides to protect our skin against the hot sting of sand that blasted us at fifty miles per hour.

The wind gradually died, and three hours later the sun reappeared as a disk turned red by the dusty atmosphere. After crouching for so long, we struggled to stand upright. Dust and sand had forced its way into everything. There was no escaping the creeping menace. Without shaking everything out as we usually did, we set a blistering pace. With shadows lengthening, we camped at 10 PM In our hurry to cook dinner before darkness fell, we forgot to feed the camels their cookies. We were soon reminded of our indiscretion when, with long necks extended and lips working back and forth in anticipation, they asked for their treats. To make it up to them, Bill gave them four apiece. They had been outstanding throughout the storm—calm, uncomplaining, and obedient. They had become such a vital part of the expedition that they were far more than animals that just carried our gear and supplies from one point to another. They were our helpers, friends, and companions.

DAY 72 > The last *aimag* of our journey, Sukhbaatar, or "Axe Hero," was named after a hero of the 1921 Mongolian revolution who died at age thirty, some say poisoned by his political foes. A statue of Sukhbaatar astride a galloping horse stands in the large main square in Ulaan Baatar. The *aimag* is sparsely populated and, like all Gobi *aimags*, sees few visitors. The land is monotonous and flat, with a few hills and mountains, and the same vista stretches on and on. Our consolation was that somewhere out there, far beyond sight, lay Ovoo, our final destination.

We rose stiff and tired from the previous two days' sprint to safety and our struggle through the storm. Although our bodies begged for rest, there could be no letup.

As light shortened the long shadows of the night we walked, shaking the kinks out of our muscles as we went. Grateful for the firm surface and cooler temperature that still hovered in the 80s, we headed southeast. We were so obsessed with making good time that at first we didn't see the two motionless animals that blended with the desert hue. Then the mother and foal moved and we recognized *khulan,* the same species of wild donkeys we had seen before. Perhaps puzzled to see humans on foot, they galloped away. Since they normally travel in herds, we guessed they were returning to where many more lived, concealed in valleys beyond the ridges. Well suited to the desert environment, they sense water flowing just below the surface and dig down to find it.

All too soon, the cool early morning hours gave way to the same heat that rose each day as a barrier to be conquered. By nine o'clock the sun's rays blasted from space, only to be reflected back from the earth for a second shot at bodies that had already suffered too much. The anti-ultraviolet fabric of our clothes, which covered us from head to toe, had kept the burning rays at bay and protected our skin, but we often had to smear a thick layer of lip salve and sunscreen on our faces and cracked lips. The sun and surrounding bleak emptiness spurred a grim need to be finished with the torture.

It was no longer possible to consume enough water to completely satisfy our thirst, which grew with every step. Our skin was dry, our throats raw from breathing hot air and dust. Coughs that had begun two weeks ago had become increasingly persistent, especially during the day. Nagging headaches now assailed us by noon. The sun had become our hated enemy, and we longed to be done with it. In its insidious way, the desert was breaking us down little by little.

But hope loomed in the far distance, barely visible through the thick haze of glare and dust. It was our first glorious sight of 4,000-foot Altan Ovoo ("Golden Hill"), a symmetrical, cone-like volcanic sacred mountain that loomed above the town of Ovoo, also known as Dariganga. It was to be a tantalizing beacon for the next four days.

In the distance a herd of animals moved slowly north, probably to fresh pasture many miles away. Six forlorn camels chased along by two boys moved with the herd, all following the eternal rhythm of the nomadic existence. The camels' humps were flat and empty of fat. It was impossible to imagine what the animals were eating. As desolate as the western Gobi had been, the region we now traveled in midsummer was even more intolerant of human or animal existence.

Water was just as much of a problem in the eastern Gobi as in the west. At least in the desert, if water was there at all, it could be found in shallow wells usually eight to ten feet deep. In parts of the green central steppes some distance north of the Gobi, however, shallow wells are often salty. The previous year we had traveled for mile after mile across green rolling steppes of inviting pasture, but we saw no animals or people living there because of the unusable salt water. Drilling deep wells to reach good water would open many square miles of grasses and herbs, but the cost of such a project is beyond the financial resources of the country.

Unlike the western Gobi's perpetually clear blue skies, the eastern skies were often decorated with white clouds that formed intricate patterns. After the gold miners told us that this area hadn't received a single drop of rain in two years, our dream that the clouds would bring rain faded.

Even though we drove ourselves hard, our protesting legs gradually moved more slowly. Earlier, averaging twenty-six miles a day was not a problem, but now, after already logging almost 1,400 challenging miles, it was a mammoth task. All morning we focused on pushing our tired bodies even harder. At least the usual wind was only a breeze and there were no storms in sight.

Later, a dust cloud crossed our path a half-mile away. We strained to see through the glare, hoping it was caused by gazelle and not smugglers. Then, with a relieved shout, Bill called, "Gazelle for sure!" A herd of animals numbering somewhere between twenty and thirty sprinted away in long bounds. Just like the *khulan*, the gazelle were camouflaged by the desert hue. Herds of these white-tailed gazelle, or *tsagaan zeer*, inhabit the eastern Gobi and the eastern steppes by the thousands. During the November and December hunting season they are hunted for their meat, which is sold commercially. Their spectacular yearly migrations depend on their being able to move unimpeded across vast areas of steppe and desert; however, their future as a free-ranging species is uncertain. Already, mining and oil drilling are opening up the region, along with proposed roads, pipelines, and a new railroad complete with a fence that will dissect gazelle migratory routes, just as the fence along both sides of the Sainshand railroad had.

During dinner we talked about the days of Genghis Khan, when his raiding armies stormed across the very plains we now traveled. To the north, in the Khentii *aimag*, believed to be the birthplace of the great leader, and all across the eastern Dornod *aimag*, the Chinese built a wall that extended far into China in an attempt to keep the rampaging Mongols out. Known in China as the Great Wall, and in Mongolia simply as the "Wall of Genghis Khan," the barrier was completely ineffective. The Mongolian generals paid off the guards, who let the masses through unimpeded. When we had visited the Mongolian section the previous year, we had found it in ruins.

South of the border lies the Chinese province of Inner Mongolia, which is separate from Mongolia (which was known as Outer Mongolia when under Chinese rule). Over several hundred years, the ebb and flow of Chinese rule engulfed Mongolia. Mongolians are squeezed between two great powers, Russia and China, and they seem to fear a Chinese invasion more so than one by the Russians.

By 1279 the Mongols had conquered China and later made Beijing their capital. The Mongol Kublai Khan, grandson of Genghis Khan, became the first emperor of the Yuan dynasty. The rule lasted until 1368, when Chinese rebels converged on Beijing and drove out the Mongolians. Once again the Mongols became a loose tribal collection of roaming warring factions who occasionally invaded China. This lasted until the eighteenth century, when Qing emperors defeated the Mongols and took control of their country.

Caught in the border wars between Russia and China, Mongolia found itself ruled in the north by Russia and in the south by China until 1911, when the Qing dynasty fell. For eight years, Mongolia remained an independent state; then it became a Communist satellite under Soviet rule, which lasted until the fall of Communism in 1990. Although Soviet rule was harsh and at times murderous, it is the cruelty to the early Mongols by the Chinese that is perhaps causing a nervous relationship. On many modern maps, the Chinese still claim Mongolia as a Chinese province.

DAY 73 > Day in and day out, we walked and walked. In an attempt to avoid the midday heat, we began walking an hour before daylight. We had traveled only a mile when suddenly both camels stopped and refused to move, their heads held high in alarm at something that prowled in the dark. In the blackness, we saw and heard nothing.

Then, suddenly, the threat was approaching us: wolves. Tom jerked backward on his lead, almost pulling me off my feet. Jerry kicked violently with his hind legs at two of the wolves, which barely dodged his lethal kicks. Instantly we spun both camels to face the danger as we yelled at the wolves. We breathed a sigh of relief as they silently retreated into the dark, unnerved by our tactics.

Thinking that the danger had passed, we tried to walk on, but the camels resisted our urgent tugs on their leads. They grunted with heads aloft, looking to their right, then abruptly lunged to the left.

"The wolves are circling us," I yelled in alarm.

"Stake the camels side by side, close together," Bill called back.

With both camels tied, we stood at their sides, each holding a trekking pole at the ready, staring into the gloom, watching for any sign of movement. Slowly the dark eastern sky faded and dawn's gray light crept over us. Four wolves slowly circled two hundred yards away in the new light. One charged a few steps toward the camels, testing us, but our yells and a barrage of rocks sent him into immediate retreat. All four wolves stopped circling, moved farther away, and sat on their haunches to wait.

Thirty minutes later, as the sun rose, they stirred and milled about, tossing hungry glances at the camels, which faced them and uttered grunts of fear. Finally, obviously agitated at their lack of success, the four wolves, led by a big male, trotted east and disappeared into the haze.

Our ordeal had lasted two hours, but it was another hour before the badly frightened camels would settle into their usual easy walk. Worried about the threat the wolves posed, I suggested that we stand guard at night. Bill agreed, although the prospect of a sleepless night didn't make our day easier. Later we passed the mostly eaten carcass of a gazelle. Perhaps our unwelcome visitors had been successful elsewhere.

In camp that night, we staked Tom and Jerry close to the tent after gathering a foot-high pile of rocks and prepared to take turns guarding the camels all night. Bill and I felt no threat; it was the camels the wolves were after.

Bill took the first one-hour shift while I slept. Both camels were couched comfortably on the ground, chewing their cuds. But I must have dozed during my watch, around 3 AM A frightened grunt from Tom, as he and Jerry leapt to their feet, brought me wide-awake. At the sound Bill stumbled from the tent, shaking off sleep. The wolves, patient and determined, had returned and were waiting, concealed by darkness. Time moved in slow motion as we stood beside the camels, our nerves taut. Tom and Jerry, just as tense and watchful, grunted and stamped their front feet. Then, just before daylight, with the danger apparently gone, the camels knelt and dozed, unafraid. The wolves had left, but we continued guarding until dawn burst over the horizon.

DAY 74 > Breakfast was a silent affair. Our groggy, sleep-deprived minds rebelled at the thought of fighting another day. Our gaunt appearance would win no beauty contests. Bill looked in the compass mirror and with a grimace remarked, "That was a mistake."

Early in the journey I had given up using the mirror. It was kinder on the psyche to not know what I really looked like. Bill looked awful, and I didn't allow myself to think what I must look like to him.

Even though we were nearing the end of our trek, I still dared not allow myself to dwell on the pain in my leg and hip. The struggle to force myself through it had become my life, and I couldn't clearly remember what it was like to be without pain, so engrossed was I by it all. But that day I told myself that the end wasn't far away and there really *was* light at the end of the proverbial tunnel. Persistence had carried me through many things in the past, and now I resolved that I would get through this too. Bill, my stalwart and supportive mate, had helped more than he could ever know. Though thinner and more haggard than when we began, he forged onward with a stride that, although weary, still held a certain spring. I couldn't imagine a better partner.

Eight quarts of water a day were no longer enough, and the effects of dehydration—headache and listlessness—were our constant companions. Arriving at yet another flat plain, we stood despondent at its edge, wondering how we could ever reach the other side, twelve miles away, through the punishing heat waves and endless tedium. It was always a psychological challenge when our route stretched before us, unbroken by anything more than a few inches high.

Tackling the plain head-on, mile by mile, we put it behind us and then hiked through a series of raised ridges of black rock.

233

Although the temperature was no cooler, it was at least a relief to look at something besides flat gravel and sand.

Just as we made camp that night, the buzz of a motorcycle ridden by a monk in flowing saffron robes caught our attention as he drove past in the far distance. Surprised to see our camp, he swerved to meet us and, after the usual salutations, told us that he was traveling to Altan Ovoo to worship at the shrine at the base of the sacred mountain. We invited him to share our camp, but he was meeting other monks at the shrine and would travel through the night to arrive on time. Well equipped for the journey, he carried a spare tire and a large container of extra fuel strapped to his motorcycle, although we noticed that he had no compass or map of any road to follow.

With a cheerful wave and good wishes for our safety he sped away, leaving two envious pedestrians watching him disappear. Though we had always wanted to walk across this desert, never wanting to desecrate such a fragile place with tire tracks or petroleum fumes, the monk's mode of travel now looked to us—baked and tired as we were—not so bad after all. All at once, the remaining miles seemed even longer.

As if the plains weren't enough to sap the last of our fading energy, we faced a stretch of wind-rippled sandy mounds that went on for several miles with no way around them. Due in part to overgrazing, migrating sand particles had blown about, caught on low shrubs, and formed these mounds, which were several feet high. The soft, ankle-deep yellow sand flowed into our boots even though we tightened the laces.

As Gobi herdsmen allow animals to overgraze the meager vegetation down to the ground, the increasingly dry desert spills beyond its borders to become larger and larger. And the Gobi is not the only imperiled desert: global warming and humans' misuse of land are increasing the size of deserts worldwide. Winds blow with abandon, eroding exposed rocks into fine particles of sand, which in turn form wide sandy plains and dunes hundreds of feet high. In the Sahara, which has vastly more sand than the Gobi, we trekked through places where entire villages had been buried.

We detested those sandy places. With the air temperature over 120 degrees, we were made even more uncomfortable by sand many degrees hotter, which reflected glare and heat into our faces hour after hour. The burning sun and reflection had swollen the backs of our hands to such a degree that we wore white gloves to stave off serious sunburn.

Second only to our dislike of the sand and heat was our dislike of the wind. Although not endless, it blew unimpeded by vegetation and very seldom impeded by topography, dehydrating the soil and vegetation so that in summer the desert resembled a giant mirage—a shimmering place of misery.

Our day ended with Altan Ovoo looming larger by the mile. Our plan called for a route that would take us to the Ganga Nuur, a freshwater lake in the 69,000-acre Ganga Lake Nature Reserve. After that refreshing treat, we would walk to the base of Altan Ovoo and then six miles to the nearby town.

DAY 75 > Loading the camels that morning went slowly. My mind floundered as I tried to think ahead to what our last steps would be like tomorrow, but the effort to concentrate was too much. It was easier to let my thoughts wander wherever they felt like going. As we hoisted the last water container onto Tom's load, Bill tightened the tie-down rope and said, with a heavy sigh that illustrated our dismal state of exhaustion, "At least tomorrow morning will be the last time we have to do this."

It felt almost like a dream, the idea that tomorrow we could stop walking. But first we had to survive the day's 117-degree temperature, although it promised to drop as we approached the cool waters of the lake.

Around midday a small plane approached. It was Chuluu, flying low to check our position, just as he had promised. We waved an exuberant "all is well," and with a dip of the plane's wings in salute, he disappeared eastward to his cousin's *ger* to arrange for

235

the camel owners, who had traveled there from their home, to meet us the next day at the prearranged coordinates.

I stared at the spot in the sky where Chuluu had disappeared, not wanting the noisy plane to leave. At this stage of our journey, even the harsh sound of an engine took on the character of a friend.

Well into the afternoon, we crossed the sandy rolling country that surrounded the reserve and its lake, and walked beneath an archway that spanned the entrance. It leaned at a rakish angle, and the gatekeeper's hut stood locked and abandoned. But it was the large lake and its sparkling cool water that held our attention. Used to lakes at home surrounded by trees and other green vegetation, we found this one striking: it lay amid a flattish sandy plain, its shores quite barren. From the entrance we descended a short slope, hitched Tom and Jerry to an iron fence that protected a natural spring close to the lake, and raced toward the water.

Stopping at the edge only to remove our boots, we dove into the lake, allowing its heavenly coolness to wash over us. We giggled and laughed like two children as we ducked beneath the surface and splashed each other. Eventually an unfamiliar coolness drove us from the lake to dry off in the hot sun. Green grass surrounded the spring, the first we had seen in a very long time. We touched it as we would soft velvet.

So engrossed were we in all the new experiences that we forgot all about Tom and Jerry. Ashamed that we hadn't taken them to the lake when we first arrived, we made up for our transgression. After a long drink, the camels were happy to walk along the shallow edge and once in a while reach down to scoop up more mouthfuls of the cool liquid. Later we fed them hay, an apple each, and cookies. We noticed people watering a dozen horses at the far end of the lake, and another horse and her foal grazed close by. We hobbled both camels, and they attacked a few shrubs with gusto, making occasional trips to the lake for more water.

As for Bill and me, we drank a quart each of the sweet water from the fenced-in spring, then pitched our tent. Too lazy to cook dinner, we ate leftover bread, some oily cheese, and an apple each, then lay on the spongy grass, which felt like a soft mattress to our weary bodies.

Of the many lakes scattered throughout Mongolia, the Ganga Nuur is one of the few freshwater lakes in the country. Genghis Khan is believed to have dipped his sword into the lake to give its pristine waters special healing powers.

All night long we listened to the calls of the night birds that inhabited the lakeshore. We were too early, though, to see the thousands of swans that visit the lake during their migration from late August to October.

DAY 76 > It was August 9, and what we hoped was our last day in the desert turned out to be the day of an unpleasant surprise.

We emerged from the tent to find the outside fabric wet with dew, something we had not seen in the extreme dryness of the desert. The lake, which appeared to cover about two-and-a-half square miles, produced its own microclimate of dampness, which accounted for the nighttime dew and the patch of green grass surrounding the spring.

With twenty-seven miles still to travel, and in the interests of an early start, we resisted another dip in the lake. We had slept well in the cooler lake climate and had been refreshed by its waters, but we were eager to meet Chuluu.

We made little conversation, each of us no doubt thinking of the journey's end, which would give us relief at last from the constant need to keep marching to stay on schedule. I tried to think back to our first day in the far west, but it seemed a lifetime ago. It seemed odd that now that we were close to the end, it was almost impossible to recall the beginning of the journey. At the beginning, the last day had seemed impossibly far off.

The day's first destination was Altan Ovoo, one of the two hundred or so extinct sacred volcanoes in the region. Due to its location in the midst of a 4,000-foot-high plateau, the mountain stands only 500 feet above the small desert town of Ovoo. Legend has it that the names of the surrounding sacred mountains and the Ganga Nuur were seldom mentioned in public, for fear of upsetting the resident spirits.

After four hours of laboring across uneven ground, we reached the base of the mountain. At the summit stood a white stupa, or shrine, which gleamed in the midmorning light. Only men are allowed to climb the steep path up the sacred mountain to worship at the new stupa, which was built in 1990 atop the ruins of the Bat Tsagaan stupa, built in 1820 and destroyed by Russians in 1937.

At the mountain's base stood a picturesque white shrine, at which several devout Buddhists prayed and spun the prayer wheel. After our long struggle across the desert, we lingered in the atmosphere of peace and devotion in that sacred place.

We reached the dusty streets of Ovoo only to find the town barely awake. The few people walking about stared at us as we led Tom and Jerry along the main street. An older man, badly stooped over his cane, beckoned us to stop. He patted Tom and Jerry in admiration and asked where we had come from. "From the far west," I answered. "Across the Gobi?" he asked, tilting his head as if to better understand.

"Yes," I replied. Taking a moment to absorb my answer, the kindly man took a crumpled piece of blue cloth from his pocket and handed it to me. "To keep you safe," he said. Taking both his hands in mine, I thanked him as I would a close friend. Bill shook the man's hand, deeply touched by his kindness.

Two young boys insisted on leading the camels and then held them while we went into a tiny shop, where we bought four chocolate bars. We gave two to the delighted boys, who disappeared into a *ger* with squeals of glee.

A mile after we left the town, it was with unspeakable joy that we entered a valley between low sand dunes where a busy stream flowed amid a wide, grassy meadow. Green life greeted us in delightful splendor. It was the Gobi's version of an oasis.

Although it was not surrounded by date palms, like many oases we had seen in the Sahara, it was nevertheless a beautiful place of flowing water, green grass, and healthy animals. I picked a tiny stalk of grass, then another, and then another, until I held a handful. Bill plucked a stalk too and slid it into his hatband, declaring that he could feel new energy pouring into his veins: "Something to breathe besides dust!"

At that moment, awash in the soft green life that reached out to welcome us, I felt like someone come back from the dead. But it was already noon and we had another six miles to go, so we resisted the temptation to linger and walked on through the green valley.

At the sound of galloping hooves, we turned to see a man racing across the oasis, calling to us to stop. He carried a message from Chuluu, who had sent it via an antiquated phone system to a friend in Ovoo, who was to watch out for us and deliver the message.

The news was devastating. Because our route was close to the Chinese border, Chuluu had to get permission to land his plane to pick us up. But the official in Ulaan Baatar who had originally granted permission to land not far from Ovoo had at the last moment changed his mind and insisted on a landing position farther from the Chinese border—ninety miles east!

In our debilitated condition and the constant heat, it would take us another five days of walking. Stunned and bitterly disappointed, we thanked the messenger, who wished us well and trotted away.

The end of the journey had been within our grasp. To have to walk another five days was almost too much for our emotions to handle. We sat on a grassy mound, too despondent and too angry with an insensitive official to find the energy or ambition to continue.

After the first wave of seething anger had passed, and we had given vent to our feelings in the most graphic language, reality took over. We had two options. We could return to Ovoo and hire a truck and driver to take us to our new meeting place, or we could continue walking.

In spite of the extra miles, we knew we had to walk to the end. It was the only acceptable way to complete our journey.

To set our new plan in motion, we first of all topped off our water supplies from the stream and drank a quart each while Tom and Jerry sloshed about in the water. Three miles later, we were out on the wide-open sandy desert, traveling northeast, once more at the mercy of the sun and wind. After the soothing atmosphere and temperatures of the lake and oasis, the desert seemed more unsympathetic than ever. We regrouped and processed our emotions as we walked, and worked on a plan to get through the next five days.

"Why not walk at night?" I suggested. "We'll be farther from the border and probably won't meet smugglers."

"No," Bill said, "we shouldn't take any risks at this stage."

"Can we safely walk five more days in this heat?" I asked. The temperatures had eased somewhat as we entered August, but were still over 110 degrees.

"When you put it that way, I guess we should walk at night. Let's give it a try."

With our new plan in place, we camped early so we could sleep for two hours before setting out at dusk.

DAYS 77–81 > The novelty of traveling under soft moonlight and twinkling stars would have been exhilarating if not for our fatigue and pain, which had built over the last seventy-six days to an unbearable level. The nearly irresistible urge to lie down and rest increased by the mile. It was only the desperate need to move my body beyond a level of pain that was almost intolerable that forced one foot in front of the other. We walked side by side, talking of home, our friends, and anything else that could take our minds off the miles yet to travel. In the rising sun, we camped to rest before starting all over again at dusk, though sleeping fitfully through 110-degree daytime temperatures left us groggy and lacking ambition to begin a new night's walk.

The moon, often veiled in dust, was no help in the blackness, which challenged our ability to navigate through a velvet curtain of darkness. To avoid detection by possible unseen eyes, we used our flashlight only for brief moments, while concealed close to a camel's side, to read our compass and GPS.

One dawn the sun rose across a ridge of barren rock that blocked our way. It would be impossible to find a safe passage for the camels in the dark. Rather than risk injury, we agreed that we should cross these ridges in daylight. After two hours of sleep, we were off to find a pass that Bill had detected through binoculars. We trudged up slopes of loose gravel, crested a summit, and then eased our way through a narrow pass, only to find more slopes and summits ahead.

Tom and Jerry, although cautious, managed the terrain better than Bill and me, emitting only a few grunts of protest. Our fatigue and the heat that reflected off the surrounding rocks made us stumble awkwardly. With the last slope and the last summit behind us, we were dismayed to break out onto another plain that was just as empty of life as those before it.

241

As the sunset painted the desert gold we stopped, ate a meal, slept three hours, and started all over again, marching through a night that was black space. Shadowy figures of increasingly larger herds of gazelle raced from us to disappear as ghosts into the night. But our lack of sleep turned us into stumbling robots, programmed to reach a still distant goal. In such a lethargic state, it was impossible to go on. With thirty-two miles to go in two days, we elected to camp early and sleep for twelve hours before the final push to meet Chuluu. After the tent was erected, we fed the camels and fell into our sleeping bags without stopping to eat.

A bright moon made navigation easier, and we stumbled over unseen objects less frequently. Around midnight, four wolves chased a herd of perhaps fifty gazelle into the night. Later we passed a *ger*, its distant white form shining in the moonlight. We envied its occupants, who were no doubt sleeping.

We stopped for breakfast and three hours of sleep before setting out at 7 AM on Day 81. The temperature swiftly rose to

109 degrees. "Let's just go for it," I urged, since we had no need to reserve energy for another day. Stopping only for compass checks, which were made easier by points of reference in the distant mountains, we took no breaks.

To quicken our pace when we slowed, we counted steps in unison, then sang marching tunes to pull each foot forward. Doing our best to ignore our headaches and dust-ravaged throats, on and on we went, determined not to miss our meeting time by even one hour. I felt like the marathon runner in the lead with a mile to go, grasping for a finish line before all energy is gone.

Following our compass and GPS, we checked our exact position each hour to make sure we didn't stray off course. Our day was spent in the transition zone between the Gobi Desert and the eastern steppes. Although barely perceptible, a change was taking place; the sand and barren desert began ever so slightly to merge with the friendlier eastern steppes that were beyond our sight. Larger groups of gazelle were more frequent. A few plants, barely green, began to appear. A mirage of mountains sprang up and then disappeared in the dust lifted high by an increasing breeze. Our spirits rose and excitement built as the end of our journey crept nearer.

Finally, at 5:30 PM, ecstatic with relief and happiness and barely able to see through my tears, I read off the final coordinate numbers of 115 degrees east longitude. It seemed that we had struggled for a lifetime to reach this moment. We embraced in a great hug of congratulations and relief.

We had challenged ourselves to the limit and had survived everything that summer in the Gobi had thrown at us. We finally stood at the far eastern edge of the great desert. According to our calculations we had traveled 1,600 miles, and although our pace had slowed over the last two weeks, we still averaged almost twenty miles per day. Our many long days earlier, in the relative coolness of the trek, had helped us at the end.

There was no need to walk farther. No need to stay on schedule or navigate through sandstorms. No more exhausting, pain-filled days. The heat that marched with us was over. And no more scorpions in our tent or boots. Thirst was about to become a problem of the past. And perhaps most important of all, we need no longer fear smugglers.

We would miss the people we had grown to love, who had taught us important life lessons, such as patience and the value of taking one day at a time. We would cherish our memories of the hospitality we had received from the Mongolian herdsmen and their families, who are some of the most rugged, kind, and resourceful people on earth.

At about 6 PM the sound of two trucks drifted across the steppes. It was Batbaatar and his family in one, and his cousin and family in the other. With great smiles of greeting they leapt from the trucks, then stopped in obvious astonishment at our disheveled appearance. In a moment everyone regained their composure and met us in a flurry of hugs and tears.

And of course they had the dreaded *airag* to celebrate our success. Out came a large container, and after bowls had been filled, it was time for toasts and salutations to everything we could think of and to everything around us, even the gazelle, snakes, and scorpions. But our experience had taught us to put the liquid to our lips without taking a mouthful. Our stories about the effect *airag* had had on us brought lively laughter from everyone. They slapped each other's backs and doubled over with tears streaming down their faces. Although this wasn't quite the reaction we had anticipated, we joined in the merriment.

Batbaatar, noticing Tom and Jerry's firm humps and bright eyes, and with obvious pride at owning these two special camels, told us that they would live a life of luxury. Four-year-old Saran claimed them as her own, and her parents nodded agreement. The camels would be her responsibility for the rest of their lives. We were delighted. More toasts followed to Saran and the camels' continued good health and long life. Finally, just as Bill and I thought that everything real and imagined had been toasted, someone remembered that we hadn't toasted Chuluu and his plane, who were still to arrive. A half-dozen more toasts later, we were finally finished and the leftover *airag* was returned to the truck for a future momentous occasion, which we suspected wouldn't be far off.

Batbaatar quietly asked us, "Were you afraid to cross such an empty, dangerous place?"

"In spite of everything," I said, "we always believed we would make it all the way."

Batbaatar softly replied, "We Mongolians have a proverb—if you are afraid, don't do it. If you do it, don't be afraid."

Soon Chuluu arrived. It was time for us to leave the desert, and time for Batbaatar and his family to load Tom and Jerry on the truck and return home.

Everyone helped load the plane with our diminished pile of gear. Bill and I went to Tom and Jerry with a cookie each, and with one last hug around their long necks and a whispered good-bye, we thanked them for helping to make our journey possible. Then we turned to the family, and with more hugs and best wishes we boarded the plane.

We took off and circled a few times over the waving figures below, then flew north, leaving our friends and Tom and Jerry behind.

As we gained altitude, I finally realized that it was all over. With eyes blurred by tears, I looked down at the passing country-side. Although relieved to be free of the trials of the desert, I felt the desert would always be part of us. I was sad to leave the people we had grown fond of, and sad to leave Tom and Jerry.

It had been a privilege to get to know some of the Gobi Desert nomads and to share in their traditional ways. We had stepped out of our life for eighty-one days to experience another culture and their mysterious land, and we had been forever changed. It was impossible to leave the desert as the same people we had been when we arrived, having waged such a hard-fought battle.

Although the Gobi's vast expanses will always remain a place of intrigue and fascination to us, and our physical journey will be indelibly stamped on our memories, it was the inner journey that was the most important. The inner journey carried us across plains, sand dunes, and mountains. It brought even minuscule objects to our notice, and caused us to grow in our understanding and respect of another culture, and of a desert that had at first seemed so inhospitable but now was part of us.

Over the roar of the plane, Bill and I held hands and mouthed the same words to each other: "We'll be back."

EPILOGUE

Once we reached Ulaan Baatar, we set about keeping our promise to Butterfly, Batbayar, and their struggling family. We had given them as many extra supplies as we had while on our trek, but we knew that wouldn't be enough to sustain them through the next winter. So we had promised them that a friend would fly in with extra supplies and clothes for the newborn baby. And as soon as we told Chuluu about the family's desperate plight, he enthusiastically agreed to help.

With his sister Jargal, we set out on a shopping spree in the main markets of Ulaan Baatar. We bought bright flowered blouses for the women, subdued colored shirts for the men, and winter *dels*, warm sweaters, hats, gloves, and leather boots for everyone. For the baby we bought a tiny winter *del* and a larger one for a year later, long pants, blankets, and a baby mattress.

Jargal took us to the food market to buy our new friends enough flour, sugar, salt, and tea for the coming winter. At the meat market we bought two whole butchered sheep, ready to be

sun-dried, and four large sheep tails. For good measure we included fruit, carrots, potatoes, and a sweet commercial curd to
supplement *aaruul*. A doctor friend of Jargal's gave us medicine,
vitamins, and special baby formula and other baby food.

We added cooking pans, utensils, and two large butcher's knives
to the growing pile. Later that day, at the carpet stall, we found two
dark green carpets for each *ger* floor to stave off the winter cold.
Four horse bridles and saddles completed our shopping.

The next day, after loading the plane, we watched Chuluu
and Jargal fly off into the desert. We didn't accompany them
because we knew the families would find it more acceptable to
receive gifts from their fellow countrymen than from foreigners,
even though they would know that we had sent the treasures.

Chuluu and Jargal found the family with no trouble and spent
three days with them. Chuluu also contacted relatives in the
northern Gobi, who invited the two families to winter over near

them, in the shelter of a low mountain range. There, humans and
animals would stand a better chance of survival, in a place full
of winter forage but protected from the full force of the freezing
Siberian winds. The family sent their thanks and blessings, and
said they would travel north to meet Chuluu's relatives before the
first snowfall.

We delayed our flight home until Chuluu returned to tell us
the details of his stay with the desert family. And then, all too
soon, it was time for us to return home. But our leaving was made
easier knowing that our special desert friends could look forward
to a brighter future, and that Tom and Jerry were receiving care
and attention beyond a camel's wildest dreams.

After we returned home I entered a lengthy period of treatment and rehabilitation for my car accident injuries. I recovered
completely, and with Bill I continue to participate in expeditions
to far-flung areas of the world to produce educational projects for
Adventure Classroom.

In the summer of 2006 we returned to Mongolia to visit the
family. We were honored to learn that they had named the baby

Helen, and that she had grown into a beautiful six-year-old girl. She was attending school and had already learned a few words of English. Her family was prospering in their new northerly location, where their herd of sheep and goats, now numbering more than four hundred, enjoyed sufficient water and pasture.

Our visit with Tom and Jerry was no less rewarding. Both immediately recognized us and enjoyed having their ears stroked, just as they had in the desert. Their life of continued retirement, under the gentle care of young Saran, clearly suited them both.

As for Bill and me, our return to Mongolia allowed us to visit friends, bask in the Mongolian culture we had come to love, and renew memories of our journey across the Gobi Desert. Although the trek was at times life-threatening, our philosophy of setting a goal, planning for success, and never giving up in spite of tough obstacles had carried us through to the end.

ACKNOWLEDGMENTS

A special thank-you to our Mongolian logistics coordinator, Chuluu, for his enthusiasm and skills. As always, we are indebted to David Burch of Starpath Navigation, whose advice helped us with a difficult navigation project. Grateful thanks to Marlin Greene of One Earth Images (www.OneEarthImages.com), who has been helpful in many ways, including with our Adventure Classroom. And to all the nomad families who offered us hospitality and friendship throughout our long trek, thank you for your kindness and for the memories.

ABOUT THE AUTHOR

Helen Thayer, born and educated in New Zealand, began climbing mountains when she was nine years old. She continued with major climbs worldwide, including Mt. McKinley (20,320 feet) in Alaska and Tajikistan's Peak Communism (24,590 feet) in the former Soviet Union.

In 1988 at the age of 50 Helen became the first woman to trek solo to the magnetic North Pole, as well as the first person to circumnavigate the magnetic North Pole region. This became the first educational project for Adventure Classroom©, a program Helen developed to bring the four corners of the world into classrooms. She has since spoken to over one million students in schools worldwide.

Helen has explored approximately 2,700 miles in the Arctic and Antarctica on foot; walked 4,000 miles across the Sahara; and kayaked 1,200 miles in the Amazon. Her wildlife expeditions include living for a year with wild wolves in a wolf study in the Canadian Yukon and trekking hundreds of miles with caribou herds in Alaska and Canada to document migration routes and habits.

The recipient of many awards, Helen was honored by the Kremlin in 1990 and 1998 for co-leading the first USA/Russia Women's Arctic Expedition and for her work as an Arctic explorer. In 1999 President Clinton honored her at a White House reception as "a woman who dared." She was named in 2002 by National Geographic/National Public Radio as one of the great explorers of the 20th Century. In 2006 she was granted the "Vancouver Award" by the Explorers Club "as an explorer who has contributed to the pursuit of knowledge and demonstrated the spirit of exploration."

Future plans include more expeditions into remote regions of the world in the quest for educational data. The author of *Polar Dream* and *Three Among the Wolves*, Helen regularly appears before corporate, educational, and nonprofit organizations.

More photos from her Gobi expedition can be viewed at the *Walking the Gobi* photo gallery at Helen's website *www.helenthayer.com*.

THE MOUNTAINEERS, founded in 1906, is a nonprofit outdoor activity and conservation club, whose mission is "to explore, study, preserve, and enjoy the natural beauty of the outdoors. . . ." Based in Seattle, Washington, the club is now the third-largest such organization in the United States, with seven branches throughout Washington State.

The Mountaineers sponsors both classes and year-round outdoor activities in the Pacific Northwest, which include hiking, mountain climbing, ski-touring, snowshoeing, bicycling, camping, kayaking, nature study, sailing, and adventure travel. The club's conservation division supports environmental causes through educational activities, sponsoring legislation, and presenting informational programs.

All club activities are led by skilled, experienced instructors, who are dedicated to promoting safe and responsible enjoyment and preservation of the outdoors.

If you would like to participate in these organized outdoor activities or the club's programs, consider a membership in The Mountaineers. For information and an application, write or call The Mountaineers, Club Headquarters, 300 Third Avenue West, Seattle, WA 98119; 206-284-6310. You can also visit the club's website at www.mountaineers.org or contact The Mountaineers via email at clubmail@mountaineers.org.

The Mountaineers Books, an active, nonprofit publishing program of the club, produces guidebooks, instructional texts, historical works, natural history guides, and works on environmental conservation. All books produced by The Mountaineers Books fulfill the club's mission.

Send or call for our catalog of more than 500 outdoor titles:

The Mountaineers Books
1001 SW Klickitat Way, Suite 201
Seattle, WA 98134
800-553-4453
mbooks@mountaineersbooks.org
www.mountaineersbooks.org

OTHER TITLES YOU MIGHT ENJOY FROM THE MOUNTAINEERS BOOKS

Beluga Days: Tracking the Endangered White Whale
Nancy Lord
An intriguing personal journey into the world of endangered beluga whales in Cook Inlet, Alaska.

The Tecate Journals:
Seventy Days on the Rio Grande
Keith Bowden
A side of the mighty Rio Grande river few people ever see. From illegal immigrants and drug runners trying to make it into the U.S., to encounters with coyotes and mountain lions, the author reveals one of North America's most overlooked regions.

Forget Me Not:
A Memoir
Jennifer Lowe-Anker
An insightful and at times wrenching memoir of love lost and love found, set against a backdrop of the world's tallest peaks.

High Infatuation:
A Climber's Guide to Love and Gravity
Steph Davis
One of the most accomplished female rock climbers in the world takes readers along as she climbs, struggles, loves, and makes it to the top.

Strange and Dangerous Dreams:
The Fine Line Between Adventure and Madness
Geoff Powter
Adventurers are among the world's most celebrated heroes, but cross a line and potential glory can become madness and death.

The Mountaineers Books has more than 500 outdoor recreation titles in print.
Receive a free catalog at
www.mountaineersbooks.org.